Praise for

FROM THE SHAHS TO LOS ANGELES

"As many as 40,000 Iranian Jews live in the Los Angeles area ... Saba Soomekh, an Iranian-born member of this community, has written an informative profile of the three generations of women in this community ... As an insider, Soomekh has a unique perspective on these three generations on the basis of her own experience, her background research, and interviews with members of each generation."

— Jewish Book Council

"...Saba Soomekh draws a compelling ethnographic portrait of what life was and is for [Jews] in Iran and the United States."

— *Canadian Jewish News*

FROM THE SHAHS
TO LOS ANGELES

FROM THE SHAHS
TO LOS ANGELES

*Three Generations of Iranian Jewish Women
between Religion and Culture*

SABA SOOMEKH

STATE UNIVERSITY OF NEW YORK PRESS

Published by
STATE UNIVERSITY OF NEW YORK PRESS, ALBANY

© 2012 State University of New York

For information, contact
State University of New York Press, Albany, NY
www.sunypress.edu

Production, Laurie Searl
Marketing, Fran Keneston

Library of Congress Cataloging-in-Publication Data

Soomekh, Saba.
  From the Shahs to Los Angeles : three generations of Iranian Jewish women between religion and culture / Saba Soomekh.
      p. cm.
  Includes bibliographical references and index.
  ISBN 978-1-4384-4383-6 (hardcover : alk. paper)—978-1-4384-4384-3 (pbk : alk. paper)
  1. Jewish women—California—Los Angeles—Religious life.   2. Iranian Americans—California—Los Angeles—Religious life.   3. Iranian Americans—California—Los Angeles—Social life and customs.   4. Jewish women—Iran—Religious life.   5. Iran—Politics and government—1979–1997.   I. Title.

BM726.S66 2012
305.48'89240794940922—dc23   2011046224

10 9 8 7 6 5 4 3 2 1

CONTENTS

ONE

WOMEN OF CHANGE

Los Angeles is home to the largest concentration of Iranians outside of Iran.[1] With the Islamic Revolution of 1979 and the consequent fall of Mohammad Reza Shah and the Pahlavi dynasty, seventy thousand Iranian Jews fled the newly forming Islamic fundamentalist country and flocked to the United States. Iranian Jews knew that with the collapse of the Pahlavi monarchy and the new regime of the Islamic Republic, there would be not only a change of government but also a revolution, during which they would most likely be stripped of their religious rights. Iranian Jews felt that due to their prominent socioeconomic status; their identification with the shah and his policies; and their attachment to Israel, Zionism, and America, they would not be tolerated under Ayatollah Ruhollah Mousavi Khomeini's new regime. Khomeini accused Jews of distorting Islam and the Qur'an; he believed they had taken over Iran's economy, and he depicted them as imperialist spies; he even emphasized the Shi'i doctrine of the unbelievers' ritual impurity (nejasat).[2] As David Menashri wrote: "Iranian Jews' previous assets turned into their liabilities."[3] Iranian Jews knew that they were now viewed as an inferior minority in Iran and must depart the country in order to escape religious persecution, so many moved to America.

The Iranian migration to America arrived in two back-to-back waves— before and after the 1979 Iranian revolution. Before the revolution, most Iranian immigrants were college students majoring in technical fields who had come to the United States in order to meet the needs of the rapidly industrializing oil-based Iranian economy. In the late 1970s, Iran surpassed all other countries in the number of foreign students in the United States.[4] Originally, many of these students had planned on returning to Iran after their studies but had chosen to remain after the 1979 revolution. After the revolution, Iranian migration consisted of exiles, political refugees, and those seeking asylum. These exiles were mostly religious minorities, such as Armenian Christians and Jews, who had experienced or feared persecution

1

in the Islamic Republic of Iran.[5] Many fled to America, specifically to Los Angeles, California.

Since 1965, Los Angeles has had the highest concentration of Iranians in the United States and has become the Iranian center after the Iranian Revolution. According to the U.S. Census Bureau, by 2000, some 75,491 Iranians were living in Los Angeles County.[6] According to *The Association of Religion Data Archives*, there are currently 202 Jewish congregations and 564,700 Jews living in Los Angeles County.[7] After the revolution, many Iranian Jews opted to settle in Los Angeles County because they knew about the already well-established large Iranian community thriving there. In 2007, the Iranian Jewish community numbered roughly 30,000 to 40,000 in Los Angeles alone. Most people came to be near their family and friends and, thus, formed the largest community of its kind in the United States.

Although Iranians are heavily concentrated in Los Angeles County, they are dispersed within the county itself. Iranian Jews and Muslims are highly concentrated in Beverly Hills, as well as in affluent parts of the west side and the San Fernando Valley. Armenians from Iran have mostly settled in Glendale,[8] and a newly emerging Orthodox Iranian Jewish community has settled in traditionally Jewish neighborhoods such as Fairfax and the Pico/Robertson area. Because Iranian Jews have dealt with prejudice and discrimination in Iran, they identify more strongly with their ethnoreligious background than with their nationality. This ethnoreligious background identification was further emphasized when the majority of Iranian Jews immigrated to America around the time of the "Iranian hostage crisis," where tensions between Iran and the United States ran high. In order to avert prejudice and discrimination from Americans, Iranian Jews stressed their Jewishness over their Persian identity.

Religion is an important distinguishing identity factor within religiously diverse nationality groups.[9] Studies of minorities within nationality groups such as Chinese, Vietnamese, and Iranian minorities, such as Armenian, Baha'i, and Jewish Iranians, found that these minorities typically have a highly developed sense of ethnic identity even before migration to America.[10] Mehdi Bozorgmehr wrote that unlike the dominant religious group, minorities in the country of origin form solidarity groups as a result of hostility from the majority and years or centuries of minority status. This has prompted ethnoreligious minorities to develop ethnic self-identity, religiosity, family unity, endogamy, social ties with co-ethnics, organizational activity, and occupational clustering, often in self-employment.[11] As a result of the discrimination Jews suffered in Iran, they formed the type of solidarity groups discussed by Bozorgmehr. They were adamant about observing Jewish holidays; they mainly socialized and worked with fellow coreligionists; family unity was stressed in Iranian Jewish homes; and Jewish organizations developed in order to serve the community. This insularity and religious cohesion of the Iranian Jewish community is also evident in America.

The Iranian Jewish identity can be characterized by its symbolic ethnicity. Symbolic ethnicity can be expressed in numerous ways, especially by a nostalgic allegiance to the culture of the immigrant generation or that of the old country. Symbolic ethnicity is a love for and a pride in a tradition that can be felt without being incorporated into everyday behavior.[12] However, for Iranian Jews, pride in their Iranian Jewish identity is expressed in many aspects of their daily life. The daily traditions they practice are characterized both by their Iranian culture and by their Jewish beliefs. Symbolic ethnicity can be directed toward the desire for a cohesive extended immigrant family, the obedience of children to their parents, or the unambiguous orthodoxy of immigrant religion.[13] Iranian Jews have a cohesive extended family: Everyone from great-aunts and uncles to second cousins are included in the most intimate family affairs. There is a strict sense of familial hierarchy and devotion to Judaism, where even the most religiously lax family respects Jewish beliefs.

Since the 1979 Islamic Revolution of Iran, Iranian Jews have become major players in the economic, social, and political life of Angelenos and have become one of the most well-established immigrant communities in Los Angeles. Their mark is felt not only in the secular sphere, but it is also strongly felt in the religiously dominant Ashkenazi community of Los Angeles. Iranian Jews attend and are involved in Ashkenazi synagogues and day schools; they have formed their own Jewish Federation, synagogues, and Jewish charity and social organizations. Slowly, with the integration of the Iranian Jewish community, Iranian Jewish scholars, and religious leaders, the Jewish communities in Los Angeles and around the world are becoming more aware of the influence that Persia[14] has had on Jewish history.

This is best exemplified with the Persian Achaemenid king, Cyrus the Great, who freed the Jews from Babylonian captivity and granted them religious pluralism. Cyrus is referred to as "God's anointed" in Isaiah 45; his "spirit" is discussed in Ezra 1; and the ecstatic joy he caused by freeing the Jews from the Babylonians is the topic of Psalm 126. His successor and great-grandson, Darius I, was responsible for the building of the Second Temple, while Iranian Jewish characters such as Zerubabel, Esther, Ezra, and Nehemiah all played important roles in Jewish history.

GOALS AND FOCUS OF THIS BOOK

The first objective of this book is to present an ethnographic portrait of life for three generations of Iranian Jewish women who lived in Iran and now live in America, exploring the political and social changes that have affected these women in regards to their rituals and religious observances, and their self-concept as Iranian Jewish women in Iran and now in America. The three focal incidents in terms of their effect on Iran and, consequently, the Jewish community, are the Constitutionalist Revolution in 1906 and the granting of the throne to Reza Shah Pahlavi (1925–1941); Mohammad Reza Shah Pahlavi taking the throne (1941–1979); and, finally, the Islamic Revolution in 1979 and the immigration to Los Angeles.

Throughout, this book examines historical events and how they have affected the religious and social lives of these Iranian Jewish women and the manifestation of the sacred within the lives of these women. Sacrality can be found in different ways for each generation of women: for the first generation of women, it is found through sacralizing the domestic sphere and having a numinous relationship with God;[15] for the later generations, sacrality can be found in the numerous social events the community has to attend, within a woman maintaining and redefining her *najeebness* (virginity and innocence), and through the way some of the *hozrei bi'tshuvah* (those who return to repentance) women observe Jewish *halakhah* (Hebrew term for Jewish law).

The comparative works demonstrate the similarities and uniqueness of Iranian Jewish women, both in their home country and in America. The lives of Iranian Jewish women are not monolithic; they vary depending on the cities in which the women were raised, their socioeconomic class, and their level of assimilation into the dominant society.

Comparisons are made among three generations of Iranian Jewish women—grandmothers, mothers, and daughters—exploring these different generations to understand how history, political change, social change, assimilation, financial mobility, and immigration have affected their religiosity, their concepts of womanhood, their intergenerational relationships, and their identity.

In particular, this volume looks at the concept of sacrality throughout these three generations and how it has changed over time. Although different generations of women have different interpretations of sacrality, one overarching theme is the emphasis placed on women's religious and social rituals and maintaining their *najeebness*—all of which uphold the community's Jewish beliefs and distinguish them from other Iranians, Americans, and Jews. The emphasis on religious tradition and *najeebness* among Iranian Jewish women allows them to create meaning in their lives, establish authoritative figures within the community, and most importantly, reinforce the collective morals and social norms held within the community.

Research shows that Judaism not only provides social control and cohesion and reaffirms social norms for the community, but more importantly, it provides a way for the women to maintain their identity in times when they are confronted with anti-Semitism, gender segregation, assimilation, and immigration.[16] Throughout generations and across borders, it has been their identification as Iranian Jewish women, whether through following the community's moral, social, and religious norms or transforming and reinterpreting them, that has enabled these women to connect with their history in Iran while embracing their present life in America.

Researchers have placed importance on rituals by asserting that women should be perceived as ritual experts; this book approaches Iranian Jewish women in the same manner, primarily focusing on the use of ritual innovation by Persian Jewish women in order to define their piety and establish their identity. With three generations of women issues are explored for each generation relating directly to the social and political climate of their time. The first generation of women (chapter 2) includes those who were raised under the reign of Reza Shah Pahlavi. The second generation of women (chapter 3) includes those who were raised under Mohammad Reza Shah Pahlavi and his secular and Western regime. Finally, chapters 4 and 5 examine the lives of the American-raised daughters of these immigrant mothers and how they establish their multiple identities in their native country.

In the traditional Iranian Jewish context, women were excluded from public religious life. When Iranian Jewish women came to America, specifically to Los Angeles, they found themselves in a situation of public observance. The women who were born and raised in Iran and immigrated to Los Angeles later in their life, meaning women who were raised under the reign of Reza Shah Pahlavi and Mohammad Reza Shah, felt this change most severely. This book focuses on the issue of change in the patterns of religious observances and religious rituals among the first two generations of Iranian Jewish women and on their self-concept as Iranian Jewish women in Iran and now in America.

This book examines the ritual practices and beliefs of Iranian Jewish women, their attitude toward Judaism and ritual observances, the importance of religious activities for them and their community, the changes in the patterns of religious observances and religious rituals that have taken place due to modernization and immigration, and finally, how modernization and demographic change affected religious change and ritual observance.

Within these issues, we explore the status of women in the family and in public life, asking how much influence rabbinical law, Muslim society, and the location of their home had on placing women in the domestic sphere; examine how influential Jewish *halakhah* was in dictating the relationship between husband and wife (i.e., attending the *mikveh*,[17] sleeping in separate beds, and other menstruating laws); and look at the rituals of sociability within the first two generations, exploring the rituals of Persian Jewish social

activities, a woman's role in these events, and the connection between
Persian Jewish social activities and religion. Finally, we examine how
women perceive themselves and their role as Jewish women in the Persian
community, exploring how their self-perception has changed throughout the
years while living first in Iran and now in America.

RECENT HISTORY OF IRAN

Iran has gone through major political and religious changes in the twentieth
century, changes that have greatly affected the status and condition of Iranian
Jews. It would be gravely erroneous to imagine Iran as a stagnant political
and social climate or to describe Iranian women's piety, rituals, and identity
as unchanging within that climate. Numerous Judeo-Persian scholars have
written about the changes that have occurred in the Iranian community
during the twentieth century.[18] The Constitutionalist Revolution of 1906
has been described as the beginning of the Iranian people's struggle for
freedom,[19] with many important measures adopted at this time, such as the
Assembly, which allowed each religious minority, except the Baha'is, to elect
a delegate to the government body. Other changes in the country included
less influence from the clergy in governmental affairs, an opposition in Iran
against the acceptance of new foreign loans, a national bank established to
provide relief from foreign financial restrictions, and a new constitution. It
was during this time that Jews finally felt some form of freedom, what Levi
calls the "Jewish Emancipation." Jews gained the freedom to work and be
educated; the Jewish *mahaleh* (ghetto) was sanitized; Jews were no longer
considered to be "unclean" by Muslims; a Jewish-Iranian newspaper, *Shalom*,
was published; and finally, Jews were no longer restricted to living in the
mahalehs and could move to other parts of the city.[20]

As a result of the First World War and inner conflicts in Iran, all
military, fiscal, and customs-related affairs had come under the exclusive
control of British advisors by 1921. It was during this period that Reza
Khan entered the arena of Iranian politics, staging a successful coup, seizing
command of the Iranian armed forces, and taking over the throne in 1925.[21]
The most effective reform Reza Shah Pahlavi established was the expulsion
of even the most senior clerics from government administration; he did not
permit them to meddle in state affairs. For the first time since the Safavid
dynasty, religion was separated from politics in Iran. During Reza Shah's
reign, many Jews prospered financially. One of the great accomplishments
of the Jews during his reign was the establishment in Tehran of the Kurosh
elementary school and high school. However, Reza Shah's extending a hand
of friendship to Hitler brought about his compulsory abdication and exile
after the Second World War.

The coronation of his son Mohammad Reza Shah in 1941 brought about a resurgence of the Jewish people of Iran. Habib Levi wrote that "the years of Mohammad Reza Shah's reign may be considered the zenith of Jewish Iranian well-being and prosperity."[22] Under his rule, Jews were prominent figures in economics, industry, commerce, higher education, administration, and the arts and sciences. Educational opportunities for Iranian Jews increased when the second shah came into power. Jewish schools, summer camps, and seminars for training teachers were opened. Hundreds of Jewish students went to Europe and America to pursue advanced studies. Jewish girls, who until a few generations earlier had received no education at all, were now on equal footing with boys and studied at all levels.[23] Levi identifies Israeli independence as the most important historical event of this period for Iranian Jews. In 1960, the shah recognized Israel and repeatedly affirmed Israel's right to exist, publicly declaring that Iran and Israel should maintain economic ties; with the implementation of various treaties, as a result, Israeli organizations engaged in a wide range of activities in Iran.[24]

In the fall of 1977, a revolutionary upheaval began with the outbreak of open opposition movements, and Jews in Iran once again found themselves threatened by their Muslim neighbors. Iranian Jews realized that their previous assets had turned into liabilities: Their prominent socioeconomic status; their identification with the shah and his policies; and their attachment to Israel, Zionism, and America were all held against them by Khomeini and his followers.[25] It is estimated that by 1978, some seventy thousand Iranian Jews had fled Iran, many of whom immigrated to the United States. This immigration to the United States is important in a religious sense because, for the first time, Iranian Jews found themselves in a secular society where they faced the challenges of retaining their Judeo–Persian identity.

Iranian Jews have chosen to maintain their Jewish identity in Los Angeles and have taken the opportunity to give their children what many of them lacked in Iran—a Jewish education. The majority of Jewish Iranian boys and girls in Los Angeles attend Jewish day schools or after-school programs. Most have a *bnei mitzvoth* or *bat mitzvot*,[26] attend synagogue regularly, and are actively involved in Jewish organizations and social events. For the first time, Jewish Iranian girls have equal status with boys in regards to religion. Because many Iranians in Los Angeles attend Reform and Conservative synagogues, Iranian girls are receiving a Jewish education on par with boys. They read from the Torah, get called for up for *aliya*,[27] recite the blessings before and after meals and during holidays, and many are taking leadership positions within the synagogue (i.e., as cantors or as temple president). In doing so, they are practicing a form of Judaism that is influenced by the Ashkenazi American Jewish movements. The question is, in this context, what happens to the female Jewish rituals their mothers and grandmothers practiced in their native Iran? Have these rituals been replaced or have they incorporated with Ashkenazi ones?

WOMEN RAISED IN LOS ANGELES

Initially, the author planned to use the same five questions posed for the women of chapters 2 and 3 for the women of chapter 4, the daughters of immigrant parents who were and are raised in America. However, it soon became apparent that this is a very different generation from those who came before, and the theme of rituals does not really apply to them because they were raised with very few religious rituals outside of the traditional Jewish ones, such as attending synagogue and going to their parents' home for Shabbat (Sabbath) dinner. This generation did not grow up in Iran experiencing the reign of the Pahlavi dynasty; they only know the Iran of their grandmothers and mothers through the memories of their matriarchs.

However, the Iranian Jewish culture is still a dominant aspect of their lives, and at times, it does not blend well with American values and cultural norms. These young women, like most children of immigrant parents, struggle to meld the culture of their parents with the American culture they live in. Thus, a more appropriate theme to investigate for this generation was the issue of identity—how these young women establish and juggle their multiple identities in their native land. How have they incorporated womanhood, Judaism, and the rules and expectations placed on them by their family and the Iranian Jewish community into their life as young Americans? The three important subjects of chapter 4 are being *najeeb* (virginal and innocent), pressures placed on young women, and mother-daughter relationships.

Today, immigrant children have constructed their own cultural world, where they are in the process of mixing different cultures in order to form their own hybrid identity. Hybridity is described as cultural creativity, the making of something new through the combination of existing things and patterns.[28] One cannot assume that one's ethnic or cultural traits are set in tradition and do not change, but rather, these traits go through an on-going negotiation that emerges when one is going through historical transformations.[29] The hybridity model describes how young Iranian Jewish women are constantly negotiating their identity as they live in a world where they respect the rules, values, and cultural norms of their parents' generation, while appropriating the American culture in which they have grown up.

SIGNIFICANCE OF RITUALS

This book places priority on examining the Jewish rituals Iranian women participated in when living in Iran and the religious rituals they practice now in Los Angeles. Catherine Bell, in her book *Ritual Theory, Ritual Practice*, traces the scholarly endeavor to use *ritual* as a term of analysis for human experience.[30] Bell wrote that many theorists of myth and ritual have looked to ritual in order to describe "religion," while social functionalists explored ritual actions and values in order to analyze "society" and the nature of social phenomena, and symbolic anthropologists have found ritual to be fundamental to the dynamics of "culture." Thus, the notion of ritual studies is meaningful not only because it is an analytical tool, but also because it has been integral to the mutual construction of both an object for and a method of analysis.[31] Rituals demonstrate the influence of religious ideas, and religious ideas are the basis of religion.[32]

In *To Take Place*, Jonathan Z. Smith describes the "gnostic" dimension of ritual, asserting that rituals are fulfilled as a means of gaining knowledge and performing the way things ought to be in conscious tension to the way things are.[33] The power of ritual lies in the fact that it is concerned with ordinary activities placed within extraordinary settings; thus, rituals provide an occasion for reflection and rationalization on the incongruence of the world and ways to rectify it.[34] Smith uses the example of Christians in Jerusalem during the fourth century to demonstrate that through the conjoining of myth to ritual, one is able to turn the profane into the sacred.[35] In an earlier book, Smith wrote that one of the basic building blocks of religion is ritual repetition and routinization.[36] He believes that "ritual is an exercise in the strategy of choice."[37] One has to decide what to include, what to hear, what to exclude, and so on; therefore, through ritual, one is establishing what kind of knowledge one chooses to learn and appropriate in one's ritual performances and routines.

Emile Durkheim also discusses the importance of rituals in *The Elementary Forms of Religious Life*, writing that religious phenomena fall into two categories: belief and rites.[38] He asserts that "rites are not purely manual operations but they bring into play the spiritual and their primary function is to act upon moral life."[39] Henri Hubert and Marcel Mauss demonstrate how ritual activities effectively sacralize things, people, or events.[40] They believe that religious phenomena and ideas derived from social activities and that, therefore, "ritual is a sociological concept and a universal category of social life."[41]

OUTLINE OF CHAPTERS

Chapter 1

This first chapter serves as an introduction to the various focuses of this study, emphasizing the importance of ritual and its place in religion for the first two generations of Iranian Jewish women in the study, and on the distinct rituals they perform as an expression of religious piety and as a system of gaining knowledge. The argument for the first two generations of women is about how they partake in ritual innovation in order to express their piety. For the last generation, the discussion centers on how these young women have appropriated both the Iranian Jewish and American culture into their lives, thus forming a hybrid identity.

The women profiled in chapters 2 through 4 discuss the following: their attitude towards Judaism and ritual observations, their ritual practices and what they believe, the importance of religious activities/rituals for them and their community, changes that have occurred in their pattern of religious observances and religious rituals, and how demographic change and modernization have affected religious change, specifically in regards to rituals.

In chapter 5, different topics are addressed in light of the changing influences on the women's lives compared to the previous generations: their understanding of being *najeeb* and whether or not they appropriate that belief into their lives, the social and cultural pressures they feel as young Iranian Jewish women raised in America, and their relationships with their mothers and what aspects of their mothers' beliefs they have appropriated and what they have changed.

Chapter 2

Chapter 2 revolves around the first generation of women, those who grew up under the Constitutional Revolution (1906) and Reza Shah (1921–1941). Because of the dearth of archival materials accessible on the subject of Iranian Jewish women, interviews were conducted, in Persian, with women from this generation. Therefore, information came almost entirely from women's voices and through oral histories of Iranian Jewish women now residing in Los Angeles.

In her book *Change within Tradition among Jewish Women in Libya*, Rachel Simon wrote that the status of Jewish women in Libya was influenced by three main sets of factors: Jewish law and tradition; Muslim law and customs; and environmental conditions in the urban and rural areas.[42] However, in her analysis, Simon does not offer an alternative women's history, because she accepts the male history based on rabbinic law, which constitutes Jewish culture. This book takes Simon's framework for analysis a step further to examine how women developed their own Jewish rituals and responded to social and political change in ways significantly different than did Iranian Jewish men.

Chapter 2 also examines Jewish customs in the home, participation in ceremonies, and the Muslim code of modesty (veiling) that Jewish women were obligated to follow and later were forced, by the secularist Reza Shah, to disregard. The chapter includes a discussion of how Susan Sered's theory of domestication of religion is linked with Iranian Jewish women: how these women received their religious education; their perceived role in Judaism and how they expressed their religiosity when they could neither read Hebrew nor attend synagogue; and finally, the Jewish rituals in which they partook, how they interpreted these rituals, and the influences of Zoroastrianism and Islam on their ritual practice.

Chapter 3

Chapter 3 focuses on interviews conducted with women who grew up in Iran under the reign of Mohammed Reza Shah, immigrated to the United States, and currently reside in Los Angeles. These women directly benefited from the secularization and modernization of the Pahlavi dynasty. Under this program of modernization, women were required to attend schools, and many Iranian Jewish women continued their higher education at vocational schools or universities. This period in Iranian Jewish society is characterized by both assimilation into the mainstream Muslim society and the insularity of the Iranian Jewish community.

Topics of this chapter include the changes that were brought about by, and the influence of, the Alliance Israélite Universelle, Western modernization efforts, new educational and vocational opportunities, and the shah's attempt to secularize Iran; how this new generation of women practice Judaism and their participation in public and religious life; their assimilation of or disregard for their mother's Jewish rituals; their memories of life under the Pahlavi regime and now in Los Angeles; their idea of what constitutes a "good Jewish woman" and what social responsibilities they must attend to in order to live up to the community's expectations of them; and finally, how they preserved their Iranian Jewish identity while appropriating the secular ideology of the shah.

Chapter 4

Chapter 4 looks at how women who were raised under the Pahlavi dynasty and immigrated to Los Angeles preserve and pass on their identity while still appropriating certain aspects of the dominant Ashkenazi Jewish culture in Los Angeles. While Iranians do attend the few Iranian and Sephardic synagogues in Los Angeles, an overwhelming majority of Iranians attend either Conservative Ashkenazi or Reform Ashkenazi temple and day schools. Thus, Iranian Jewish immigrants are experiencing a notably different Judaic environment than that which was practiced in Iran. The Judaism with which they are now familiar in Los Angeles is an egalitarian one rather than the male-dominated Judaism practiced in Iran.

The move to egalitarianism has altered the household roles of Jewish men and women, forcing Jewish institutions to redefine the role of a woman and include her in the community of Jews. Women have joined the religious elite, and, thus, the Judaism that was family based has had to adapt to new patterns of women's involvement, either by incorporating changes and developing new religious expressions or by rejecting the need for adaptation and reinforcing traditional gender-based religious barriers.[43] This chapter examines how the religious roles of women in the Iranian Jewish community have changed with this move toward egalitarianism. Does egalitarianism within the Iranian Jewish context mean a woman has equality in the synagogue, but that she must still appropriate a traditional gender-based role in the home and within the family?

In *Women as Ritual Experts*, Susan Starr Sered conducted fieldwork among a group of women who frequent a senior citizens' day center in Jerusalem in 1984 and 1985. The women are of several ethnic groups: the majority is Kurdish; there is a sizable minority from Turkey; and several are Yemenite, Iranian, Iraqi, and Moroccan. They have lived in the same part of Jerusalem for fifty years. Sered chose these elderly women for her study because they have already experienced most or all of the religious events that are connected to the life cycle. Illiterate and functionally illiterate women were chosen in hope of learning what women really believe and do, not what rabbinic authorities and books have told them they are supposed to tell strangers. Sered's book is an important model for this study because she wrote about the meaning of religion and religiosity for a group of women whose religious life is conducted for the most part in the female domain, among other women, and is not a part of "official Judaism." Like the women in Sered's study, the religious lives of Iranian Jewish women are mostly revealed through nonverbal gestures, rituals, daily experiences, and life stories.[44]

Sered wrote that the daughters and granddaughters of the day center women who were born and raised in Israel have embraced a completely secular form of Judaism. They do not participate in any religious rituals, though many of the older women say they use the cooking of traditional dishes in order to preserve the Jewish identity of their children and grandchildren.[45] One would assume that members of the Iranian Jewish community in Los Angeles would face the same problem of secularization now that they live in a pluralistic country, yet the opposite is true. A majority of the Iranian Jewish interviewees in this study believe that Judaism is one of the most important aspects of their lives, and attending synagogue, observing Shabbat, and partaking in the Jewish holidays is given top priority.

When looking at modern pluralistic societies, two questions must be untangled if one is to understand the changing characteristics of the Jewish community: (1) How are changes in religion linked to other processes of transformation? and (2) What are the implications of the new emerging Judaisms for the cohesion of the community?[46] For the first time in Iranian Jewish history, the community has a choice of partaking in "new emerging Judaisms" which did not exist in Iran (i.e., the Reform, Conservative, and Orthodox movements in America). It is important to look at the effects that the dominant Ashkenazi community has had on these women's attitudes toward Judaism and the way they observe and partake in Jewish rituals. How have the Reform, Conservative, and Orthodox movements affected the religious and social cohesion of the Iranian Jewish community in Los Angeles? Are these women performing the same rituals as those of Iranian Jewish men, and how do they view the Jewish rituals practiced by their matriarchs? Chapters 3 and 4 will look at the newly emerging Iranian Orthodox community and how this deep sense of religiosity is seen among the rest of the community. This discussion continues to examine the processes of the *domestication of religion* as Iranian Jewish women experience political, social, and demographic change.

Chapter 5

Chapter 5 explores how demographic change has affected first-generation young Iranian American Jewish women and how they establish and juggle their multiple identities (Iranian, Jewish, and American). The voices of this generation provide a summary of the events that led to the immigration of Iranian Jews to Los Angeles and a discussion of the community's social, economic, and religious lives. The discussion focuses on several questions in regards to being *najeeb*, social and cultural expectations placed on young women, and their relationship with their mothers: How have womanhood, Judaism, and the rules and expectations placed on them by their family and the community fit into their life as young Americans? Because a mother holds great significance and influence in a Middle-Eastern household, what is the relationship of these young women with their mothers? What aspects of their mother's lives do they choose to emulate, and what do they choose to reinterpret in order to fit into what they see as a more modernized American society? And finally, how have these women embraced American society without compromising their Iranian Jewish traditions and beliefs?

Chapter 6

Chapter 6 summarizes the lives of these three generations of women and discusses how Iranian Jewish women in present-day Los Angeles have responded to the forces of social and political change that dramatically affected Iranian Jewish society and, thus, women's identity. Ultimately, this book concludes with insight into the affect modernization and demographic changes have had on the *domestication of religion* and the establishment of one's identity.

THE WOMEN OF THIS STUDY

The women interviewed for chapters 2 and 3 were from two major cities in Iran—Hamadan and Tehran. Hamadan was selected for numerous reasons. It holds great importance in Judeo–Persian history because the Esther/Mordecai story takes place there,[47] and, thus, Iranian Jews, believe their history in Iran grew in this city. Also, unlike other Jews in Iran, Iranian Jews of Hamadan did not live in Jewish ghettos,[48] and, thus, the Jews of Hamadan were more integrated in the community. The Alliance school and numerous missionaries settled in Hamadan and, therefore, Hamadanian Jews developed solid knowledge of their Jewish traditions and were exposed to other religious traditions.

The second group was women from Tehran because it is the capital of Iran and, unlike Hamadanian Jews, Tehrani Jews lived in ghettos and were less integrated into Iranian society. This difference allowed juxtaposition of the two communities. In addition, both communities are highly accessible in Los Angeles, making it convenient to conduct multiple interviews. The first generation of women was born in the 1920s and 1930s; these women are included in the "Generation of the Constitutional Monarchy." The second generation of women was born between 1948 and 1963, and is featured in chapter 3, "All the Shah's Women." The women interviewed in chapter 4, all born between 1973 and 1990, were raised in Los Angeles and live in Beverly Hills, West Los Angeles, or the San Fernando Valley. They are also featured in chapter 5, titled "Jewish American AND Persian." Thus, the voices represented come from people who are both positional and representational, with the dynamic of the narrative coming from the oral stories of the women.

The author is a member of the community being studied. Born in 1976 in Tehran, Iran, she and her family escaped to Los Angeles in 1978; thus, she falls within the third generation of Iranian Jewish women. As a woman in the community, she came to realize that the voices, life stories, happiness, and traumas of Iranian Jewish women are never openly discussed. This book strives to correct that oversight and looks at the history, rituals, and everyday lives of Iranian Jews from a woman's perspective.

Initially, it was difficult to convince women of each generation to agree to be interviewed. Because the community is very secretive, and the threat of gossip is a major issue, they demanded promises that their actual names would never be revealed. The women from the first generation were, at first, the most reluctant—and then gradually, as the interview took place, became the most open. When initially approached, the first-generation women were shocked. Many responded by saying, "I have nothing to talk about; my life was so boring," or, "It is too bad my husband isn't alive; he has more to say than I do." They were not accustomed to anyone showing an interest in their lives. But in their houses, often talking over numerous cups of tea and Persian pastries and fruits—typically forced onto the author's plate whether she wanted them or not—the women would open up and talk for hours and hours. (Some interviews lasted up to four hours.)

Perhaps the reason the first-generation women were so open and told such personal stories—often involving their sexual encounters or disputes they had with their parents, husbands, or in-laws—was that most of the people they mentioned in their life stories were deceased; thus, perhaps the women felt liberated in being able to talk about their lives without having to worry that anything they said would cause family drama. They were so excited to talk about their childhood and life in Iran that, many times, the women would quickly run around their homes, showing family pictures, jewelry they had received from their in-laws, their *ketubahs* (Jewish marriage contracts), and even their wedding dresses.

Often, their daughters or granddaughters would call to request a copy of the interview tape or a transcription because they wanted to learn about their mothers' and grandmothers' lives. It became quite evident that it was rare for later generations to sit down with their matriarchs and ask them what their lives were like in Iran.

The women in the second generation were also very open and honest and enjoyed discussing their memories and experiences in Iran. They were delighted about the opportunity for Iranian Jewish women's voices to be heard. Often, they got personal in regard to the difficulties they had experienced with immigration or with pressures placed on them by their families, in-laws, extended families, and the community. There were times when the author had to turn off her tape recorder and comfort the woman being interviewed as she cried uncontrollably over past regrets, pressures to maintain her status, or feelings of sadness. This further demonstrated how much pressure these women experience; having to be a "super mom" has taken an incredible emotional toll on them.

Women in the third generation were the most reluctant to open up about their lives and trust their stories to this book, also demanding that their actual names not be used and that they not be identifiable in any way. Perhaps it is because these women are young—some newly married, other single—they had to be more conscious of protecting their reputations and of not offending their families, friends, and in-laws. Thus, discussion about topics such as sexuality, being *najeeb*, and double standards in the community were guarded. However, there were some women who were excited to voice their opinions and to have an outlet for many of the frustrations they experienced as members of the community.

Overall, the author found all the women to be very inviting, and she is grateful for the gift of their time. In a community where gossip can make or break a person, the author truly appreciated how forthright and honest these gracious women were with her. All of the first- and second-generation women expressed how proud they were of the author—an Iranian Jewish woman who was pursuing a PhD and choosing to write about her own community—and thus, they really wanted to support her research. Additionally, the author's family has an excellent reputation in the community, and many of the women were willing to be interviewed because they knew her grandmothers, mother, aunts, and others.

For the third-generation women, perhaps it helped that the author is a member of their community and of their generation, and not a random outsider coming into their lives, and, thus, they did not find the questions to be invasive. It likely helped that while she is a member of the community, she is also something of an outsider, having lived outside of the community for ten years while away at college and graduate school. Also, on a social level, she rarely attends Iranian Jewish functions, and the majority of her friends are not Iranian. Thus, the women believed they could talk to her openly because she could relate to them; at the same time, because she lacked a presence in the social aspects of the community, she would be unable to identify the people they discussed. They were able to maintain a level of anonymity and did not worry that she would go back to the community and gossip about them.

TWO

THE GENERATION OF THE
CONSTITUTIONAL MONARCHY

An elderly Persian woman makes a dramatic gesture of opening her arms widely as the Torah is lifted out of the Ark. She then places her hands over her eyes, says a blessing, and kisses her hands. She most likely neither understands the prayer service nor the rabbi's sermon, yet she will walk, get a ride, or take the bus in order to attend synagogue every Saturday. In the same synagogue, her daughters, granddaughters, and great-granddaughters will also partake in the prayer service, with each generation developing a greater understanding of the liturgy and sacred text than the preceding generation.[1]

This scene represents a typical Saturday morning in some Ashkenazi, Sephardic, or Iranian synagogues in Los Angeles. Women, along with their children, grandchildren, and great-grandchildren, describe themselves as having been pious Jews in their native country of Iran and now in the Diaspora. Whether they are in a conservative Shi'i country like Iran or in a pluralistic society like America, religion is a major component of their lives. How can we interpret the way elderly women, who are illiterate in Hebrew and excluded from a male-dominated Jewish culture, define their own piety? If the religious aspects of Judaism were never taught to them, how do they know what to do for the holidays? How do they define their Jewishness? This chapter explores Iranian Jewish ritual life as understood by elderly women in order to examine how Persian women, who once lived in Iran and now live in Los Angeles, express their piety and participate in the Jewish community.

This chapter discusses how women from the Persian cities of Hamadan and Tehran recall their lives in the Old Country. Born in the 1920s and 1930s and growing up under Reza Shah (1921–1941), they became mothers during Muhammad Reza Shah's reign (1941–1979) and came to Los Angeles during the last years of his reign and during the early years of the Iranian Revolution.

Hamadan holds great importance in Judeo–Persian history. The story about Queen Esther and her uncle Mordecai took place in Hamadan.[2] Thus, Iranian Jews believe their history grew in this city. Also, unlike other Jews in Iran, the Jews of Hamadan were not forced to live in Jewish ghettos and, therefore, were more integrated into the community.[3] The Alliance school and numerous missionaries settled in Hamadan, thus exposing Hamadanian Jews to other religious traditions as they gained knowledge of their own Jewish traditions.

The most popular schools in Hamadan were the Alliance Israélite Universelle schools, which opened in 1898. The Alliance schools taught the students French, Hebrew, and Persian. The aims of the Alliance schools were to (1) work everywhere for the emancipation and moral progress of world Jewry; (2) offer effective assistance to Jews suffering from anti-Semitism; and (3) encourage all circulation publications to promote this aim.[4] The Alliance schools were based on the modern French tradition of nationalism; therefore, their vision of Iranian Jewish emancipation was to educate and promote the prosperity of Jewish communities, so they would remain loyal to their respective nations and live in harmony with the Gentile majority.

The Alliance schools also encouraged the adoption of modern European social manners and hygiene, as well as the secular and liberal ideals of the French Revolution.[5]

The women from Tehran, the capital of Iran, provide a good contrast to the Hamadan Jews because the Tehrani Jews were forced to live in Jewish ghettos and were, therefore, less integrated into Iranian society. Because they were forced to live in the ghetto and did not assimilate with Muslims, many Tehrani Jews were more religious than Jews from other parts of Iran.

Both communities are now established in West Los Angeles and Beverly Hills. Thus, the body of this evidence comes from people within the community, with the dynamic of the narrative coming from the oral stories of the women. At times, those who were interviewed recollected with great agony the domestic life they had lived in Iran, while at other times, they romanticized their past, remembering life in Iran under the Pahlavi dynasty as being pleasant. It appeared that the women's romanticization of their lives in Iran and their downplaying of the difficulties that they experienced as Jewish women under the Pahlavi regime means that they have chosen to remember the shah and the Iran of their past with fondness and reverence.

This chapter explores the extensive ritual and social structures of Iranian Jewish women with regard to four interrelated topics: women's ritual practices, the relationship between husband and wife, the influences of non-Jewish culture, life under the shah, and life in Los Angeles. Although women were excluded from the traditional Persian Jewish cultural domain, they practiced a well-developed religious life by turning their day-to-day profane activities into sacred acts. Through the domestication of religion,[6] these women were able to sacralize their daily lives, ensure the safety of their loved ones, establish themselves as good Jewish wives, and show their respect to God.

THE DOMESTIC SPHERE

To understand the role of Jewish women and their ritual practice, one must focus on the area in which women exercised the most power and authority— within the domestic sphere. The duties of a housewife and mother were so important that rabbis exempted women from time-bound *mitzvot*.[7] Rachel Biale states in *Women and Jewish Law* that a number of modern writers have legitimized this position by stating that the Mishnah (oral Torah) takes into consideration the woman's domestic responsibilities.[8] Biale wrote that women in traditional Jewish societies were encumbered by the demands of children and home, which dictated a woman's timetable. Therefore, time-bound *mitzvoth* would interfere with her responsibilities and unreasonably burden her. According to the Orthodox perspective, women are bound to the domestic role for spiritual reasons and are set apart from the clock that dictates the lives of men. Therefore, the demands of her husband and children take precedence over the commands of God.[9]

As in most traditional societies, the role of Middle Eastern women was centered in the home and family. Although Middle Eastern Jewish women were traditionally segregated from men who practiced Judaism in the public sphere, they were still able to form their own Jewish experience. Parvin Paidair asserts that Middle Eastern women are the backbone of social systems such as the family and community; they help sustain and change them.[10] The matriarchal role in Iran enabled women to develop a relationship with God and become ritual experts in their community.

Anthropologist Sered argues that when looking at a woman's religious world, one theme that emerges in many ethnographic descriptions is the domestication of religion[11] and proceeds to discuss the domestication of religion as a process in which people personalize their religious tradition and its rituals, institutions, symbols, and theology in order to safeguard the health, happiness, and security of the people with whom they are linked in relationships of care and interdependence.[12] Sered explains that for the elderly women, every activity is potentially sacred. For these women, food preparation for Shabbat, the holidays, and charity is a religious pursuit.

Sered's domestication of religion applies to Persian women because they have been excluded from the study and formal prayers of Judaism, and their religious world is concentrated within the sphere of their home, kitchen, holidays, and familial duties. They see the profane activities of cleaning the house or preparing food as a sacred act of ritual devotion. While their husbands' religiosity stems from their synagogue attendance and the study of the Torah, the women's religiosity stems from their domestic duties, and union with God comes from being an altruistic wife and mother.

WOMEN AND RELIGION

Although many Jewish women were illiterate in Hebrew and, therefore, unable to study the Torah and other sacred texts, they still considered themselves to be devout Jews. Raphael Patai, a Hungarian Jewish ethnographer and cultural anthropologist, wrote that although many Jewish girls grew up without learning to read and write Hebrew, they were not ignorant of Judaism. He stated that, quite to the contrary, their mothers taught them the benedictions, prayers, and other religious matters that pertained to the lives of women and to the kitchen. Thus, the chain of Jewish tradition was upheld among women. It was the women who watched "assiduously over the observance of Jewish rituals."[13]

In historical and ethnographic accounts of the religious lives of women, a link has been established between women's religious lives and women's domestic or interpersonal concerns.[14]

Sered wrote that the most effective strategy available to women within a male-oriented religion is to sacralize their own female life experiences. She wrote that for women, "food preparation is sacred because it embodies, concretizes, dramatizes, and ritualizes the central elements of Judaism."[15]

RITUAL PRACTICE

Iranian Jewish women were involved in many ritual activities that demonstrated their devotion to God and to their family. Ritual activities revolving around the Sabbath, Rosh Hashanah, Yom Kippur, Passover, tomb pilgrimage, the laws of *niddah*,[16] celebrating *nowruz*,[17] and lighting *esphan*[18] were done not only as a way of communing with God but also as a way of enacting their role as spiritual guardians of their family and protectors of their loved ones.

Rabbi David Shofet from Nessah Synagogue, an Iranian synagogue in Beverly Hills, was born into a family of twelve generations of rabbis. His father, Rabbi Hacham Yedidia Shofet, was a revered religious and political leader in Iran. Rabbi Shofet practices an Iranian style of Judaism, developed more than twenty-five hundred years ago, that balances elements of Conservative and Orthodox traditions.[19] He states that although Iranian

Jewish women in both Tehran and Hamadan received little education, and the economic status of Iranian Jews was bad, still the religious life of Iranian Jewish women was very rich.

Speaking about Iranian Jewish women under the Pahlavi monarchy, Rabbi Shofet stated, "They did not have a very close relationship with the practical aspect of religion. Judaism to them is not only a belief but it is exemplified through a series of actions and *mitzvoth*. Most of these *mitzvoth* are related to the home. Keeping Shabbat was primary for the women;[20] 90 to 95 percent of the homes kept Shabbat."[21]

Shabbat

Lighting the Shabbat candles is the quintessential ritual required of Jewish women. According to Jewish sources, women are commanded to light candles on the eve of Shabbat because women must amend for Eve having "put out the light of the world." Elaborate Jewish texts describe the time and manner in which the candles must be lit. According to the law, two candles must be lit in each household, and the woman who lights the candle must recite a formal Hebrew blessing ("Blessed art Thou, Lord our God, King of the universe, who has commanded us to kindle the Sabbath lights").[22]

A majority of women said that Shabbat is the most important holiday celebrated in the home. As young girls, they said their Thursday and Friday mornings were spent helping their mothers and, later, their mothers-in-law with cooking, cleaning, and lighting the candles. It was a labor-intensive process, yet they saw it as an act of consecrating the home. Homa, a ninety-year-old woman from Hamadan, described Shabbat in her home: "Our whole family got together and ate the food that my mom and all the ladies in the house prepared the day before. We lit the Shabbat candles; we didn't work on Shabbat. We always had a Muslim housekeeper, so we never had to touch fire or even the *samovar*[23]—the housekeepers did it for us."

She took great pride in mentioning that her family would not touch fire or even the *samovar* during Shabbat, thus emphasizing that her family followed Jewish *halakhah*; however, she was unaware that, under Jewish law, even her Muslim housekeeper should not use electricity on Shabbat in their Jewish home. Jewish law states explicitly as a general principle that one may not ask a non-Jew to do anything on the Sabbath that Jews themselves may not do.[24]

In The *"Shabbes Goy,"* Jacob Katz discusses contemporary *halakhic* literature in regard to observant Jews hiring non-Jews on the Sabbath. According to the rabbis, it is only permissible to have a non-Jew work for a Jew on the Sabbath if great loss or damage might be incurred by their business if it were to close on the Sabbath.[25] Thus, *halakhah* does not permit servants to work on the Sabbath in a Jewish home. Yet the women interviewed were not aware of this and still believed they were following the law. This demonstrates how little women knew of *halakhah*. Instead, they followed traditions that were passed on to them by their mothers and grandmothers.

Many of the women lit candles yet did not recite the Jewish prayer over them because they did not know the official blessing. Thus, they would say their own blessing. If they were praying for the health of a loved one or remembering the passing of a loved one, they lit more candles, one for each person, and again they supplied their own blessings.

Most of the women interviewed said that they did not know any official holiday prayers, but whatever little they had learned was from their fathers or husbands. Thus, it was the fathers, grandfathers, and husbands who taught their wives and children about the Torah and *halakhah*, mostly after coming home from synagogue. This knowledge was reinterpreted and personalized by the women of the household and then passed on to their daughters and granddaughters.

This is what Rabbi Shofet calls *Torah she-be'al-peh*, translated as "oral Torah." *Torah she-be'al peh* refers to the oral tradition of law, which was given concurrently with the *Torah she-be-ketav*, the written Torah. Rabbi Shofet said, "Every woman married with a certain amount of knowledge. It is an oral tradition of the Torah that was passed down to daughters; they learned from *Torah she-be'al-peh* what they can or cannot do. They [the daughters] were raised next to their mothers, they were raised next to their grandmothers and, thus, they learned from them; what ever they did, they followed and imitated. It is a kind of continuation of an oral and not written Torah."

As Moshe Shokeid wrote, "Flexibility of meaning and interpretation of symbols and norms seems to be an important feature of the ritual domain."[26] These women performed rituals that have been reinterpreted by their matriarchs and then passed on to them through an oral tradition. However, under the secularization policies of Mohammad Reza Shah (1941–1979), many of the ritual traditions were not passed on to the next generation. Chapter 3 discusses how these traditions were seen to be too religious and outdated by the next generation of Jewish women, who chose to assimilate into Persian society rather than maintain the religious rituals that they saw as being cumbersome.

Parvin, an eighty-year-old woman from Tehran, described her Shabbat dinners as being nonreligious. She believes her family was not religious because her father studied in Paris and her family was considered to be *roshan-fekr*, "enlightened, educated." When women use this word to describe their family, they are typically implying that their family was more Westernized and modern than were most traditional Middle Eastern families.

In their understanding, Westernization led to enlightenment, which they saw as being the opposite of religious. Parvin said her father never went to synagogue, that he was not concerned with religion, and that, thus, her mother never lit the Shabbat candles. Yet every Friday night, although they did not celebrate Shabbat, her mother still found time to make a time-consuming dinner with typical Iranian Jewish foods, such as *ghondi*, *ob-ghoosh*,[27] and certain stews. Thus, for her family, although they did not celebrate Shabbat by lighting the candles and saying the prayers over the bread and wine, they still upheld their Jewish identity through her mother's Jewish meals.

The anthropologist Mary Douglas wrote about the "pre-coded messages" carried by food and meals. Douglas sees in food a pattern of social relations being expressed. Sered, who has been influenced by Douglas, believes an individual forms his or her deepest attachment to tradition in the domestic sphere. It is primarily in the kitchen that the child internalizes his or her identity as belonging to a certain group with its particular history, beliefs, and customs.[28] Thus, for Parvin, although she grew up in a secular and *roshan-fekr* environment, her mother's Jewish meals on Shabbat trained her to identify herself with her Jewish culture.

Shabbat is the most sacred holiday in the Jewish community. Both men and women look at this time as being incredibly holy, yet this holiness, according to Sered, is manifested in different ways for the two sexes. For women, Shabbat means being with the family, preparing meals, and petitioning God while lighting the Shabbat candles. According to Sered, "cooking is the essence of the Sabbath and holidays."[29]

Significance of Food

Cooking traditional Shabbat foods was an important way for women to maintain their Jewish identity in the home. The Jewish Persian cuisine is complex, incorporating a blend of spices, fruits, nuts, and herbs. It took days for women to purchase, clean, cut, chop, and cook the stews, rice, and meat dishes; this activity made the profane act of cooking into a sacred activity. While the Iranian men distribute the food and sit at the head of the table, without the women, the Shabbat table with its ritual foods would not exist.

The preparation of food functions as an integral element of daily healthcare, and it also holds symbolic significance because it is seen as maintaining ethnic identity.[30] This argument is based on the fact that, due to Jewish dietary laws, food preparation can be understood as a religious ritual, and through food preparation one is preserving Jewish identity and tradition. Sered asserts that food preparation epitomizes women's interpersonal and familial approach to religion and allows women to fulfill *mitzvot* and be connected to the Jewish liturgical calendar and the Jewish symbol system.[31]

Not only was it important to make traditional Jewish meals on Shabbat and other holidays, but it was also important to maintain a kosher home. The laws of *kashrut*[32] are first discussed in the book of Leviticus; the actual instructions for implementing these laws appear in the Talmud[33] and the sixteenth-century Shulhan Arukh.[34] The rules of *kashrut* provide a way to make the profane act of eating into a sacred ritual act.

In *Cosmos and History*, Mircea Eliade argues that the archaic world knows nothing of "profane" activities; every act that has meaning participates in the sacred. Thus, every responsible activity in pursuit of a definite end is, for the archaic world, a ritual. However, Eliade states, since these activities have undergone a long process of desacralization and have, in modern societies, become profane, we group them separately.[35]

Eliade uses the example of the task of cooking and maintaining a kosher home as a way for women to commemorate their mythical past and honor the Mosaic covenant. Cooking and the laws of *kashrut* are a way for women to ensure the health of their loved ones and to pass on their Jewish ethnic identity while forming a relationship with God.

With regard to foods and herbs, Eliade believes that no food is precious in itself; it is the participation in and repetition of certain gestures and words that isolate it from the profane world and consecrate it.[36] Sered suggests that the "perception of 'holy' may not always necessarily *stand out* against the everyday world of experience—the holy may be totally embedded in the everyday world."[37] By keeping a kosher home, the mother of the house raises the menial task of food preparation to a level of sacrality. She brings the holy into her everyday world.

The separation of milk and meat is the most prominent distinguishing mark of the Jewish home; the family becomes directly involved, and through this separation, the kitchen receives its Jewish character. The laws concerning the consumption and cooking of milk and meat together are based on the one verse that is repeated three times in the Torah: "Thou shalt not seethe a kid in its mother's milk" (Exod. 23:19, 34:26; Deut. 14:21).[38] Many of the religious and nonreligious women said that as children, and later as wives, they bought only kosher meat for their home. They never mixed meat and dairy together.

Iranian Jewish women took the laws of *kashrut* very seriously. It is written in the Shulhan Arukh (88:10–11, 93:1) that meat may not be cooked in a pot used for dairy, and dairy foods may not be cooked in a pot used for meat. Thus, one should have separate dishes for milk and meat.[39] Only one of the women interviewed separated dishes for dairy and meat.[40] One woman stated, "*That* is too fanatical for us. No one in Iran used to separate their dishes; that is something Iranian Jews who have become Orthodox have learned from Ashkenazi Jews when they moved to Los Angeles. But we did keep a kosher house, and we never brought unkosher meat into our home." This Jewish law is just as important as keeping kosher; however, it seems that Iranian Jewish women have allowed tradition to dictate which *halakhic* laws to keep and which they regarded as being "too religious."

Keeping kosher was so important that Iranian Jews would never eat food from a Muslim, Christian, or member of the Baha'i faith. Although Muslims and Jews have very similar dietary restrictions and procedures for the slaughter of animals, even the most nonobservant women said they would not eat food given to them by a Muslim. Under the Pahlavi regime, many women said they did not experience anti-Semitism, yet as Shohreh, a seventy-three-year-old Tehrani woman said, "We still wouldn't go over to our Muslim neighbor's house and eat their food or drink tea with them. We were cordial with them, but at the end of the day, they thought our food was *najes*[41] and we definitely thought their food was impure, too. My father worked in the bazaar, and even though he had a lot of Muslim colleagues and friends, he still wouldn't even drink their tea."

Hamideh, a seventy-one-year-old Tehrani woman who had many Muslim friends in her youth, remembered that eating at her Muslim friend's home "was never an issue because people didn't socialize in that way. You wouldn't go over to your friend's house, anyway. We were good friends, but we never ate each other's food."

Another Hamadani woman recalled that even though she had many Muslim neighbors, "At that time, we didn't socialize too much with each other. If we ate their food, we would be in so much trouble. We didn't even want the oil of their food in our house."

Passover

Having a kosher home was incredibly important, especially during Passover (Aid-e-Nissan or "Holiday of Nissan"),[42] the most important annual holiday for women. More than any other holiday, Passover was the most labor intensive for women. According to Jewish law, it is necessary to remove forbidden grains from one's home in preparation for Passover (Exod. 12:15–20). However, Iranian women believed they had to renew the home completely. They started preparing for the holiday four to six weeks in advance. Many women stated that they would "clean the house from top to bottom." Everything was cleaned to make sure it was not *hames*[43] for Passover.

The Shulhan Arukh (451:4–5) states that one must make utensils kosher for Passover. Cooking utensils are made kosher by boiling, while those used for broiling over an open fire must be heated until they are red-hot or until they become so hot that a piece of paper would be singed if touched to the utensil.[44] The women took koshering the utensils very seriously. Sahar, a woman from Hamadan, explained that her mother taught her to: "clean everything for Passover. We started by repainting our house; we washed the carpets, and then all the sheets, pillows, and blankets. We changed all of our pillows, taking the feathers out and refeathering them. Every plate had to be new. My mother would get boiling hot water, put it over a fire, and immerse every plate and utensil. Even the stones that she used around the firewood had to be cleaned and koshered for Passover."

Sered wrote, "Jewish women have made a cult of Passover cleaning. Investing weeks creating an immaculate house is one of the most important measures of a pious woman."[45]

Beyond the cleaning of the house, Passover was labor-intensive also because "kosher for Passover" food did not exist; thus, the women would constantly reclean their food in order to make it suitable. Every spice had to be made kosher for the holiday. Farideh, an eighty-six-year-old Hamadanian woman, said:

> There was no kosher salt for Passover. We had to purchase blocks of salt, grind, and dry them. We had to do that for the salt, pepper, and zarchoobeh[46]—all these things, that was just the beginning. We then got the nuts for the charoset,[47] brought them into the house, removed all the dirt and leaves from them, and then cleaned them three or four times. Everything was like that. All we did for weeks was clean the house and constantly clean and grind food. It was too much to ask someone to do."

The women stated that the most difficult ritual task during Passover was cleaning the rice, an integral part of Iranian meals. Although Ashkenazi Jews include rice among forbidden grains on Passover, Middle Eastern Jews do not. The women described the process of thoroughly checking each grain in order to make sure nothing dirty was in it. Some women said they went through the rice numerous times in order to ensure there were no rocks, stones, or dirt. These women believed that this was their way of doing something pleasing in the eyes of God. They did not attend synagogue, so while their husbands were praying to God, they cleaned as a way of showing devotion.

The holiday of Passover occurs during the same month as Nowruz, the Persian New Year. Many Jewish women expressed their frustration about watching Muslim women beautify themselves in preparation for Nowruz while they would be, as one woman put it, "slaving away." She said, "Do you know how unfair it was, how frustrating it was to watch Muslim women come and go as they please and make themselves beautiful for Nowruz while our hands were dry and chapped from washing and cleaning, while our backs were permanently bent from bending over and cleaning the floors and the clothes? When I look back at my life then, I don't know how I did it. I don't know how my mother and grandmother did it." Yet she was not resentful. She explained, "It was my duty as a wife and mother to do this, and I didn't think about it. That is what a good Jewish wife does; this was our duty for our family, and this is my duty to God."

Even though many women complained about their Passover duties, many said they liked doing the cleaning; they enjoyed seeing their home clean. Further, Soraya, explained, "This is what was expected of a Jewish woman; we didn't even question it." Although many women expressed how labor-intensive preparing for the holidays was, the act of cleaning, washing, and grinding had religious significance for these women.

When asked if they still perform that task today, they replied that they do not. Some say they would still if they had the energy, while others acknowledge and have accepted that Jewish law does not require going to such extremes in preparing your home for Passover. A majority of the women now attend synagogue on the first two days; because they are able to worship in a traditionally male way, they do not feel that they must show their religiosity through the domestic sphere. Synagogue attendance has replaced domestic tasks. Sered wrote that widowhood and old age have forced "the women out of the domestic sphere into the public sphere for the performance of certain religious rituals."[48] Now that they live in Los Angeles, the women have a more lax approach to preparing their home for Passover, yet a thorough cleaning job is still expected and has remained a woman's duty in the home.

This decline in domestic rituals among Los Angeles Iranian Jews reveals the changing attitude of women, especially now that they attend synagogue. Neither their daughters nor their granddaughters go to such extremes during Passover. As Nahid, a fifty-five-year-old Tehrani woman, reveals, "I don't need to prove my religiosity to God by killing myself in the home like my mother did. And I don't need to show my husband that I'm a good Jewish wife by exaggerating the cleaning during Passover. I would rather be at synagogue with my family than on my hands and knees scrubbing the floor, making it kosher for Passover."

For the second and third generations of Iranian women, there is a similar decline in domestic rituals. Many of these women have a better Jewish education than did their mothers and grandmothers and, therefore, know what is required of them according to Jewish law. Furthermore, the traits that a Jewish wife must possess have changed. For the first generation, in order to be considered a proper wife, a woman had to devote herself to her family and to the domestic sphere. For the second and third generations of women, the domestic sphere has been replaced with the social sphere. Religious rituals have been replaced with the social obligations in which women must participate within the Persian Jewish community. Although the duties of a wife and mother are still important, what makes a good Jewish wife are not the religious rituals she performs in the house but, instead, the many social rituals to which she must attend.

For the first generation of women, Passover not only held religious significance, but in a traditional Shi'i society where Jews were considered to be *najes*[49] by Muslims, it was a way for Jewish women to display their cleanliness to their Muslim neighbors. The Shi'i Muslim tradition considered Jews as unclean and polluted like dogs, pigs, urine, and feces. Contact with Jews was shunned because the mere touch of a Jew would make a Muslim ritually impure.[50] Thus, many women said they felt it was important personally, and for their grandmothers and mothers, to prove their own purity; preparing for Passover and other Jewish holidays was a way to distinguish themselves from the Muslim community. Farideh, a seventy-eight year old from Tehran, said that the Passover was important because, "It was also the Persian New Year and all the Muslims would be getting ready for the New Year and clean everything, and the Jews wanted to do something to show that they are not below Muslims, that they are not *najes*, and that their homes are cleaner and more pure than theirs."

Rosh Hashanah and Yom Kippur

Due to the household work that women do, very few of them attend synagogue during Shabbat or any other holiday except Rosh Hashanah[51] and Yom Kippur.[52] Most of the women said that as children they had stayed at home with their mothers in order to help them and their grandmothers to prepare for the holidays. Some said as children they attended synagogue weekly with their father while their mother stayed home to prepare for the meals. But a majority said that once they became mothers, they did not have time to attend synagogue except during Rosh Hashanah and Yom Kippur. According to Rabbi Shofet, "There were some ladies who went to Beit Knesset[53] every day. But look, if the mother has five kids, how can you ask her every morning to go to Beit Knesset? But most of the women who lived in the *mahaleh* of Tehran would go to synagogue every Saturday morning."

The women living in the *mahaleh* of Tehran tended to be more religiously observant than were those living outside the Jewish ghetto. Thus, where most women outside of the ghettos barely attended synagogue, those from the *mahaleh*, according to Rabbi Shofet, attended quite regularly. However, *halakhah* does not require women to attend synagogue. According to Rabbi Shofet, "Women are not obligated to pray. This is the system of *halakhah. Halakhah* does not ask women to perform the same religious practices as men. It is very obvious that a woman has different duties and functions; the most important is to keep the house and to prepare the kids. They didn't want to obligate her to put another burden on her shoulders."[54]

So why is it that every woman interviewed, from the most nonreligious to the most observant, expressed that the most important time or the only time they attended synagogue was on the High Holy Days? "Well," said Rosa, an eighty-seven-year-old woman from Tehran, "these were the most spiritually significant holidays because you are atoning for your sins and asking God to forgive you for them. My grandmother would go to synagogue all day; she would wear a white dress and a white veil. It was traditional for religious women like my grandmother to dress in all white." Even the most nonreligious women from the most *roshan-fekr* families would attend synagogue during these two holidays.

However, Rosh Hashanah and Yom Kippur not only held religious significance for Iranian Jews but also held social significance. This was the time when mothers of young men and women were involved with matchmaking. During the nineteenth and early twentieth centuries, parents arranged the marriages of their children. A young man's mother initiated the marriage by visiting the family of the available daughter. After the girl had been selected, the mother went to the *hammam* (public bath), when she knew the girl would be there. That was the mother's opportunity to see whether the girl had any deformities or skin diseases that would indicate poor health.[55] However, by the midtwentieth century, women were no longer using the *hammams* as a way of viewing potential daughters-in-law. Instead, during the High Holy Days, mothers had the important task of matchmaking for their young sons and daughters. This is a time when everyone, from the wealthiest to the poorest, from the most nonreligious to the most observant, attended synagogue with their children; it was an opportune time to show off daughters and send the word out about sons.

Nahid, a seventy-year-old woman from Hamadan, explains what it was like to go to synagogue and meet a potential suitor:

> As a child I used to hate going to synagogue during *Yom Kippur*. It would be so crowded and hot. All the women would have to sit in a smaller area up in the balcony, and no one had the patience to deal with us children. They would always tell us to go away or be quiet. But once I got older and in my teens, all the girls would

look forward to going to synagogue on Yom Kippur because it was the only time to see boys our age or older. Our mothers would parade us around, and if a woman was interested, she would come up to my mother and ask for our family's last name and my mother's permission for her son to meet me. This was a time to show off your kids and, as a mother, take the role of matchmaking very seriously.

In Persian, this act is called *chastegaree*;[56] this is when the mother of a boy approaches the mother of a girl and inquires about their family. If the mother approves of what she hears, she will then ask the girl's mother if her son has permission to be a suitor for her daughter. If the mother agrees, the young couple will go on numerous chaperoned dates in order to decide whether they are a suitable match. A sixty-five-year-old Hamadani woman said: "During my mother's generation, they had arranged marriages, so the groom would show up one day, and they would meet each other for the first time at their wedding. During my generation, we had *chastegars*.[57] Although we had a bit of a say in the situation, it was still up to our families to approve of the relationship."

Thus, the holidays of Rosh Hashanah and Yom Kippur not only held spiritual significance, but they also provided an opportunity for young girls to show themselves to their community and see boys, while it also gave their mothers an opportunity to find suitable spouses for their children. Farideh Golden recalls in her memoir, *Wedding Song: Memoirs of an Iranian Jewish Woman*, that during the holidays, many families scrambled to have their daughters sit closer to the main sanctuary (the men's section), either on the front row of the balcony or in the yard, to be seen by the young men inside. Still, she adds, it was the other women who were the judges. They viewed the new crop and passed the information to families with sons.[58] This tradition is still maintained today among the Persian community in Los Angeles.[59]

HUSBAND AND WIFE

What was the relationship between women and their husbands? According to Arlene Dallalfar, the traditional family culture in Iran is both patrilineal and patriarchal. The extended family is a significant social unit, and within the family, each individual's role is defined by his/her age and gender. The head of the household, the father, has the ultimate authority over his wife and children. The mother's role revolves around her social responsibilities to her extended family.[60] She must take care of her husband and children, and she must look after her own parents and siblings, while also maintaining a strong alliance with her in-laws. In the early twentieth century, Iranian Jewish women married at a very young age, either when they reached puberty or by the age of fifteen or sixteen.

A majority of the women had arranged marriages; many discussed how overwhelmed they felt by being a bride at such a young age. Most of the women said they had grown to love their husbands, but as one eighty-one-year-old Tehrani woman said, "We really didn't know our husbands. Basically, we married the man our parents thought would give us the best life, the man who came from a family with a good reputation. There was no such thing as dating or finding your soul mate. Besides, what did we know about soul mates? We were so young when we got married; I was sixteen, what did I know about who would be the right man for me for the rest of my life?"

The attitudes of the women in this study depended on the fate of their husbands. If they have or had a good husband, they spoke of marriage with utter delight. If their husband caused a lot of hardship for them, they would not speak ill of him in order to maintain respect for him; however, they discussed how difficult marriage is for the woman of the family. Many of these women's husbands who were at least ten to twenty years older than their wives have passed away. These women, when they spoke of their husbands, used the Persian word *shoma* (a polite form of "you") when referring to them. It connotes respect; thus, it is the way younger generations address their elders. It also connotes a sense of formality, the way a shopkeeper would address a client.

The women felt that because of the age difference, they had to show respect to their husbands, who were seen at times as more like father figures than spouses. The women said that it would have been disrespectful to address their husbands in an informal way. "You have to understand," said Jillah, a seventy-nine-year-old Tehrani woman, "I was so much younger than my husband [they were fifteen years apart], and I got married at such a young age. He was more of a paternal figure for me than a spouse. I was his wife; thus my duties revolved around the home and making sure I maintained a Jewish home. He was the husband; he went to work all day and provided for us."

Jillah left school by sixth grade. She said: "My husband was responsible for teaching me a lot. I didn't have time to go to the synagogue, so when my husband would go and make *aliyah*, (be called to the Torah in the synagogue), he would come home and say that every prayer he said was for me, that he prayed on my behalf. My children learned about Judaism through my husband. After he would come back from the synagogue, we would all sit together and learn about Judaism, the Torah, and our Jewish identity."

Influence of the Matriarchs

Through their husbands, these women learned about the Torah and other literary aspects of Judaism. However, through their mothers and grandmothers, they learned about ritual. Along with teaching their daughters how to cook Jewish foods, keep kosher, and clean the house in a way appropriate for Jewish rituals, mothers also taught their daughters how to pray. Manijeh, a sixty-nine year old, said, "I didn't need to go to synagogue to show my love to Him. I regularly pray on my own and speak to God on my own daily; I don't have to be a part of a synagogue to have that relationship with God." When asked how she had learned to pray, she said: "I learned how to pray to God from my mother. She would pray twenty-four hours a day. From the second she got up to when she went to sleep, she was always praying. I am like that." However, the prayers are not the traditional prayers from the *siddur* (Jewish prayer book) but instead prayers women utter during their own personal dialogue with God. When asked what they pray for, all of the women responded with the same answers: they pray for the health, safety, and happiness of their family members.

Niddah

Mothers also taught their daughters the rules of *niddah*, a state of marital separation when a woman is menstruating. By extension, a woman is said to be a *niddah* when she is in this state.[61] A woman's menstrual period is regarded as lasting a minimum of five days. After these five days, the woman counts seven "clean days" and then immerses herself in a *mikveh* (ritual bath). During the days of menstruation and the seven "clean days," it is proper for a husband and wife to sleep in separate beds.[62] All of the women said they did not have intercourse with their husbands when they were menstruating. Most would sleep in separate beds or even in different rooms. Some women not only separated from their husbands during this time, but many said that their mothers-in-law (with whom they were living) would not allow them to cook dinner because they were in an impure state. However, there are no Jewish laws that forbid a woman to touch silverware or food because she is menstruating.

Birth also renders a woman *niddah*. Before she may go to the *mikveh* for her required immersion, a mother must wait a minimum of seven days for a male child and fourteen days for a female child.[63] Many of the women in this study said they refrained from coming out of their birthing rooms for a lot longer than what is *halakhically*[64] prescribed. They considered themselves *niddah* for a month if they gave birth to a boy and almost forty days if they had a girl. Again, this demonstrates how little women knew of the actual

Jewish rules and instead followed traditional customs that many times had no textual standing.

Only the women from the *mahaleh* of Tehran would then immerse themselves in the *mikveh* of the *mahaleh* after they were finished menstruating. However, the Hamadani women did not even know a *mikveh* existed. "That," said one Hamadani woman, "was something we learned about from the Ashkenazim when we moved to Los Angeles." She would go to the *hammams* (public baths) after she finished menstruating.

According to Jewish law, *hammams* cannot take the place of a *mikveh*.[65] However, Iranian Jewish women were barely aware of Jewish law. They practiced Jewish rituals in the same way that their mothers and grandmothers had learned or reinterpreted them. Thus, very few women were aware of having to wait seven days before purifying themselves. Some entered the *mikveh* or *hammam* right after they had finished menstruating, or they made up how many days they would wait before their purifying bath. Many, especially those from Hamadan, did not know that they were to immerse themselves in a specific body of water (*mikveh*) and, instead, believed that taking a shower was a legitimate way of purifying themselves. This demonstrates that women did not have knowledge of *halakhah*, yet they still practiced the laws of *niddah* as taught to them by prior generations.

Although Iranian Jewish women were ignorant of the Jewish laws, they gained literacy through the teaching of their mothers and grandmothers. Thus, they might not have practiced the rules of *niddah* correctly, but what mattered to them was that they actually did practice it.

The lack of knowledge in regard to *halakhah* has led many women to believe that many of the social customs they would practice are embedded in religious law. One woman referred to this as "blind faith," saying, "Women didn't have knowledge of what they were doing; they just did it because their mothers and grandmothers did it. They didn't know why they were doing certain rituals due to religious reasons or social reasons; they didn't know the meaning behind *tefillah*,[66] or Jewish laws. If they did, it would be better. They just acted out everything with blind faith."

Significance of Virginity

When women got married, they had to prove their virginity to their mother-in-law by showing her a bloodstained sheet after the wedding night. This practice became mostly obsolete in Iran by the 1960s, yet the importance of virginity was, and still is, incredibly important. The women from the first generation said that they grew up believing that showing a bloodstained sheet was a religious custom that they must follow; that somewhere it was written in the Torah that this is something they must do. "What did we know," said an eighty-three-year-old Tehrani woman, "of what was really Jewish law or just a social practice? We didn't even question this; who would we even ask—the male rabbi? We were told Jewish girls have to be virgins when we marry, and proof of our virginity was just a part of this belief. We didn't dare question it, especially to our mothers-in-law."

The tradition of proving a woman's virginity was customary all over the Middle East. Raphael Patai wrote that when the bride and groom in Meshhed went to their bedroom the night of their wedding, some ten or twenty women from both families sat down in front of the closed door of the wedding chamber. The women had a popular tradition of ululating to prevent sounds from the wedding chamber from being heard outside. The next day, the women would show the bride's bloodstained sheet to all the guests and then the bride's parents kept it.[67] As in the Iranian Jewish community, it was customary in Tripoli for the Jewish bride's mother to remain in the groom's house the night of the wedding. She attempted to make sure that intercourse took place so that the groom would not falsely complain that he had not found the hymen. As a precaution, the bride's mother took her daughter's dress, spotted with the hymen's blood, as proof of her daughter's virginity.[68]

Relationships with Mothers-in-Law

Because most women lived with their in-laws when they got married, the relationship between a young bride and her mother-in-law was hierarchical. Each woman's relationship with her mother-in-law depended, as one Tehrani woman said, on whether her mother-in-law was a good woman or "if she was just evil and wanted to make the life of her daughter-in-law miserable." Jalleh, an eighty-two-year-old woman from Hamadan, explained that when she got married, "Everyone lived together and the daughter-in-law was brought into the house. The mother-in-law was the most important woman in the household, while the daughter-in-law was way below her."

Another Tehrani woman said, "You have to forget the customs and rituals that your mother taught you and appropriate those of your mother-in-law. For example, I did not come from a very religious family. When I was menstruating, my mother-in-law would not let me cook or clean the dishes because she thought I was impure. That was completely foreign to me. I also had to learn how to make Jewish foods her way, as opposed to the way my mother and grandmother taught me."

Divorce

Beyond the taboo associated with divorce, Jewish women did not opt for a divorce because of economic factors. Leah R. Baer wrote that the wife was financially dependent upon her husband. It was not until 1966 that Iranian Jewish women were granted inheritance rights, and even then a son would inherit twice as much as a daughter.[69] Many women had very little education and no means to support themselves. Further, it was not socially acceptable for a woman to live on her own; if a woman did get a divorce, she would have to return to her father or brother's home and, most often, take the role of a housekeeper who worked under the supervision of her sister-in-law. Baer wrote that due to family honor, prestige, and social embarrassment, divorces were extremely rare for women in Iran. When marital problems arose, family members and a *mollah* (religious leader) counseled the couple.

One Tehrani woman explains the economic difficulties and stigma attached to Jewish women if they got a divorce:

> Two of our Muslims friends were divorced; I mean it was completely unthinkable on our part as Jews. We would never get a divorce, maybe because we stuck together or maybe for economic reasons, too. My cousin married into a family that was horrible to her. She left her mother-in-law's home and moved back to her father's home. When her father passed away, she realized she had to go to her brother's home and be a maid for her sister-in-law. She had no way of supporting herself, she knew no one would marry her because of the stigma attached to her, and she did not want to be below her brother's wife, so she went back to her husband. She realized being a maid for her sister-in-law was a lot worse than spending the rest of her life with her husband.

Although many women felt stuck in marriages they did not want to be in, the idea of living with their parents or siblings and taking on the role of a maid servant was less appealing to them.

The women expressed their beliefs that Muslim women had an easier time getting a divorce. One woman said: "Muslim women had more autonomy over their money and their inheritance; thus they had more freedom. Jewish women did not have an alternative, so they stayed in awful marriages." The women also expressed that Muslim women had the opportunity to explore their femininity and sexuality. Jewish women, according to a Tehrani woman, "were brought up to be wives and mothers. We were not supposed to interact with boys or draw attention to ourselves. We were taught to fear men and to fear our sexuality. It was different with [Muslim women]. We were taught that we should only be with our husbands and be virgins when we got married. They didn't have the same rules to follow." Asked if she had ever spoken to a Muslim woman in regards to her virginity, she said no. Thus, her comments were not coming from her own personal experience and interaction with Muslim women, but instead, from her romanticized assumption of what life was like for them.

Najeeb

Maintaining one's virginity and being *najeeb* was an important trait for all Iranian women, no matter what religious background they came from. Arlene Dallalfar wrote that for Iranian women, family honor was directly linked to their virginity, modest behavior, and avoidance of contact with men, except those from their *khanevadeh* (family). In addition, the women mentioned that there were various forms of physical restrictions placed on their activities by the men in their families.[70]

The first- and second-generation women in this study believe they were brought up to fear men and to fear their bodies. Giti, an eighty-one-year-old Tehrani woman, describes how as a child, she and her cousins were taught to be ashamed of their bodies and have negative associations with sex and nudity. She said:

> I had one aunt who, when her granddaughter's skirt went up, said, "Make sure no ones sees your *abe*,"[71] meaning her body is bad, negative, or something she should be ashamed of, where our Muslim neighbor would refer to her daughter's private part as her *yas*[72]—a jasmine, a flower, something to cherish and of which to be proud. That was the difference between raising a Jewish girl and a Muslim girl in Iran. The Jewish child learns that her sex is something to be ashamed of, while a Muslim child compares her body to a flower. You will see yourself that Muslim girls are free and comfortable with themselves, while Jewish girls are supposed to be fearful and introverted, even in their own homes.

Numerous women expressed this sentiment, saying that Muslim women were more assertive and more inclined to beautify themselves, whereas Jewish women had to be unpretentious and modest, making the home and family the top priority. One woman said, "During Passover and the Iranian New Year, the difference between Jewish and Muslim women became very evident—Jewish women during Passover were running around with live chickens under their arms or worse, with a slaughtered chicken and blood flowing all over her. Meanwhile, a Muslim woman was getting her eyebrows and hair done, and her face threaded." Many women told me that just by looking at the way a woman would dance, one could tell if she was a Muslim or a Jew. "If you looked at somebody dancing," said one woman, "you can easily tell if it was a Muslim woman dancing or a Jewish woman because Jewish women were so intimidated, there was no flow or rhythm to their movement. But a Muslim girl, she was not intimidated. She knew how to move her hips and her hands and be incredibly seductive. They were taught to be seductive, and we were taught to be fearful."

Many of the women felt that Muslim women did not have the same social restrictions as Jewish women. They felt that a Jewish woman was raised to be nonsexual and plain. She was supposed to be altruistic, giving herself selflessly to her husband, children, and extended family. As an expression of altruism, a woman might have sacrificed her happiness by being in a nonloving marriage in order to save her family's reputation. A secular Muslim woman was seen as sexually confidant, and her needs took priority before her husband and children; she did not care about her family's reputation, nor did she possess maternal instincts.

The Muslim women about whom the Jewish women spoke do not concur with these views of themselves. Minou, a seventy-three-year-old Muslim woman who lives in Orange County with her daughter's family, asked if there is any validity to the description promulgated by Jewish women responded that there is not. "Look," she said, "I grew up in a *roshan-fekr* [enlightened] household, and my parents were not religious at all. However, I had the same social restrictions placed on me as Jewish women did. I did not go out with boys—I could not even speak to them. I had to marry the man my parents wanted me to marry, and divorce held the same stigma. My job as a wife and mother was just as important to me as it was for them."

Minou does admit that being a part of the religious majority afforded her more freedom in certain aspects. "The Muslim community is not as close as the Jewish community," said Minou. "Therefore, we didn't have to worry about people gossiping and speaking badly about us. At the end of the day, the amount of freedom you had depended on your parents and, I think, your financial income. The women who came from wealthy families had more freedom than women who did not. I grew up thinking wealthy girls and Armenian Christian girls had the most freedom."

Jewish women think that Muslim women had more freedom, while Muslim women think Armenian Christian women had more freedom. Since these religious groups rarely socialized with each other, it is evident that these women are living with a romanticized notion of what life must be like for women from different religious or socioeconomic backgrounds. All of the Iranian Jewish women interviewed said that even if they had Muslim friends, they did not socialize with them nor become too close to them. Thus, the chances of a Jewish woman knowing about the sexual and familial issues of Muslim women are slim. However, as Minou mentioned, because the Iranian Jewish community was so close and insular, a Jewish woman had to be more conscious of her behavior in order maintain the family's reputation.

TOMB PILGRIMAGE

Although Muslims and Jews had very little social interaction under the reign of Reza Shah, they had many parallel religious practices, including the ritual of pilgrimage (ziyarat). The most popular pilgrimage site for Iranian Jewish women was the tomb of Esther-Mordechai in Hamadan. The Jewish community believes that this is where Queen Esther and her uncle Mordechai were buried;[73] the original monument of Esther was probably built around the seventeenth century.[74] The most auspicious time to visit the tomb was in winter, during Purim. The pilgrim would also visit the tomb of the prophet Zekharia, near the bazaar, and conclude with a visit to the tomb of Habakkuk in nearby Tuserkan.[75] The women in this study said that women went to the Esther-Mordechai tomb and prayed for the health of their families. Because maintaining the family's well-being was a woman's task, more women visited the tomb than did men.[76]

Mahin, a Hamadani woman in her late eighties, describes her memories of attending the tomb as a young girl in the 1930s: "It was mostly women who would go there and pray; majles was also held there. Women would go and pray for things they wanted—their daughter to get pregnant; they would go and pray for the health of their family members. So they would go in, bow their head; they would say prayers for themselves, and after 1948, for the state of Israel. The prayers would mostly resemble the following: "Esther and Mordechai, you saved the Jews in their time of peril; please help me and save my family." They would then give money to the attendant and be on their way."

By visiting the Esther-Mordechai tomb, women were attempting to improve their lives or the lives of their loved ones. They brought the sacred into their mundane world; it became a reality that permeated their daily existence. Iranian Jewish women, like Muslim women, practice the concept of Namaz—the process of praying to God, embarking on a sacred pilgrimage, and making a monetary donation; in return for which, their prayers will be answered. Women visit the shrines and give money not only to commemorate an event or a person, but also to change their futures. Religious historian Jonathan Z. Smith asserts that rituals are performed in order to perfect an imperfect situation.[77] Thus, by visiting a saint's tomb, women enact their quest for power in the vast horizons of sacred space, untouched and unspoiled by human authority and its hierarchies.[78] Going to the Esther-Mordechai tomb not only heightens spirituality for Jewish women, but more importantly, gives women the right to ask the saints to intercede on behalf of their families. Thus, women domesticate the public realm and become specialists in spiritual guardianship.[79]

The women interviewed said they had made pilgrimages to the tomb to preserve the health of their families. However, many women reported that if they were praying for a specific cause, such as the health of a child or husband, they would not only go to the Esther-Mordechai tomb, but they would also sacrifice a goat or a chicken and donate the meat to charity. One woman said that she would pay someone to sacrifice a chicken or a goat for her when her children were sick, and she would also sacrifice an animal before Yom Kippur. When asked where this tradition originated, she replied, "It is written in the Torah to spill blood." Asked where, specifically, this is written, she said she did not know, but she knew it was a part of Jewish law to sacrifice animals to ward off "the evil eye." She is one of many women who practice superstitious rituals but do not distinguish between superstition and Jewish law.

The tomb was important not only because women could offer *namaz*, but it also served as an important gathering place for women from Hamadan and all over Iran. One Hamadani woman explained that fifty to sixty women might visit the small tomb to sing *tefillot*[80] and to listen to a woman teach about the lessons of Torah. Two or three women would sing from the Torah and tell Jewish stories. At that point, women could ask questions. After the Torah session, the women could do a group prayer for that person who was sick. When asked where the female Torah instructors learned how to read Hebrew and gained familiarity with the Torah, the women said that they learned this information from their husbands or fathers. This demonstrates that male family members had an important role in teaching women about the written words of Judaism, while women played an integral part in propagating the oral and ritual side of the tradition.

A Shi'i ritual that was appropriated by Jewish women in Iran was the wearing of a *chador*—a loose robe. For centuries under Muslim law, Jewish women had to wear headscarves. Many women said that it was incredibly difficult for their mothers and grandmothers to take off the scarves when Reza Shah banned them in 1936. Reza Shah's decree forbade women to appear on the streets in a *chador* and scarf. The shah ordered the police to remove these articles from any women who were wearing them.[81] As Tali, an eighty-five-year-old Tehrani woman, told me, "My grandmother felt naked without it. It was incredibly difficult for her to take it off. I never had to wear a *chador*, and most of the younger generations were so happy to take it off, but our grandmothers and mothers felt that it was a part of the Jewish tradition. They didn't know anything else." Because Jewish women were not familiar with *halakhah*, and wearing the *chador* was deeply embedded in their collective experience, many believed that it was required by Jewish rules about modesty.

Zoroastrian Influence

Not only did Shi'i Islam have an influence on Judaism, but the Zoroastrian religious tradition also greatly affected many rituals that Jewish women practiced in Iran. The two most evident Zoroastrian rituals that have been appropriated by Jews are celebrating Nowruz and lighting *esphan*.[82] *Nowruz* is the Iranian New Year, which is celebrated on the first day of spring, during the same time as Passover. In Persian households, a special cover is spread onto a carpet or on a table.

This ceremonial setting is called *sofreh-ye-haft-sinn* (also, *haftsin*). This literally is translated to "seven dishes," each one beginning with the Persian letter *sinn*. The symbolic dishes placed on the table consist of *sabze* (sprouts), *samanu* (creamy pudding), *sib* (apple), *sanjed* (dry fruit of the lotus tree), *seer* (garlic), *somaq* (sumac berries), and finally, *serkeh* (vinegar). Other elements and symbols are placed on the table. A book of tradition and wisdom is laid out: Muslims use the Qur'an; secular Muslims put out the poems of Hafez (Persian poet); and Iranian Jews place the Torah on the table. A few coins symbolize wealth, and a basket of painted eggs represents fertility. A Seville orange floating in a bowl of water represents the earth floating in space, and a goldfish in a bowl of water represents life. A flask of rose water represents cleansing power. Nearby is a brazier for burning *esphan*, which is a sacred herb whose smoldering fumes are said to ward off the evil eye (described below). There is a pot of flowering hyacinth. On either side, there is a mirror, which represents the image and reflection of creation, and two candelabra holding a flickering candle for each child in the family.[83]

While the more observant women said they did not celebrate Nowruz because it was not a Jewish holiday, many of the women in the study did celebrate the holiday, yet made it Jewish. They recall their mothers setting the *haftsin*[84] table, yet, instead of using a Qur'an, they placed the Torah on the table. They still celebrate Nowruz and do not feel that they are violating Judaism in any way. One seventy-three-year-old Tehrani woman said: "It is not as if we were worshiping another God or doing something that was against our religion. We are welcoming Spring and by placing the Torah on our table, we are saying, 'Yes, we are celebrating an Iranian holiday but emphasizing our Jewish identity.'"

Another ritual that everyone practiced in Iran was the lighting of *esphan*, the seeds of wild rue that women placed over fire, mainly the stove, said to keep the evil eye away from home and loved ones. When the *esphan* starts popping, the fire is turned down, and the honored person smells the scent of the herb. At that point, the mother or grandmother says a prayer asking God to repel the evil eye from that specific person or the family. She then stretches her hand out over the recipient's head, circling her hand over the head three times, and, finally, she taps the recipient on the shoulder three times. "As far as I can remember," said an eighty-one-year-old woman, "my mother and grandmother would light *esphan* to protect all of us in the home. I did it for my children, and I do it still for my grandchildren. If I go to a party, and my children or grandchildren are complimented and talked about, I light *esphan* when I get home because I don't know if that person is being sincere in her comments or is giving me the evil eye."

All of the women interviewed, from the most religious to the most secular, continue to do this ritual weekly. They stressed the importance of lighting *esphan* and believe that it is their duty as matriarch to be the guardian of the house. While the most observant women do not celebrate Nowruz, because they feel it is not a Jewish holiday, they still do not hesitate participating in a weekly ritual of repelling the evil eye, which has its roots in the Zoroastrian tradition. This shows the significance these women place on protecting their families from, in their view, the jealousy and negativity of others. These women truly see the ritual of lighting *esphan* as one of the most important duties of a mother or grandmother.

Women as Intercessors

The women see themselves as intercessors; they pray, perform rituals, and petition God in order to ask for protection for their loved ones and to ward off the evil eye. By observing Jewish holidays, keeping a kosher home, attending tombs of saints, and lighting *esphan*, women are ensuring that they gain favor in God's eyes, and in return, he will protect their families. Many of the interviewees believe that any negativity that has befallen family members, such as poor health or infertility, is due to some type of curse that was placed on their family due to jealousy or the evil eye. Thus, as spiritual guardians, it is their matriarchal duty to piously pray and observe religious and evil eye rituals in order to break that curse and find favor with God. One great-grandmother explained:

> My granddaughter had a hard time getting pregnant. I don't know why, none of the women in our family had a hard time having children, but she did. I think it was because someone put a curse on her. She is very beautiful and has a very handsome and successful husband. People were jealous. Every time she would go out, her mom and I would light *esphan* for her. I would go to Temple every Saturday and put my hands on the Torah and ask God to let her

get pregnant. I would give *tzedakah*[85] so that He would see I am pious and sincere in my request. After a year and a half of trying, she finally got pregnant. You see, God heard my prayers and broke the curse placed on her.

FROM THE SHAH TO LOS ANGELES

Many Iranian Muslim feminists criticized Mohammad Reza Shah and his regime for forcing women to embrace modernity, secularism, and Westernization. Parvin Paidar believes that the shah turned women into Western puppets and forced Westernization on them, at the expense of the indigenous culture. She argues that it was really the upper-class women who benefited from modernization in Iran and that the shah took up "the woman's question" as a way of manipulating and controlling the women's movement and its leaders. She argues that Iran, under the Pahlavi regime, was still very patriarchal.[86]

The women in this study had a very different opinion of the shah and his form of modernity. Every single woman spoke highly of the shah. They loved the fact that he modernized Iran and, most importantly, that he gave Jews freedom to flourish in Iranian society.

Under the shah, many Jews left the *mahalleh*, assimilated more into Iranian culture, and were able to practice their religion in a less anti-Semitic milieu. One woman referred to this as "the golden age of Iran" for the Jews. The Pahlavi regime changed the life of Jews. Parvin, a ninety-year-old Hamadani woman, described how life changed for her when Reza Shah came into power: "I was born under the Qajar dynasty; I was seven when Reza Shah came into power. Before he came, they would call Jews *najes*[87] or Juhud.[88] All the attitudes changed when the shah came into power. He let Jews get out of the *mahalehs*, allowed us to go to schools and get jobs and be represented in society more. He didn't allow the anti-Semitic *mullahs* to control the country. What was most important to us was that the shah helped Israel a lot. Most of Israel's oil came from Iran."

Not only was the shah's view of Jews and Israel important to these women, but his position in regard to women was heavily lauded as well. All the women interviewed felt that he had liberated Iranian society from misogynistic Islamic views toward women. While many Muslim women felt humiliated when the shah banned the *chador*, Jewish women embraced the Western clothes that he endorsed. Many took advantage of the educational and vocational opportunities. As one woman said: "I would never say that he was a feminist, but when you saw women becoming doctors and lawyers, it became obvious that he fought for women's equality." Another woman commented: "We know he was not perfect. He tried to enlighten everyone, but in a traditionally Muslim society, it was hard to change people's embedded beliefs. No, the shah did not make a woman equal to a man—even in America women are not treated equally with men. But he made a Muslim woman equal to a Jewish woman. He did take us out of our veils and into a more modern society."

While women had more opportunities under the Pahlavi regime, all the women agreed that secular Muslim women took better advantage of these opportunities than did Jewish women. As one Hamadani woman put it, "Not all the Jewish families were enlightened. Jewish men did not give their wives and daughters as much freedom. A lot of them believed that a woman's place was in the home; freedom wasn't given so easily to Jewish women from more traditional societies." While many of the women discussed how much freedom the shah gave them, in reality, not too many took advantage of the opportunities.

Thus, the fear propagated among Iranian Jews under the Pahlavi regime was not anti-Semitism, but instead, the fear that their children would assimilate too much. This fear was proven valid by the fact that Jewish life changed tremendously under the shah, and many Jews did not want their religious identity to hinder their assimilation. "People became less religious" said one woman, "because they didn't want others to know they are Jewish and look down on them or not give them a job. Names were changed, not specifically to Muslim names, but to Iranian names so you weren't immediately categorized under a specific religion."

All the women in this first generation discussed how fearful they were when the Jews began to become more integrated into Iranian society; their biggest fear was that their daughters would marry a Muslim man. Even women from the most secular families disapproved if their daughters intermarried. Many sent their children to Jewish schools because "there was too much freedom under the shah, and we didn't want our children intermixing too much with Muslims."

Beyond sending their daughters to Jewish schools, many of the women instilled values in them that they considered to be proper for a Jewish woman. These values consisted of being *najeeb*, nonsexual, and fearful of the outside world. Ironically, these are many of the traits that these women resented, yet still passed on to their own daughters. And shown in the following chapter, their daughters also resented these traits that they were forced to appropriate. The fear of assimilation and intermarriage was evident in many Jewish communities in the Middle East. Thus, although Iranian Jewish women welcomed the shah and his forceful implementation of modernity, many feared that that their children's Jewish identity would be lost under the new umbrella of secularism.

IRANIAN JEWISH SCHOOLS

Many women attended private Jewish elementary schools that were less concerned about teaching their students about Judaism and more concerned about teaching Iranian Jews to assimilate. The most popular school both in Tehran and Hamadan was the Alliance Israélite Universelle schools. One student of the Alliance school in Hamadan explained: "I went to the Alliance school in 1910. They had *mullahs* who would teach us Hebrew. They taught us French; the school left a great impression on the Jews of Hamadan. They really taught us how to be dignified and more up to date." Homa, an eighty-year-old woman who went to the Alliance school in Tehran, thought that the school was "very good": "From preschool on, we learned French. We had a book that would teach us the French alphabet, we read stories in French, and sang songs in French—we even performed plays in French. After that, they also taught us Hebrew and Persian, but I don't remember ever getting any religious instruction. They never taught us about religion. We just learned how to read and write Hebrew."

Rabbi Shofet explained that although the Alliance school educated and advanced the Jewish community of Iran, the people paid a price for it. "Alliance actually didn't emphasize the Jewish tradition. They did a good job preparing Jews to come out of the ghetto and to address their economic needs, but on the other hand, we paid a dear price because the Alliance schools didn't emphasize religion." As a result, the community as a whole became less religious. He states that the schools "knew about religion, they knew that on Shabbat one should not work. But they also knew that in Iran, one must work on Shabbat in order to have a successful business. They must be ready to work and not be so confined by Jewish law. The school taught that no one should say, 'I will sacrifice my work for my religion.'"

This new wave of secularism was also propagated under the regime of Mohammad Reza Shah. The men who attended the Alliance schools benefited more from the jobs available to them and were able to assimilate into Iranian culture, and as a result, they lost their religiosity. Because the husband dictated his family's level of religiosity, if he embraced the new secularism promoted by Jewish schools and the Pahlavi regime, his wife and children also had to embrace that ideology. The woman had to take on her husband's degree of religiosity.

The Alliance schools adopted a policy of enrolling non-Jews, in an attempt to facilitate the assimilation of Jews within the predominantly Muslim society. They hired Muslim teachers in an attempt to weaken certain social taboos, mainly to break down the segregation of Jews based on the notion that they are *najes*.[89] "For the first time," said one former Hamadani student who is now seventy-nine years old, "we had Muslim kids who wanted to be in our schools. We even had some Muslim teachers. The Muslim students didn't care that this was a Jewish school, because there was very little Judaism involved outside of learning how to read Hebrew. All the religious instruction we got was at home, not at school." Because the Alliance schools were known to have the best French education in Iran, up to 10 percent of the students enrolled were not Jewish. For the first time, Jewish children found themselves as equals with their Muslim neighbors.[90] This forced Jewish students to interact with Muslims in the school system.

IMMIGRATION TO LOS ANGELES

Immigrating to a secular country like America has only made the women more religiously observant: they light Shabbat candles weekly; they only eat kosher meat; and most observe all religious holidays. Further, synagogue attendance definitely increased for Iranian Jewish women when they moved to Los Angeles. Even though most of these women do not drive, attending synagogue for them is so important that many take the bus or walk long distances. Understanding neither the Hebrew prayers nor the sermons unless they attend Nessah Synagogue[91] does not deter them.

The most important reason to go to synagogue is to see the Torah come out of the ark. During this time, the women stand up, bow down, reach their hands toward the Torah, and then place their hands over their eyes as they silently move their lips and say their own prayers. One woman said, "I know I don't understand the prayers; and I know I don't understand Rabbi Wolpe's[92] sermon well—but it doesn't matter to me. The most important reason why I am there is to see the Torah and to be able to kiss it when it comes out of the ark." The act of saying a silent prayer is seen in the Bible. The book of Samuel mentions Hannah and her prayer to God to grant her a son: "She spoke in her heart; only her lips moved, but her voice could not be heard."[93] Just as Hannah presented herself before the Lord, silently praying for an offspring (Sam. 1:11) and pouring her soul before the Lord (Sam. 1:15), these women stand in front of the Holy Ark, silently praying, only lips moving, asking God to grant them their wishes.

Another woman goes to synagogue weekly because she is making up for lost time. She regrets not having been able to attend synagogue in Tehran because of her familial duties, but she said, "Now that my children are grown, and I don't have the same duties as a wife and a mother, I like to go every week and take that time to do what my husband had the privilege of doing while I was busy tending to the house."

These women do not have to work as hard as they used to in order to prepare for Jewish holidays. Physically, they can no longer work hard, and modernity has made life much easier. The elaborate home rituals they participated in are no longer a sufficient way to show religious devotion. Therefore, the religious domestic realm has been replaced with synagogue attendance as a way of showing religiosity. The month-long preparation for Passover is now replaced with actually attending synagogue during Passover.

For some, attending synagogue not only provides spiritual relief, but also provides social benefits. Most of the women are widows; many have said that going to synagogue each week gives them an opportunity to get out of the house and socialize with other women in the same life stage. In fact, sometimes the women socialize too much. In many synagogues with a large Iranian congregation, it is very common to see the older women sit together and socialize. At Sinai Temple and Nessah Synagogue, the older women generally talk throughout the service. But when the Torah comes out, they turn serious and focused in their own prayers and petitions to God.

The women in this study also take pride in their grandchildren who attend Jewish day schools and, thus, are very knowledgeable about Judaism. They believe that one of the many benefits of living in America is being able to send children to Jewish school. Many expressed their joy in attending their grandchildren's *bar* or *bat mitzvah* service and simply watching them recite the prayers over the wine, bread, and candles during Shabbat. These women gleamed over the fact that their granddaughters had *bat mitzvah* services and were just as knowledgeable in Judaism as were their grandsons. Fereshteh said: "I never had the chance to learn about Judaism, to read from the Torah, to be included in all aspects of Jewish life. Now my granddaughter has a *bat mitzvah*, and she gets to go up there and sing and read and get close to the Torah. This is only something we experienced once we came to America, and I am very grateful for it."

In fact, many women stressed how important it is for their granddaughters to take advantage of being able to read from the Torah, expressing their disapproval of the Orthodox and Hasidic movements because they do not give women equality with men. Because of their desire to have their grandchildren brought up in an egalitarian synagogue, many choose to attend Conservative synagogues because they allow girls to have a *bat mitzvah* service in which they read from the Torah. It seems that most of the women liked the Conservative movement[94] because it took an intermediate position between the Reform[95] and the Orthodox movements.[96] Many said that Reform synagogues were too liberal for them: "What's the point," one said, "of being Jewish if you change so much of the Jewish rules?" On the other hand, they said the Orthodox movement "was too religious for them."

One woman who attends Rabbi Shofet's Orthodox Nessah Synagogue said, "I go to Nessah because it is Persian; it is easier for me to understand what is going on, I feel comfortable there, and I like Rab David [Shofet]. But my daughter and her children are members of Sinai Temple, and I prefer that they are there because I want my granddaughter to have the full *bat mitzvah* experience; I want her to read from the Torah, carry it, and be included in all the rituals that her brother participates in." Another woman passionately expressed the importance of raising her granddaughters in an egalitarian synagogue. She said: "Why shouldn't they [girls] read from the Torah. Why should they sit behind the men in a synagogue? Those were things practiced in Iran, and now that we are in a modern society, we need to embrace a new way of looking at Judaism. We didn't have any of these opportunities, and I don't want my granddaughter to miss out on it like we did. Is a woman not equal to a man before the eyes of God?"

Iranian Jewish women living in Los Angeles have not become more secular in a pluralistic environment; instead of abandoning their faith, they are taking advantage of the numerous movements found within American Jewry in order to allow themselves and their granddaughters a place within Judaism. Along with synagogue attendance, many of the women have spent their time volunteering for Jewish organizations, such as ORT,[97] Magbeet,[98] and Hadassah.[99] All of the ladies expressed the importance of being a part of an Iranian Jewish charity. Even the women who do not participate in these organizations have still attended many luncheons or events. For these women, it is important to support the state of Israel and give charity to Jewish people. These charity luncheons also serve as a social gathering, allowing the women to socialize outside the parameters of the home and synagogue.

Many women also attend *dorehs*, social gatherings. A *doreh* can refer to any type of get together; within the Jewish community in West Los Angeles, *dorehs* consist of weekly gatherings of couples attending each other's homes and women meeting once a week during the afternoon. Many of the women attend a weekly *doreh*, where they will meet one day out of the week, each time at a different woman's home. The *dorehs* consist of eight to thirty women; the hostess of that week will make an elaborate lunch, with many different salads, pastries, and teas. After the lunch, they then gather around the table and play cards, specifically the game "Rami."

The older women no longer have a *doreh* group because many can no longer physically attend them. However, most of the women under the age of seventy still maintain a weekly gathering. Seventy-seven-year-old Layl still meets with her *doreh* group. Instead of meeting at each other's homes and making lunch, however, the women now meet at a new restaurant each week. "One week," she said, "we'll go to Santa Monica and eat there by the beach. Another week we will go and see a new Iranian movie. We rarely go to each other's homes because we no longer have the energy to cook and entertain. It is easier now just to go out and see each other."

Though these women do not cook and clean the way they used to in Iran, they have replaced their busy lifestyles within the home with synagogue attendance and an elaborate social network of charity events, women's gatherings, and of course, taking care of their families. These women are still active both within and outside the home. Many still take the time to attend *dorehs*, make Shabbat dinner, attend synagogue on Saturday morning, and for those who are physically capable, attend numerous weddings and *bar* or *bat mitzvah* services and parties. Living in Los Angeles, they still stress the importance of maintaining traditional cultural values while advocating egalitarianism within Judaism.

The members of first generation of Iranian Jewish women have lived through the Constitutional Revolution, the Pahlavi dynasty, the Iranian Revolution, and reestablishing their lives in Los Angeles. From their childhood to their role now as grandmothers or great-grandmothers, their lives have been dedicated to their immediate family, their extended family, and to God. Every menial task was carried out as a religious pursuit; thus, the most secular activities became sacred through the manner in which they were performed. The women believe that their lives were centered on ensuring the health and safety of their loved ones while also using the domestic sphere to propagate their Jewish identity to their families. These women learned from their mothers and grandmothers that sacrality does not only come from the synagogue and from studying the sacred texts but, instead, can radiate from the domestic sphere. However, now that these women live in Los Angeles, synagogue attendance, and not the home and kitchen, is the way women choose to embrace God, thus making them advocates of egalitarian forms of worship.

The following chapter discusses why the religious rituals these women practiced were not passed on to their daughters, the second generation of women, who grew up under the secular regime of Mohammad Reza Shah. There is a decline in religious ritual, and emphasis is placed on social rituals and acculturating into the dominant secular Iranian culture. There is a new definition of what constitutes a proper Jewish woman; in many ways, she still has to follow the same rules as her mother. She has to be *najeeb* when she gets married and dedicates her life to her husband, children, and extended family. However, there are social pressures, which are now added on to her role as a Jewish wife, and, thus, she must strive to find the balance between her Jewish and secular worlds.

THREE

ALL THE SHAH'S WOMEN

A middle-aged Iranian Jewish woman is gracefully socializing and greeting the seven hundred guests at her daughter's wedding. She has spent the past year preparing for this event, while also planning the numerous parties that are thrown for the couple before the wedding. She has carefully picked every guest who is in attendance. They are from her immediate family, in-laws, distant relatives, business associates, close friends, and people she must invite in order to maintain her hierarchical position within the community. She hires the best Iranian band and kosher caterer and has her dress made by a well-known Iranian seamstress. She has turned a bland wedding hall into a lush garden, with tens of thousands of dollars spent on decorative flowers. Not only is this wedding party a celebration of her daughter's marriage, but it also demonstrates the woman's wealth, hospitality, and social position in the Iranian Jewish community of Los Angeles.[1]

A majority of Iranian couples spend their weekends at events such as weddings, the numerous social functions that take place before weddings, and *bar* or *bat mitzvah* celebrations. The women in attendance dress in beautiful gowns and accessorize with expensive jewels, including the now-popular canary diamonds. The guests socialize with each other while dining on kabobs, rice, and sushi, which has become a popular food to serve at parties. The guests are likely to know each other's family histories—what town one's grandfather is from, whose brother married into what family, and whose business made a profit this year and whose went bankrupt. Weddings and other events are not merely social gatherings. There are social obligations and economic considerations involved in throwing and attending parties, and, thus, they serve a greater function within the community. They are a way for families to demonstrate their financial position—the bigger, more elegant, and more exotic a party, the wealthier a family is perceived to be. Social gatherings bring the community together. Members of the community have the obligation to throw a social event, to attend social events, and then to repay the host by throwing another event. It is a delicate balance among hosting, attending, and repaying. And it is the woman of the house who is responsible for maintaining and preserving this balance within the community. It is her obligation as an Iranian Jewish wife and mother to take care of her family—a responsibility that encompasses everything from housework to socializing with the right people. From her youth, she is raised to develop traits that make her a "good Jewish wife"—an ideal that many women embrace and yet simultaneously find overwhelming. What was life like for these Jewish women in a modernized Iran, and what is life like for them now in Los Angeles?

This chapter focuses on women born between 1948 and 1963, who grew up during the secularization period of the Mohammad Reza Shah (1941–1979) and then immigrated to Los Angeles, as they recall their lives under the Pahlavi regime and how their lives changed—and remained the same—after their emigration to the United States. What constitutes a "good Jewish woman," and what was life like for her growing up under the shah and now living in Los Angeles? How did women preserve their Jewish identity while appropriating the secular ideology of the shah, and how do they preserve and pass on their Iranian Jewish identity to their offspring while still appropriating certain aspects of the dominant Ashkenazi Jewish culture in Los Angeles?

This study includes forty women from Hamadan and Tehran who grew up under Mohammad Reza Shah and became wives and mothers under his regime. The women currently reside in Beverly Hills, West Los Angeles, and the San Fernando Valley. They come from different socioeconomic backgrounds and degrees of religious observance. Some of the women have professions outside of the home, but most are stay-at-home mothers and grandmothers. While the women are diverse in many ways, what unites them is the importance they place on their Jewish identity and their devotion to their families.

SECULAR WOMEN

Unlike the women described in chapter 2, the women who grew up under the shah and moved to Los Angeles did not prioritize religion or practice religious rituals. They were raised in an Iran that wanted to modernize and separate itself from its religious past, and these women wanted to embrace that modernization. They cherished and protected their Jewish heritage and identity but believed it should be separated from their public lives—they did not want their Jewish identity to separate them from other Iranians.

In his attempt to modernize and secularize Iran, Mohammad Reza Shah wanted religion to be a private affair and did not want it to define his citizens. He wanted Iranians to be nationalistic and show more allegiance to their country rather than to their religious institutions. The shah wanted to Westernize and secularize Iran and looked to the European countries as a paragon of what his country should be.[2] In his attempt to transform Iran, the shah tried to improve the position of women, yet he did not alter the existing balance of power between men and women. Iran was still a patriarchal society, and modernization failed to fully integrate women into the process of national development and bring about gender equality.[3] While some scholars are very critical of the shah's modernization attempts and believe his position on women was a halfhearted attempt to create equality between the sexes,[4] the majority of Iranian Jewish women interviewed had a very different opinion of the shah, his regime, and the life they led in Iran. These women appropriated the Westernized and secular lifestyle the shah propagated and did not practice any of the religious rituals that defined their mothers' generation. However, now that they live in a pluralistic society in America and are influenced by Ashkenazi Judaism, they have the means and the desire to learn and practice Jewish texts and rituals, which they have embraced wholeheartedly.

This chapter explores the identity and social structure of Iranian Jewish women with regard to four interrelated topics: the shah's modernization attempts, women's ritual practices, the influence of non-Jewish culture, and life in Los Angeles. The chapter discusses the idea of *najeeb* and what defines a "proper Jewish woman" and how those ideals have changed over time, and how, by upholding the Jewish community's expectations of women yet appropriating certain aspects of the dominant culture and ideology of their time, the women were able to maintain their Iranian Jewish identity and heritage when they lived in a secular Iran and are able to maintain it today in an Ashkenazi-dominated Los Angeles.

Modernization

The second generation of women raised under the reign of Mohammad Reza Shah (1941–1979) was heavily influenced by modernization, which was associated with Westernization. Paivin Paidar wrote that Western countries, particularly the United States, considered Iran an ally. Thus, there was an effort by the modernizing state to transform backward "Muslim" society into the image of the modern West.[5] Modernization theory held that the state was expected to introduce Western institutions in the Middle East, reversing "backwardness" and creating a Westernized society in that region. Modernity entailed the secularization of the state, industrialization, urbanization, the nuclearization of the family, education, and paid employment. Thus, secularism and modern institutions replaced traditional sources of identity, such as ethnicity and religion.[6]

Mohammad Reza Shah continued his father's policy of reform and development by focusing on the country's infrastructure. In 1961, he initiated a program of land reform, followed by a series of reforms focused on rural development, health, and education. These reforms, which he referred to as the White Revolution, had only limited success. During the next ten years, government propaganda portrayed revolutions as generally positive social phenomena. By 1973, oil prices had skyrocketed, and the government launched a new propaganda campaign. This campaign, the Great Civilization, promised Iranians that within a few years Iran would reach a level of industrialization equal to that of Japan, if not greater.[7]

The shah ignored his advisors' recommendations of slower growth and a more thoughtful spending policy that would take into account the country's limited resources and infrastructure. The Great Civilization campaign led to rampant inflation, high rates of urbanization, and extreme socioeconomic inequality. Class distinction and national identity became primary, with aristocratic, religious, and ethnic privileges being replaced with new measures of social status, such as educational level and influence in state agencies. A new class was formed of professionals, army officers, bureaucrats, and entrepreneurs.[8]

In his attempt to transform Iran from a dependent society to a modern independent nation state, Reza Shah Pahlavi gave women the vote in 1963. The state's policies on education and employment improved the position of women but did not affect the balance of power between men and women. The overall proportion of educated and employed women increased; by 1976, the rate of literacy among women was 35.7 percent, and 11.3 percent of urban women had entered the workforce. However, women's opportunities to enter higher education were much more limited than were men's. In 1976, only 30 percent of students in higher education were women. Women were encouraged by state policies to take up "feminine" professions and faced discrimination and lower pay if they attempted to enter traditionally male-dominated professions. Women were also absent from top decision-making jobs. Although Mohammad Reza Shah attempted to involve women more extensively in his modern state, he was not able to effectively bring about male–female equality, and modernization failed to fully integrate women into the process of national development.[9]

THE FAMILY

In the domain of the family, the shah changed many laws. The *Family Protection Law* of 1967 and 1975 curbed the excesses of male power in the family through the creation of a family protection court. Women had more of a say in regards to divorce, custody, and polygamy. The minimum age of marriage was raised to twenty for men and eighteen for women. Abortion was legalized in certain circumstances. However, Nahid Yeganeh argues that the improvements brought about by these reforms were limited. She believes that familial changes under the Pahlavi regime only scratched the surface of the problem of male-female inequality. The Family Protection Law continued to construct women as male property and concentrated on curbing excess male power in the family rather than fundamentally redistributing it. Yeganeh states that the Pahlavi gender policy did not aim to remove patriarchal relations, but merely modernize them.[10]

Few Jewish women were concerned that the shah's reforms did not fundamentally change gender relations. Custody matters were not an issue because very few Iranian Jewish women applied for divorces. Polygamy reforms did not affect them because polygamy was not a Jewish practice. Nor were abortion rights a concern because of the very strict enforcement of being *najeeb*. Other reforms that the shah implemented, such as increased education and employment opportunities and the shift to a secular-modernized state, made him incredibly popular among the Jewish community, especially among women.

HOW THE JEWS BENEFITED FROM MODERNIZATION

Between the end of the Second World War and the Khomeini revolution, the Iranian Jewish community went from being an oppressed and poor community to being an affluent and well-integrated one.[11] Upper-class Jews were a new phenomenon that developed in the 1960s as Jews benefited from the financial boom caused by the oil industry. Almost overnight, many Jews became prosperous, achieving prestigious positions and becoming an increasingly integral part of Iranian society.[12] A majority of the women of the second generation who came from affluent or *roshan-fekr* backgrounds discussed how their families appropriated the lifestyle the shah promoted— modern, secular, and European—and, thus, became less religious. However, although many affluent Jewish families became less religious, they still maintained their Jewish identity.

When describing Jewish practices and identity in Iran, Leah Baer, a Jewish sociologist, wrote that Iranian Jews did not have categories or labels such as Reform, Conservative, Orthodox, or Unaffiliated, all of which have been part of the American Jewish experience. They did not have the philosophies and "dos and don'ts" that certain movements impose upon their members, yet Iranian Jews in the past were at ease with the philosophy and practices of their religion. Their Jewishness was defined in terms of "who you are" rather than "what you do." Some families had to conceal their Jewishness, but they never denied it. They valued and protected their

Jewish heritage and identity. They taught their children that they were Jews, and even though many did not go to Jewish schools or attend the *knisa* (synagogue) on a regular basis, they still felt their Jewishness. Baer wrote that Jewish observance was learned in the home, with all the family closeness, warmth, and love that accompany such instruction.[13]

Delaram, a sixty-two-year-old Tehrani woman, grew up in what she described as a *roshan-fekr* family. Her father was an attorney, and her family socialized with many non-Jewish people. Delaram remembered that she was not aware of people's religion growing up. She said, "My parents were dedicated Jews, but they were not fanatical about Judaism. I didn't grow up in a religious household. We were Jewish and observed the Jewish holidays, and God forbid any one of us children would marry a non-Jew. We had a strong attachment to our Jewish identity but did not practice it strictly in the home."

Sima, a fifty-one-year-old Tehrani woman, recalled that when she was growing up

> everyone wanted to be Europeanized. Under the shah, my father's business became successful, and we lived in a neighborhood with upper-middle-class Jews, Muslims, and Armenian Christians. No one discussed religion anymore. You didn't want to identify yourself through your religious tradition. Instead, we took pride in being Iranians who had the luxury to travel to Europe and buy the newest designer clothes and go to private schools. Religion was not an issue anymore; only during the Revolution did it become an issue again. However, we always knew that no matter how much we assimilated, we are still Jews and will always be seen by Muslims as Jews.

The desire for upper-middle-class Jews to assimilate into the dominant nonreligious Iranian society is very similar to the way Western and Central European Jews felt in the nineteenth century. Jewish emancipation in Europe led many women to rethink both their religious roles and their religious status. Ellen Umansky wrote that by the nineteenth century, Jews participated in the economic, cultural, and political life of Western and Central Europe. Thus, the "medieval Jewish mindset," which embraced the notion that religion provided an all-encompassing framework for one's life, was shattered. Judaism was viewed as one of the many aspects of one's existence, and Jewish institutional and educational beliefs had to be adjusted in order to conform to the spirit of the modern age. Wealthy Jewish women were the first to take advantage of the opportunities that emancipation provided, enabling Jewish women to study, to move beyond the home, and to seek new means of self-expression.[14]

Similarly, the Pahlavi regime's attempt to modernize and secularize Iran allowed Jews to participate in most aspects of Iranian society, and many Jewish women wanted to embrace a more secular and Westernized community. However, there was a limit to how much the Jews appropriated Iranian culture. The assimilation of Jews into secular Iranian culture under Mohammad Reza Shah is comparable to the assimilation of Jews into German society during the nineteenth century.

When looking at German culture and the Jews, Jacob Katz wrote, "Jews have not assimilated into 'the German people,' but into a certain layer of it, the newly emerged middle class."[15] They were expected to conform to the standards of the German middle class through occupational restructuring, religious reform, and the adoption of German manners, language, and culture.[16] The Jews were not distributed across the whole range of middle-class professions and occupations; they married among themselves and remained exclusively bound to their own community.[17]

Like the German Jews of the nineteenth century, Iranian Jews under the Pahlavi regime were expected and encouraged to appropriate secular Muslim culture. Yet no matter how *roshan-fekr* and modernized they became, the Jews of Iran never truly assimilated into Iranian society. There were limits placed on how successful they could become in their professions, and, like German Jews, they remained exclusively bound to their own community and Jewish identity.

Thus, no matter how secular a family became, intermarriage was still a taboo subject. When asked whether her *roshan-fekr* family approved of intermarriage, Sima said, "Absolutely not. No matter what, no matter how secular we were, we still held on to our Jewish ethnicity, and I would never bring that stigma and embarrassment to my family." A majority of the women assimilated into the dominant secular Muslim/Westernized culture, yet they still said it was very important—to them and to their families—to marry a co-religionist. Naderah, a sixty-three-year-old Tehrani woman, explained, "There was always the worry of marrying a non-Jew in every Jewish family, especially because society intermingled more. But very few women did. It was as if your child died if they married a non-Jew. No matter how educated, nonreligious, and assimilated a family was, you still didn't marry a non-Jew. It was considered to be a curse on the family."

Assimilation

Attempting to assimilate into the secular Iranian culture was important for Jews; one way of showing one's assimilation was by having Muslim friends and acquaintances. For example, Giti, a fifty-three-year-old psychotherapist, said, "Everybody was proud of saying 'Oh, I have a lot of Muslim friends.'

Why? Because it meant that you were accepted into Iranian society. You had a sense of pride in having secular Muslim friends." The more religious Jews at this time tended to come from a lower socioeconomic background; therefore, by saying one had many Muslim friends, it was a way of connoting affluence. Having Muslim friends meant that one came from a secular and, thus, more modernized and *roshan-fekr* family.

Religion was stigmatized under the Pahlavi regime. "Anyone who was too religious," recalled Mehri, "was considered to be old-fashioned and of date." She explained: "It was not as if only the Jews became less religious, but Muslims and Christians did, too. There was a lot more freedom under the Pahlavi regime, and, thus, there was less religion. I feel that when Judaism was being attacked, like it was under our parents' and grandparents' generation, there was a sense of closeness and a desire to keep the faith in order to maintain strength and togetherness. But when you have more freedom and openness, society became a little bit looser and less strict."

Mahin, a successful writer and journalist, discussed life in Iran and why Jews became less observant, stating that by the 1950s and 1960s, her mother had ceased to observe many of the rituals she had observed when Mahin was a young child. For example, Mahin's mother did not spend a lot of time preparing and cleaning the house during Passover like she once had. Mahin remembers that by her late teens, her parents ate nonkosher meat in restaurants and did not observe Friday night Shabbat rituals. Asked why her mother had become less observant over time, she replied: "This was the trend of life in Iran. The whole country and population was embracing modernity and assimilation. People didn't want to be different from each other. Jews didn't want to be different from Muslims, and Muslims didn't want to be different than Christians. It was politically correct to be a more nationalistic Iranian than to identify with being solely a Jewish Iranian."

What did it mean to be a more "nationalistic Iranian"? According to the women, it meant that they took pride in the secular and modern Iran—the Iran that invoked the spirit of the non-Islamic ancient Persian Empire, the Iran that embraced European ideals and aesthetics. Many women discussed wanting to change their Jewish-sounding names in order to hide their Jewish identity. Mehrzad stated that as a teen, she paid money to have her identity card changed, so it no longer identified her as a Jew. She remembered:

> I was embarrassed to have it say on my identity card that I am the daughter of so-and-so, the Jew, who is now living in the Jewish quarter. I left my elementary French school and went to a co-ed French high school, and it was politically correct to not tell people you are Jewish—it was like hiding your identity. I went to the center

that issued ID cards myself and bribed them to take my Jewish identity out of my card. They put some stamp on that section, so you couldn't read it. The denial of identity was so strong at that time that even as a young girl, I paid money to change my identity.

Other women discussed naming their children non-Jewish Iranian names in order to help them assimilate more easily into modern Iranian culture. Some women made a conscious effort not give their children Jewish names, but others claimed they were just following the trend of their time and named their children popular names from the pre-Islamic Persian Empire. Why did Jewish women try to hide their Jewish identity, change their names, and give their children non-Jewish names? Mona, a fifty-one-year-old Hamadani woman, said, "I didn't want to be a second-class citizen. If people knew in your school or workplace that you are Jewish, they automatically treated you like a second-class citizen. In our homes we were Jewish, but in public we were Iranians."

Privatizing Religion

Being Jewish in the home but Iranian in public meant that these women valued and cherished their Judaism and practiced it to some degree in their homes, but in their public life at work or at school, they mostly wanted to be seen as just Iranians—not Jewish Iranians. Thus, their religiosity consisted of lighting the Shabbat candles on Friday night and having a traditional Shabbat meal. Many women said they would go out after they had Shabbat dinner with their families, meeting girlfriends at coffee shops or even going out to dance. Because they had to attend high school or college classes, few of the women attended synagogue on Saturday mornings. (Friday was the only day that Iranians had off.)

The rules of *kashrut* were kept in the home, but very few women observed them outside of the house. As Jews were enjoying their upward mobility, they were taking advantage of all the leisurely pursuits that became popular under Mohammed Reza Shah's reign, such as movie theaters, cabarets, discos, and restaurants. Therefore, while eating kosher meat was observed in the home, eating nonkosher meat at popular chelo-kabob[18] restaurants became very common. Merna, a fifty-seven-year-old Tehrani woman, explained: "My dad worked with a lot of non-Jews, and I remember my parents having to constantly entertain them and take them out to dinners. They would always take them to chelo-kabob restaurants. Of course they had to eat nonkosher meat outside of the house; there was no way they could wine and dine their clients and maintain the rules of *kashrut*. It would have definitely hindered my father's business. But inside our house, my mother was very strict in regards to only having kosher meat."

Many women also said that their fathers would take off from work on Saturdays and observe Shabbat by not working. But starting in the 1960s, said the women, their fathers began working on Saturdays and would transgress the rules of the Sabbath. Thus, according to Mahin, she and her family would "keep kosher in the house, light the Shabbat candles, say the prayers, eat traditional Jewish cuisine, but we would only go to synagogue on major holidays and eat unkosher food and had some non-Jewish friends. We thought we were so *farangi*."[19]

A fifty-nine-year-old woman born and raised in Tehran, said:

> Can you believe that in Iran we barely practiced the way we do here [in Los Angeles]? We were strictly kosher in the house but would go out to eat all the time. The only time I would go to synagogue was on Yom Kippur, but we observed that holiday very strictly, not even using electricity or touching fire. We would have Shabbat dinner, and that was about it. I think the most Jewish thing we did was associate with Jews, study at Jewish schools, and we would never consider marrying a non-Jew. But the reason why my parents sent me to Jewish day school (Ettefaqh) was not for religious reasons but for social and academic ones. It was a great school, and they did not want me to socialize with non-Jewish people, especially non-Jewish men!

Thus, for her and many of the Jewish women interviewed, religiosity consisted of maintaining a kosher home, celebrating the Sabbath together, and attending synagogue, mainly during Jewish holidays. All of the women agreed that the most important aspect of maintaining their Judaism was socializing with and marrying Jews, yet they were still able to successfully integrate into secular Iranian society. Thus, they took advantage of the economic mobility the shah allowed the Jews to achieve, while simultaneously maintaining an insular Jewish community.

Many women stated that although the shah tried to end discrimination against Jews, in reality, people still maintained anti-Semitic views. Some believed that the shah did not do enough within the written law to curb anti-Semitism. Many women told stories of their husbands being demoted in their jobs or not getting the jobs that they were qualified for because they were Jewish. Thus, for many women, changing their names or hiding their Jewish identity not only allowed them to assimilate more into Iranian society, but it also allowed them to avoid hostility in the workplace. Although hostilities toward the Jews never truly faded from the Iranian

Muslim psyche, the mood among most Iranians was a desire to leave behind their religious differences and support the shah in his attempt to modernize and Westernize Iran.

"The Great Civilization"

After 1963, the Pahlavi regime began to reconstruct the image of Iran as "the Great Civilization," invoking the non-Islamic ancient Persian Empire—an empire that would be prosperous and compatible with Western civilization.[20] The shah built glamorous holiday resorts, casinos, hotels, palaces, high-rise buildings, and stadiums. Iranian pop music and entertainment were promoted, and the mass media dominated people's lives. The traditional Iranian lifestyle was discouraged; the lifestyle of the royal family was presented as a paragon for ordinary people and imitated by the newly rising, luxury-seeking, and consumerist upper and middle classes. Thus, it became fashionable for well-to-do Iranians to shop at expensive Western stores and to take seasonal holidays in Western ski and beach resorts.[21] Middle- and upper-class Jews tried to emulate this Western lifestyle, and even Jews who came from a lower socioeconomic class and maintained an observant Jewish lifestyle supported the shah and his modernization attempts. A majority of Jews embraced all things European and believed that the Western lifestyle that the shah promoted was far superior to their traditional Iranian Jewish one.

Those who wanted to preserve the traditional Iranian lifestyle were the Islamists. They saw Westernized members of the urban upper-middle and middle classes as promoting imperialism, family disintegration, moral degeneration, and cultural erosion. Western women were seen as the embodiment of all social ills. The Muslim clergy and their supporters saw all upper-middle- and middle-class women who were unveiled, nontraditional, and progressive as being obsessed with Western fads and fashions and referred to them as "Westoxicated." Modern women were stereotyped as being frivolous and Westernized and were condemned as *fitna*,[22] the erotic agents of social and moral disorder.[23] Jewish women, on the other hand, were happy the clergy did not have a say in their lifestyle, and they embraced the non-Islamic Pahlavi regime. They loved that the shah modernized and Westernized Iran and attempted to purge it of its Islamic influence.

One way the shah tried to modernize Iran was through employment and land reform. In 1967, the shah outlined a full platform for reforming Iran, in which he would implement land reform to abolish the feudal landlord and peasant system and to improve employer–employee relations, to prevent the exploitation of labor and grant working men a share in the profits of their labor. He wanted to eliminate illiteracy in order to allow the common people to defend themselves, exercise their rights, and rid Iran of rural backwardness and establish equilibrium between the rural and urban centers of society. Finally, he wanted to establish the recognition of equal rights for women.[24]

Status of Women

With regards to the status of women, the shah made a speech on October 6, 1967, at the opening of the newly elected parliament, saying:

> One of the most important results of this program was the freeing of Iranian women from many unfair restrictions and granting of rights to them equal to men. We all know that until the amendment of the Electoral Law, the Iranian woman was treated in the same manner as the mentally unbalanced or financially insolvent, and was deprived of her right to vote or contest an election. This meant that nearly half the Iranian population had no say in its own affairs. Our revolution gave millions of Iranian women their human and natural rights; so much so that even in this gathering there are a number of women sent in by the nation to sit beside their brothers and discharge their national duties. At this point, it is not out of place to recall one of the most important laws passed by the outgoing House. That is the *Family Protection Law*, which, I hope, will play an effective role in stabilizing the family and provide our society with needed security.[25]

It seemed that the shah believed in equal rights for both men and women. However, he supported traditional gender roles and wanted Iranian women to uphold an image of domesticity. The shah tried to present his family as a paradigm of the modern, nuclear, nonreligious family, and many Iranian Jews looked to the Pahlavis as the ideal family unit. The shah, as the model Iranian man, was powerful, masculine, single-minded, moralistic, protective, and the head of his family. He believed in the participation of women in society, but he did not tolerate women "who tried to imitate men." He disliked the ideas of Western feminism and felt that Iranian women should not waste their time on such nonsense. He said he was not influenced by any woman in his life, and he respected women as long as they were beautiful, feminine, and moderately clever. Thus, he believed that a woman's natural role was primarily as a wife and mother, but if a woman needed to take up other roles, society should give her the opportunity to do so.[26]

In this regard, Mohammad Reza Shah was influenced by his father and other male voices that said there should be limits on women's progress in society. The traditional role of women in Iran is centered on the family structure. Male and female roles are organized in a hierarchy based on sex, age, and experience. A traditional Iranian woman's place is in the home. Because her role and activities are limited to familial and domestic spheres, she has no identity outside of the family. She is identified by her connections to her male kin—thus, her status comes from being a daughter, sister, wife, and mother.[27]

One progressive male voice that influenced Reza Shah was Ahmad Kasravi. He endorsed Reza Shah's policy of unveiling and educating women, but he expected women to receive special instruction in the domestic sphere. He believed that a woman's most important job was as a wife and mother, and he did not support women's inclusion in the workplace unless they were indigent or the nation was at war.[28] The general consensus in Iran was that women should work, but they should not take men's jobs. Most people believed that women should be encouraged to have families, and married women should return from their offices to tend to their domestic responsibilities. This was the shah's view toward women and the ideology the Jewish community appropriated from his regime.

Heideh, a journalist under the shah's regime, believed that the shah was very hypocritical in regards to women's rights. She said:

> He gave women the right to vote, and some family laws were passed during his regime that gave women the right to divorce and guardianship over the kids, and meanwhile, he came to the U.S. and gave an interview to Barbara Walters and others in which he proclaimed that women are second-class citizens. It was obvious that deep down he didn't believe in women. But for looking good internationally, he wanted people to know that he was very liberated and Westernized and that he believed in equal rights for women when, in fact, he did not. In my opinion, the shah loved Iran but hated the people. He wanted to have a big and powerful Iran, but he hated all the people who lived within the country. If he could, he would have been the king of France, so he tried to make Iran a dominant figure within the Middle East while trying to get the approval of the Western countries.

JEWISH WOMEN'S VIEW OF THE SHAH

While many criticized the shah for his luxurious lifestyle, a majority of the women interviewed admired the wealth and pageantry of the Pahlavi regime. In October 1971, the shah celebrated the twenty-fifth centenary (2,500 years) of the Persian monarchy in air-conditioned tents in the desert near Persepolis. The estimated cost of the party was $200 million. This was one of the most lavish displays of wealth in history. Food and artisans were flown in from France and Switzerland; dignitaries from around the world attended. The event became a symbol of decadence that many Iranians resented.[29] However, a majority of these women recalled watching the event on television and wishing they could be there. They were not concerned with the amount of money spent on the event and the social problems within the country. The Pahlavi regime portrayed an image of royalty and wealth, and Jewish women wanted to emulate that life.

Shahla, an author who was raised in Tehran, explained that in Tehran, "you had the just-out-of-the-ghetto/provinces Jew, who tended to be more religious. You also had your middle-class Jews and then your upper-class Jews. My family was a bit better off than the middle-class Jews and not so well off as the upper-class Jews." Shahla's father was half French and came from a fairly dysfunctional family. When asked why her mother's parents, who were more religious and traditional, allowed her mother to marry her father, she said, "Because he was a lot better off financially than my mother's family, and my father, because he was half French, had blond hair and green eyes. In Iran, people forgive a lot if you have money or looks." Thus, Shahla's family exemplifies the mentality of that time. Her maternal grandparents were willing to overlook her father's family's reputation and his nonreligious upbringing because they believed that his wealth and his half-European descent were more important.

Very few of the women interviewed were critical of the shah, and a majority expressed deep reverence for him and his family. They believed that he emancipated the Jews, allowed them to leave the *mahalehs,* and provided opportunities for them that had never been seen before in Iranian history. However, this majority also said they had felt deceived by the shah when the revolution occurred. Many women felt that they were living a "fairytale" life in Iran. Shahnaz explained:

> There was no political openness in Iran, so we didn't know that people were unhappy and not living the life we were living; the media never portrayed any of that. We were never allowed to know what was really going on in the country; they only showed the information they wanted to show. So as Jews, we never questioned anything. All the propaganda they were feeding us only supported our fairytale life. For us Jews, we were comfortable making money and not being attacked. That was all we cared about. We had no idea what was going on in the poorer parts of town; we didn't have any discussion with religious Muslims to see how they felt. This was a time in my life that I was just living in a cloud; I wasn't in

touch with reality. I thought everything was okay and easy. As a woman, I wasn't exposed to a lot of challenges.

Many women expressed the same sentiment as Shahnaz. They never expected the revolution to occur; they felt cheated by the regime they had so adamantly admired; they did not know that people were suffering under the shah, nor had they dealt with any challenges that would prepare them for the biggest challenge of their lives—uprooting their families and escaping to America. "The Great Civilization" was perceived differently by various categories of Iranians. The real experience of many urban Iranians consisted of a daily struggle against high inflation, a shortage of basic foods, a severe shortage of housing, and high urban and rural unemployment. The government's agricultural policies created a mass of rural unemployed migrant workers living in rapidly developed shantytowns on the margins of the cities. Most of the top jobs in the civil service and in government-controlled services, such as national radio and television, went to those connected with the court. The state bureaucracy, which had an extremely tight hierarchical structure, was steeped in corruption and bribery. Thus, the lower classes, who were dealing with state-run organizations, often felt frustrated and humiliated.[30]

Most people in Iran were unaware of the overall feeling of dissatisfaction and discontent because the Pahlavi regime used its means to control the press and the media. Beginning with Reza Shah, restrictions on freedom of the press become more severe than in any previous period in Iranian history. The Pahlavi regime could set in motion any idea and policy it desired. It could formulate any ideological stance, and the regime used the press to project its image and ideology to the Iranian public.[31] There were many magazines and newspapers that were influential in spreading the Pahlavi propaganda, while those that criticized the Pahlavi regime were censored.[32] Under Mohammad Reza Shah, there was even more censorship of the press and media. Many women expressed a lack of knowledge of the disparity of wealth and corruption that was occurring in the country.

Delaram, who received her master's degree from Tehran University, acknowledged the shah's political wrongdoings; however, she believed that she personally benefited from the time of the shah. She saw questions of his allegiance to feminism as being pointless, because even if he was not a true feminist, he still enabled women to pursue education and careers, and that is all that mattered to her. In addition, she added, even if he did not completely believe in women, "He put his wife in charge of raising his son, so it was a woman in charge of raising the future king of Iran. If he looked down on women that much, he could have easily found someone else to raise his son."

Not only was the shah admired, but also his wife, Queen Farah, became the paragon of the emancipated woman. She possessed everything the shah considered attractive in a woman: She was beautiful, feminine, and elegant. All of her clothing and jewelry came from top European designers. As a wife, she was devoted and subservient, and as a mother, she was altruistic and selfless. She believed her prime responsibility in life was to look after her husband and children, but her role as the queen required her to take on interests outside of the family. Thus, she left the serious business of the state in the hands of her husband and took up "feminine" pursuits such as social welfare, education, art, and culture.[33]

Many women admitted to liking Farah and wanting to emulate her style. Nahid called her the "Jackie O of our generation. Everyone wanted to copy her hairstyle, her clothes, and her jewelry. She did a lot for the country, especially within the promotion and preservation of Iranian art, architecture, and culture." Helen, less impressed with Farah, said: "She mostly used all of her power, money, and position for herself. She used to have a lot of campaigns showing everyone that she cared about poor kids and that she cared about architecture, preserving monuments, and all those things. But in reality, she was living for another world, the European world. She would do all these things to please the French people and other Westerners. She wanted to get their attention, to have her picture in European magazines. She only cared about her image in the outside Western world."

Helen, a journalist under the Pahlavi regime, had more insight and criticism of the shah and Queen Farah than did the rest of the women interviewed. Because of her job, she had many personal encounters with the Pahlavi family and formulated an unbiased, less romanticized opinion of the regime. However, for many of the women, their knowledge of the regime came from the public media, which was controlled by the Pahlavi family; therefore, they did not question the propaganda that permeated the country. In general, the women who had careers outside of the home had a less positive view of the shah. They were grateful that he gave them an opportunity to attend universities and have jobs, yet they also single-handedly experienced the sexism and hypocrisy of his regime. They did not believe the shah was as much of a liberating figure as many of the other women claimed.

"Very few Jewish women worked in Iran; at most they attended university and then got married and became housewives," said Simin, a former secretary at the U.S. Embassy. "So how do these women know how liberating the shah was? They didn't experience the limitations he put on women in their jobs. Yes, he gave us jobs, but he didn't give us equality." As with Jews in Iran, there were limits on how successful women could be in their professions. Most female high school and college graduates took up employment in the service sector, with an estimated 53 percent of women employed in urban centers working in the service sector as teachers, nurses, clerks, administrative assistants, and secretaries.

> Women had little opportunity to enter highly specialized and prestigious professions such as medicine and law. They also dealt with a lot of discrimination in the market and at work; they had to be more highly skilled than men to gain employment. They were inhibited by stereotyping at work and were given fewer opportunities for promotion because they were regarded as less knowledgeable, less serious, and less hardworking than men. The women who made significant progress at work were considered to be different from the average woman.[34] Women also dealt with sexual harassment in university and at work and were expected to earn promotions by flirting and bestowing sexual favors on their male superiors.[35]

A majority of the Jewish women interviewed did not work after high school or college. Most were married immediately after graduation and did not have careers outside of the home. These women said that Muslim women took advantage of the careers the shah offered, but it was considered improper for Jewish women to work, and they felt it emasculated their husbands. In response to the statement that women who worked were more critical of the shah, they said that the shah did the best he could do in a country steeped in a patriarchal culture. Nahid, a fifty-five-old Hamadani woman, said, "There was only so much the shah could do in a society that has been plagued by the Islamic male-dominating culture; thus, he was slowly changing the country. No, the shah didn't make a woman equal to a man, but at least he made all women—Jew, Christian, and Muslim—equal to each other."

Her sister Tali asked, "Was there equality for women in America in the 1960s and '70s? Didn't women in the West deal with the same type of problems? It was not only in Iran that professional women dealt with harassment, but all over the world women were and still are treated this way."

A majority of women interviewed have a romanticized and nostalgic view of their life growing up in Iran. Some even get very defensive of the shah, quickly defending him, his policies, and his family. Although they did not deal with the anti-Semitism and sexism of their mothers' generation, it still existed during Mohammed Reza Shah's time. Thus, the memories these women have chosen to preserve in their hearts and minds are adequately described by one woman when she said, "My life in Iran was a fairytale. I lived in a cloud. I had nothing to worry about." Yet deeper inquiries into these women's lives revealed that they were not living in a completely worry-free environment. Constantly having to hide their Jewish identity and abiding by the rules of *najeebness* could not have been easy, yet the collective memory of life under the shah is one of utter happiness.

Avishai Margalit wrote, "Shared memory can be an expression of *nostalgia*. Nostalgia is an important element of communal memory . . . An essential element of nostalgia is sentimentality. And the trouble with sentimentality in certain situations is that it distorts reality in a particular way that has moral consequences."[36] Margalit went on to discuss how shared memory is torn between two worldviews, critical history and myth. He wrote, "The two worldviews are committed to different ontologies, to different explanations, and to different notions of cause and effect."[37]

For many of those interviewed, their memories of Iran and the shah are filled with sentimental nostalgia for a world that many would say never really existed but was a myth created in their memories. Discussing widespread dissatisfaction with the shah's regime, many of the women expressed little criticism of the shah, and many spoke highly of him and his wife. Either they did not believe that he was solely responsible for his own downfall, or they were not concerned with how he treated the poorer classes, as long as the Jews were experiencing economic freedom and living in a less hostile environment. Sahar, a sixty-year-old Tehrani woman, responded: "For centuries, the Jews were treated poorly by the Iranian government; we were forced to live in *mahallehs*, had our rights taken away from us, and we had no choice but to live a lower-class life, and no one came to our rescue. No one cared about us outside of our own community. So why, when we were experiencing religious tolerance and economic mobility from the shah, would we speak out against him for a group of people who never spoke up for us?"

Many of the other women shared the same sentiments as Sahar, stating that as long as the shah's policies did not hurt the Jewish community or hinder their mobility into the upper-middle classes, they do not care about other people's criticisms of him.

RITUALS

Chapter 2 examined the place of religious rituals in the lives of women who were raised under the constitutional monarchy and became mothers and grandmothers under the Pahlavi regime. These women's ritual lives ensured the health and safety of their loved ones, propagated their Jewish identity to their families, and allowed them to form close relationships with God. They learned from their mothers and grandmothers that sacrality comes not only from the synagogue and from studying the sacred texts, but can radiate from the domestic sphere, as well. However, the rituals these women practiced, which had been passed down from their grandmothers to their mothers and finally to them, were not passed down to the second generation of women—those who were raised under the secular regime of Mohammad Reza Shah and are now raising their children and grandchildren in Los Angeles. A decline in ritual occurred, yet the women of the second generation have a strong sense of maintaining their Jewish identity and living up to the expectations required of them as Jewish women.

As mentioned earlier, the modernization and secularization policies of Mohammad Reza Shah propagated a less religious lifestyle, while allowing women to participate in the public sphere more freely. Mohammad Reza Shah's relationship with Israel was amicable. In 1960, he recognized Israel's right to exist and publicly declared that Israel and Iran should maintain economic ties. The Israeli national carrier, El-Al, had regularly scheduled flights to Tehran. Many Israelis helped implement and build various projects in Iran, and Iranian Jews traveled freely between both countries.[38] "This was a time," remembered Naderah, "that we felt comfortable being Jews in Iran. Of course, we didn't promote our religious affiliation, because as much as the shah tried to make people religiously equal, there was still a lot of hostility toward Jews. But we didn't experience the hostilities our parents and grandparents did with Muslims calling us najes[39] or Juhud.[40] It was really rare when they did."

One would expect that during this religiously open time, Jews would embrace their religion more; however, for a majority of Jews, assimilation took priority over religious practices. Many explained that while they were in their teens and early twenties, they saw their mothers become more lax toward domestic religious rituals. Merna said:

> As a child, my mother would not let us eat unkosher meat out of the house. We would light the Shabbat candles, and she was obsessed with cleaning before Passover. But slowly, as I grew older (in the 1960s), she became less devout with certain things. We ate kosher meat in the house, but it would be okay to now eat at chelo-kabob restaurants. During Passover, she was still obsessed with cleaning the house from top to bottom, but on Fridays, we would light the Shabbat candles, but that was all. Friday was our day off, and we had school the next day, so we treated it like a weekend. It became more of a time for our family to get together and less of a religiously focused night.

Asked if her mother's lax religious devotion had anything to do with their rising economic status, Merna admitted that as her father's business became more successful and they moved to a wealthier and more assimilated neighborhood, her family became less religious. Many of the women believed that the wealthier Jews tended to be the more assimilated and less religious. However, some women disagreed with this statement. According to Helen, "Families that were religious before the shah stayed religious no matter how wealthy they got, and families that did not stress religion in the home became more assimilated throughout the shah's reign." Among the women interviewed, those who came from more affluent families were not raised in religiously observant homes, and those who came from a religiously observant background tended to live in less assimilated and wealthy neighborhoods.

RELIGIOUS OBSERVANCE

A majority said that they did not light Shabbat candles when they lived in Iran; however, they did celebrate Shabbat by having a family dinner. They kept kosher in the house but would eat nonkosher meat in restaurants. The only times they would go to synagogue were during Rosh Hashanah and Yom Kippur. Most would celebrate Passover, but they would not clean the house to the degree that their mothers did. All the women interviewed said they would clean and rid the house of *hames*[41] foods, but none admitted to "torturing" themselves the way their mothers had during this holiday. Some said they celebrated Sukkot (Feast of Tabernacles) or Tu'B'Shvat (Jewish Arbor Day) with their families. Very few women made the pilgrimage to the Esther-Mordecai tomb, and the few who went were very young and could barely remember the visit. Finally, in regards to the rules of *niddah*, most of the women said they refrained from sexual contact with their husbands when they were menstruating; however, none attended a *mikveh* or slept in a separate bed.

Thus, the shah's secularization policies heavily affected the religious observance of these women. The attitude of a majority of Iranians Jews toward religion, specifically those from the upper to upper-middle class, was that it was antiquated and projected an image of someone who is not *roshan-fekr* and modernized. Women did not want to live a life like the matriarchs before them. They did not want to be associated with the images they were raised with of their mothers and grandmothers on their hands and knees scrubbing the floors and cleaning the house as a way of showing maternal devotion. They wanted to move away from the image of the woman in the *mahalleh* and participate in the exciting world the Pahlavi regime propagated—modern and European—where socializing, beautifying oneself, and assimilating into Iranian secular culture signified one's class and education level.

The women of the first generation did not pass down their domestic rituals to their daughters, yet they did pass down traits that they believed a "good Jewish woman" should possess in order to maintain her Jewish identity. A majority of the second-generation women told me that although they were not ritually observant, Judaism was still an important part of their lives. "I didn't grow up participating in Jewish rituals; very few people did under the shah's time," said Farnaz. "But from the day I was born, I knew that I am a Jewish woman, and I must possess traits that are required of a Jewish woman. My mother always told me that we are not like Muslim women; we have to be aware of our family's name and reputation."

NAJEEBNESS: SECOND GENERATION

Mothers taught their daughters from a young age that they must be *najeeb* (virginal and innocent). While many rituals were not passed down to daughters of this generation, the most important trait a woman should possess, especially in a time of assimilation with non-Jews, was her *najeebness*. According to the women, being *najeeb* not only meant maintaining one's virginity, but as Yaffa explained, "I couldn't date anyone until it was for marriage. I was not allowed to go to movies or parties. I couldn't even speak to boys. It was an extremely closed environment; I just socialized with my family; it was very private."

All the women—from those who grew up in religious families to those who came from secular and assimilated ones—said possessing *najeeb* qualities was one of the most important traits their mothers taught them. That was what defined a Jewish woman—how innocent and pure she was. Because under the assimilated Pahlavi regime there were fewer religious rituals being practiced, and Iranian Jewish women had more exposure and contact with non-Jews in the public sphere, *najeebness* was stressed as a way to maintain their Jewish identity, an identity that stressed moral and virginal behavior, and to hinder relationships between Jewish women and men, specifically non-Jewish men.

For the first generation of women, being *najeeb* was important because it was expected of women to maintain their virginity and innocence. However, this generation of women had very little interaction with the Muslim community; thus, *najeebness* was not used as a way to maintain a woman's Jewish identity. However, there is a transformation of the meaning of *najeeb* for the second generation of women, growing up under the shah's regime; it was now used as a way to maintain a woman's Jewish identity in an assimilated culture and to protect her and her family from rumors of immorality and negative gossip.

MARRIAGE

Another common characteristic of the Jewish community was the significance of marriage. Traditionally, Iranian women have had little say in regard to their betrothal or marriage. Even if a family has a daughter's interest at heart (in addition to other considerations such as status, wealth, and power), one cannot presume a correlation between her notion of a "desirable husband" and the choice made by her family.[42] The women in this study said that their families' preferences heavily influenced whom they married. They also said they were taught that the most important role in their lives was that of wife and mother. Many women said that having an education and a career was not emphasized, but getting married to a man from a reputable family was. "We were taught," said Shahlah, "that, yes, a lot of women are now working, but having a home and family should be a Jewish woman's priority. Being a career woman was not promoted, but being a wife was, and this was the tradition that was passed down from our mothers' generation to ours."

Desired Qualities of a Jewish Wife

The traits a Jewish wife should embody did not change across generations. Women had to be good cooks and maintain clean homes; they had to be selfless and devoted to both their own families and their husbands' families. Women said that, just like their mothers, they had to make everyone else— from their children to their husbands and in-laws—their top priority and put their own needs and wants last. Josephine recalled, "I was taught to be the keeper of the house, to keep the tradition of the home and family. As Jewish women, we were taught to maintain the family, to be the nurturers."

Several of the women voiced a sense of resentment about having been too altruistic and neglecting themselves too much. One fifty-year-old woman said: "My mother's generation had it really hard; they sacrificed all their happiness for everyone else. Everything they did in their life was to please others. And they passed that trait on to us, and there was a sense of guilt if we could not live up to being a 'super wife and mom.' I was always taught to put my own needs and aspirations aside for my family, or basically, that the only needs and aspirations I should have [are] for a family. Pursuing a higher degree or a career was not even an option."

Thus, under the secular regime of Mohammad Reza Shah, religion took a backseat to assimilation and modernization, yet Jewish women maintained their identity through their *najeebness* and later by being devout wives and mothers.

Education played a very important role in maintaining the Jewish identity, while at the same time helping second-generation women assimilate into Persian secular society. Early twentieth-century Iranian texts held that a woman was not capable of running her household well unless she acquired a certain amount of intellectual and cultural knowledge. Thus, many Iranian thinkers petitioned for the education of women because they felt that women who lacked education were not able to carry out their role in society and in the family.[43] The family was seen as the foundation of the country, and the mother was the foundation of the family. Thus, "her intellectual development or underdevelopment becomes the primary factor in determining the development or underdevelopment of the country."[44] The mother was no longer seen as just the vessel for the growth of the fetus, but her educating and nurturing roles became more important and began to overshadow her function as a womb.[45]

Mothering came to be defined as nurturing and educating.[46] Reza Shah and Mohammad Reza Shah regarded women as central to the future of the nation because of their role as biological reproducers, educators of children, transmitters of culture, and participants in national life.[47] Members of the Jewish community under Mohammad Reza Shah sent their daughters to the best schools they could afford. However, they maintained the same mentality as the liberal reformers of the early twentieth century, believing that a woman should receive an education in order to adequately fulfill her role as a mother and wife.

EDUCATION

Many of the Tehrani women went to Jewish elementary schools and high schools. Although these schools taught classes related to Judaism, they also promoted and prepared students for assimilation. One of the most popular Jewish schools was the Ettefaqh school. The Ettefaqh taught students from elementary to high school. The co-ed student body consisted of mainly upper-middle-class to upper-class Jews, and many non-Jewish students enrolled in the school due to its formidable educational reputation. The typical school day started with students attending tefillot[48] classes. After tefillot, students took both Hebrew and English-language courses, and then the usual school curriculum courses were offered. Muslim students took classes in Qur'anic studies and studied Arabic.

Many women who went to the Ettefaqh school said that the Jewish education was very liberal and lax, and they barely remembered anything from their studies. As one woman said, "People went to Ettefaqh because it was a bilingual school—not because it was a Jewish school. It was the most popular school to send your child; thus, it almost became a status thing. Plus, everyone around your daughter was Jewish, so it was a safe environment." Jewish parents also sent their daughters to the Kurosh[49] school, which was more religious than Ettefaqh. The Alliance school still existed at that time, located mainly in the outskirts of the city. The students who attended both Kurosh and Alliance schools came from a lower socioeconomic background and tended to be more religiously observant. By 1970, there were eighty different Jewish schools in Iran, yet they were not very successful in educating their students about Judaism.

Most students were unable to translate Hebrew words or texts, and many Hebrew teachers could not speak Hebrew correctly. Therefore, it was nearly impossible to hold classes in Hebrew, so lessons were conducted almost entirely in Persian. Most teachers had only a superficial knowledge of Jewish subjects.[50] As a result, the younger generation lacked a historic and religious knowledge of Judaism.

By 1970, as Jewish children got older, they received less Jewish education, both in quantity and in quality. Children in elementary school did not take their Jewish education seriously. Students did not treat their Judaic studies teachers with respect, and they were often disorderly, exhibiting behavior that they never practiced in front of their Muslim teachers.[51] There seemed to be a lack of seriousness and support for a Jewish education. Prospective rabbis abandoned teaching positions in Iran because of the lack of communal observance.[52] The Iranian-Jewish scholar Amnon Netzer describes Jewish youth as living desolate Jewish cultural lives. In 1973, Ezrah Spicehandler, the past director of Hebrew Union College in Jerusalem, asserted that Iranian Jews, specifically those from Tehran, had hardly any traces of authentic Judaism.[53] Many routinely drove to synagogue and dined in nonkosher restaurants. Even the synagogues were not practicing correct *halakhah*; as early as 1951, money was collected in the synagogue on Shabbat and other holidays for the needs of the synagogue and community. It was believed that the Jewish community in Iran did not receive a suitable modern Jewish education.[54]

Netzer accused the Jewish leadership of being too involved with the physical welfare of the community and neglecting to provide it spiritual guidance. He believed that when the Jewish community achieved some financial independence, the community leaders missed an opportunity to channel funds and energy into hiring good Jewish educators. Some believed that Iranian Jews needed a Persian-Jewish school because none of the existing institutions included Persian-Jewish history, customs, or culture in their curricula. The overarching criticism was that the Jewish heritage and culture were not being passed down from generation to generation.[55]

Most parents sent their daughters to Jewish schools not because the religious education was good, but because they feared their daughters would assimilate too much by interacting with Muslims, and they wanted to ensure that they would have Jewish friends. Because of the quick rate of assimilation, parents feared their children would marry Muslims or that Muslim men would seduce their daughters, and they would no longer be *najeeb*. Their parents believed they would be protected from Muslim society in Jewish schools, while still achieving a secular and Jewish education. Such schools gave women more freedom to socialize outside the home because their parents knew they were only socializing with Jews.

Yasi, a forty-five-year-old Tehrani woman who attended the Ettefaqh school, explained: "I had a very rich social life in Iran. Every weekend we were going to the discothèques or having dance parties in people's houses. I didn't have to be chaperoned because my parents knew that everyone I was socializing with was Jewish. They knew all the kids and their family. Anyone who went to Ettefaqh came from a good family, so they had nothing to worry about it. I'm still friends with all those people."

Mehri, on the other hand, attended a French school and had a very strict upbringing. She recalled: "The girls who went to Jewish schools were surrounded by the same Jewish families that they have known forever, so, therefore, they had more freedom than I did. There wasn't such a fear that their daughters would be out of the house without their brother or a male cousin. But I went to an all-girls school, and my parents were very strict because they were so worried that a non-Jewish man and his lifestyle would seduce me. They also worried that if I did go out to parties and socialize, I would ruin my reputation."

Jewish families that were not ritually observant did not send their daughters to Jewish schools; instead, if they could afford to, they sent them to English or French Christian elementary and high schools. Nouri went to a French school for girls because it was a "very protective and sheltered school that taught a lot of discipline, manners, and the French language. My parents came from a very nonreligious background, and they thought it was more important for me to speak French than to know Hebrew. Instead of being off on Fridays, Sundays were our days off, and I was used to reciting the Christian prayers because the school was run by nuns." When asked whether her parents were fearful of her converting to Christianity, she said, "Some people did convert, but the fear of conversion was before the shah's time; my parents did not fear that I would convert to Christianity but that I would assimilate too much with secular Muslims and, God forbid, marry a non-Jew."

Other women were sent to boarding schools in London, Paris, and Switzerland. Although their families allowed them to go away to school, all the women said that they had to maintain a *najeeb* lifestyle. "That was the biggest shock for me," said Pari, "being in a school away from my family and really seeing the way the Europeans lived. We had a lot of Muslims and Christian girls at the boarding school, and the Jewish girls were the ones who were so afraid of doing anything, and if they did it, it was done in secret. We were brought up with the idea etched in our heads that we had to maintain our virginity and to not ruin our reputation." The girls who attended secular or Christian schools saw very few—if any—religious rituals practiced in their homes. Their mothers were not ritually observant under the shah, and neither would they be when they became wives and mothers. Their Judaism came from, as one woman explained, "the feeling of being Jewish, knowing you will marry a Jew, and identifying with the Jewish people." However, it did not come from ritual observances, such as lighting the Shabbat candles or keeping kosher.

CAREERS

As mentioned earlier, few Jewish women had careers. Most went to high school and were married shortly thereafter, while some were married immediately after college. Many said that they wanted to pursue a career; however, this was not something most Jewish women did. Mitra explained: "Muslim women took advantage of career possibilities more than Jewish women did. My family feared their daughter having a career within a male-dominated, Muslim atmosphere. Even though times were changing, my parents still held on to very traditional beliefs. They felt that if I worked, people would think we didn't have enough money. And once I was married, my husband told me that I didn't need to work, that he would take care of the financial stuff while I take care of the home. Honestly, I think he would have felt threatened or emasculated if I worked."

Many women shared stories similar to Mitra's; as much as their families wanted to acculturate into Persian society, there was a tremendous fear that their daughters would be seduced and objectified by Muslim men. Thus, Jewish women were discouraged, if not forbidden, from socializing outside the home or having careers that would take them away from the home.

Delaram received her bachelor's degree in English by the time she was nineteen and was hired to teach English language courses at Tehran University. She said, "Muslim families, during the time of the shah, encouraged their daughters to get careers and an education, but the Jewish family standards held the girls back from making progress." Delaram's family feared that because of her education and career, she would not get any appropriate chasteghars.[56] Delaram remembered her mother telling her, "If a chasteghar comes, and you have to teach a class, don't tell him that you are a teacher at Tehran University at the age of nineteen. They would think you are twenty-seven years old or older and not want to marry you. He would feel threatened by your intelligence." Delaram believed what her mother said to her was true and said, "It was not my family who wanted me to downplay my intelligence, but they knew that I lived in a society that didn't want a woman to work or be smarter than a man; thus, in order to marry within the Jewish society, I had to live by their standards. And I did marry a man who I downplayed my academic ambitions with, and the marriage was a total disaster."

None of the women interviewed were encouraged to work; they were encouraged to get married and start families immediately after school. All were married between the ages of eighteen and twenty-three. Sahar recalled: "Many of my Muslim friends worked even when they were married and had kids. That was unheard of for Jewish women. If a woman worked, especially when she had kids, people thought her husband was having money problems, and it was immediately assumed that she was not a good mom and wife. There wasn't that mentality that a woman would actually have a career for her own intellectual stimulation." Shohreh, one of the few women who worked in Iran while married, explained: "Muslim women were more active in their rights than Jewish women were. Jewish women grew up thinking that they are not required or allowed to do anything outside of the family and home. If a woman was active in the community, it was not through a career but through charity work or benevolent work, giving money to raise dowries or helping orphans. That was the extent of their involvement. They were not involved politically or socially in the life of Iran." Shohreh was a writer for a popular women's magazine in Iran. Unlike other Jewish families, her parents were supportive of her career. She believes this is because they come from an educated background in which poetry, literature, and writing were encouraged.

SIGNIFICANCE OF APPEARANCE

Appearance was very important to the women who grew up under the Pahlavi regime. Their mothers' generation was taught not to focus on physical traits, but the generation living in the shadow of Queen Farah and the Western media learned that physical beauty was a high priority. Many of the women in this study had nose reconstruction. A few women openly discussed their operations, saying that they did not get nose jobs "to hide my Jewish identity but just to be more attractive." Sahar, who changed her nose at age twenty-two, said, "A lot of women, both Jewish and non-Jewish, during the time of the Pahlavi regime, went under the knife to get a less Semitic nose. No one wanted a big nose on a petite face." The fact that many Jewish women were undergoing rhinoplasty demonstrated their desire to fit into the Westernized standard of beauty that became popular under the shah. It also demonstrated that they had the financial means to undergo plastic surgery for purely aesthetic reasons.

Rhinoplasty became popular during Mohammad Reza Shah's time; it is still popular for Iranian women in Los Angeles today (which will be discussed in the next chapter) and for women who live in the Islamic Republic of Iran. Having rhinoplasty is still regarded as a status symbol in Iran. Because Iranian women are required by law to cover their heads and wear loose clothing to hide the shape of their bodies, facelifts and rhinoplasty have become increasingly popular.[57] As the youth of Iran are becoming increasingly interested in the West, nose procedures have "become an obsession for young Iranians." Women who have not had nose jobs will wear tape on their faces for the attention it brings. Iranians attribute this trend to the longstanding desire for facial beauty in their culture; they also note that although Iran is politically closed off from the West, Westernized standards of beauty and fashion have once again become popular among Iranian youth.[58]

Rhinoplasty is a procedure that reduces one's ethnic visibility and conforms to the standardized beauty of a specific society. Of the eighty-nine patients Frances Macgregor interviewed in New York, all admitted to wanting a nose that was less associated with a minority group.[59] She wrote that a majority of her patients were Italian Catholics and Jews who came from upper-lower and lower-middle socioeconomic classes.[60] According to the author, two of the most important social and cultural factors that drive the desire for surgery are the relationship between patients and their social and cultural milieu and the extent to which the values of their society exert pressure on them to conform.[61] Many of her interviewees said they wanted nose jobs because of economic and social challenges, such as obtaining a job, getting ahead, making friends, and finding opportunities for marriage.[62]

Of the forty-six patients in group 1 of Macgregor's research, twenty-seven were Jewish. Most found fault with what anthropologists refer to as their "Armenoid" nose: one characterized by considerable length and height, convexity of profile, and a depressed tip with a downward-sloping septum. The Armenoid nose is a feature of many Jews, Armenians, Syrians, Greeks, Turks, and people from the Mediterranean and Eastern Europe. However, it has become stereotyped and caricatured in many societies as a "Jewish nose" and selected as a symbol that differentiated Jews from non-Jews. Many Jews in Macgregor's study were dissatisfied with their noses because they felt that the nose was a visible cue to their ethnic and religious group, and they perceived it as having negative or stigmatic connotations. They wanted to undergo rhinoplasty in order to achieve an appearance that would more closely conform to the majority.[63]

Under Mohammad Reza Shah's regime, Iranian society began to appropriate a more Westernized standard of beauty, which led many affluent Iranian Jewish women to seek nose jobs. Dr. Siavash Safavi, a plastic surgeon in Iran, said, "It's very particular to Iranian girls that by adolescence a main goal is to be beautiful. It's a value in our culture. There is education and everything else, but beauty is right up there in every class."[64] Just like the Muslim women in Iran, the Jewish community placed—and still places— a woman's beauty as her most important asset, along with being a good wife and mother. Therefore, women were encouraged to focus on their physical appearance and were discouraged from having careers, because work was seen as debilitating to one's home life.

Shohreh, who was a journalist before she got married, said, "My husband was very happy because he always wanted a woman that worked. Also, he held a high position in government and wanted a woman who didn't look Jewish. He had to attend a lot of cocktail parties, and he loved being with a woman who didn't look Jewish but looked Muslim. That was popular at that time, not to look Jewish." Thus, Shohreh's husband found it advantageous to his own career to have a wife who not only was a journalist—which suggested that she might be Muslim—but also did not look Jewish.

RESPONSIBILITIES OF A WOMAN

Traditional gender roles were encouraged, and women were not supposed to take jobs that were meant for their husbands. Although the second generation of women did not do as much domestic work as their mothers did, a woman's place was still within the home. Dori, a forty-eight-year-old Hamadani woman, explained that she did not go through the same time-consuming process of cleaning her house for Passover that her mother did, yet she was expected to be a stay-at-home mother and take care of her family. For the first generation of women, domestic work was a way of proving one's religiosity in a male-dominated Jewish culture. However, proving one's religiosity was not an issue for the second generation of women. Their concerns did not revolve around religion; they were more concerned with fulfilling the standards the Jewish community placed on wives and mothers. Dori recalled:

> For a long time, I felt guilty about not preparing for the holidays like my mother did. I don't go through the same process of preparing for Shabbat or Passover like my mother. I used to, when I first got married, but I realized that I'm making a mistake because I was suffering, I was torturing and abusing my mental and physical body for what? To go that extra mile because it is what Jewish women did? I used to feel guilty, but now I realize that it is not forty or fifty years ago, and I don't need to follow her. I have a brain, and

I don't need to follow her and do things that don't make sense anymore. I stopped, and I don't want to pass this guilty feeling on to my kids, either.

Many women like Dori realized that they did not want to, as many women put it, "torture" themselves like their mothers in regard to domestic work. The home was still the domain of the wife; however, the domestic rituals of the first generation were seen as being outdated. They were no longer necessary to prove one's religiosity, because religion was not the focus of second-generation women.

Women were not only responsible for their children and husbands, but as daughters, they also had to take care of their own parents and maintain a good relationship with their in-laws. Iranian Jews are accustomed to respecting extended family, displaying loyalty, and demonstrating closeness to their relatives.[65] A woman was responsible for maintaining all these relationships on behalf of her immediate family. One of the most important responsibilities a woman has is to make sure her parents are taken care of. Women visit their parents daily. They help purchase groceries for them, take care of their homes, drive them to their appointments, and do other chores. When parents need something, they call their daughters before their sons. Jillah, who has three brothers and a sister, explained: "In Iran and in Los Angeles, my sister and I did everything for my parents. Anything they needed or anywhere that they needed to go, we helped them. The sons help their parents financially, but it is the daughters who do all the work. You know, in Iranian culture, everyone wants a boy. But my mom used to say, 'What's so good about a son? When you get old, it is your daughter who takes care of you, not your son.'"

Along with the responsibilities of one's own family, women also had to maintain relationships with their mothers-in-law and their husbands' siblings. Unlike their mothers' generation, these women did not have to live with their in-laws after marriage, yet a hierarchical relationship still existed. In the traditional Iranian family, the wife's position, when it was not securely anchored by the birth and raising of a son, was vulnerable in relations with in-laws—particularly with the mother-in-law, whose right to tyrannize the wife seemed to be compensation for her own experiences as a bride.[66] A woman had to show a lot of reverence and subservience to her husband's mother—almost more than to her own mother. A woman's toughest critics were her mother-in-law and sisters-in-law.

Kevah Safa-Isfahani wrote about the *baziha* (games) Iranian Muslim women perform among each other. They are a way for women, who live in a male-centered structure of hierarchy, to articulate their desires and frustrations in their roles as brides, wives, and daughter-in-laws. One particular game, Abji Golbahar (Sister Golbahar), is played so a bride may convey her frustrations and dislike of her in-laws. In the game, the wife picks up various pieces of clothing she is washing and asks herself to whom they belong. As she identifies them, she expresses her feelings about their owners.

The husband evokes the most affectionate and glowing images. The husband's male relatives also merit affectionate expressions. But the tone shifts radically when it comes to the husband's female relatives. The game ends with the wife throwing her mother-in-law's clothes and calling her husband's sister a snake, scorpion, and other unflattering names. The *bazi* (game) represents the wife's frustration and resentment toward the figures of the mother-in-law and sister-in-law. It also takes chores such as washing and transforms them into choices made by the wife. Thus, the *bazi* seems to infuse autonomy and subjectivity into chores that are usually done with resentment.[67] None of the women interviewed played these games, but they understood the frustration the women felt. All of the women expressed how important it was to show respect to the women in their husband's family and to make sure that they have their approval.

"That is who you always had to impress," said Nasrin. "When I was about to get married, I had to show my in-laws that their son married a *najeeb* woman in order to maintain my respect and the respect of my family's name. Yet I also had to have traits of being worldly, I had to be beautiful, and I had to prove to them that I am a good Jewish wife—always keeping a clean house, being a good cook, a good mother, and an attentive wife." Many women said that if a woman's parents and her in-laws both invited her family over for Shabbat dinner, it would be more proper and expected of her to accept the invitation of her in-laws rather than that of her own parents. One always had to show the highest reverence to her mother-in-law and to her husband's sisters, especially if they were older. The women believed that the reverence given to in-laws was a trait that was a part of their culture and was not practiced as much among Muslim women

INFLUENCE OF NON-JEWISH CULTURE

Many of the women interviewed said they were raised with Muslim friends and grew up in assimilated neighborhoods. Thus, they had a more realistic understanding of Muslim women and their families, in contrast to the first generation of women, who barely socialized with Muslim women. However, even though the second generation had more contact with Muslim women, they still expressed sentiments similar to the first generation of women regarding the differences between Muslim and Jewish women. Many women believed that secular Muslim families did not emphasize being *najeeb*. Muslim girls were allowed to date and socialize with boys outside of their family. The Iranian Jewish women believed that because Muslims were the majority in Iran, Muslim women did not have to worry about being part of an insular community in which there was a lot of gossip and always a fear of ruining one's family's name. Thus, many of the women said that Muslim women had more freedom outside of their homes and were more comfortable with their sexuality.

Anita, who attended a French private school and had many Muslim classmates in Tehran, recalled:

> Muslim women had more rights than we did. They were more comfortable with their femininity and sexuality. Everything for a Jewish girl was "no, no, no." It was not okay to be comfortable with our sexuality, our bodies, or to be comfortable in our own skin. I love to be a woman, but I have learned, especially being a Persian Jewish woman, that being Jewish and a woman is a double burden. There wasn't any freedom. We were always told, "Don't talk like that, don't sit like that, don't laugh like that, walk straight, etc." Muslim women were more sexual; they didn't have any of the boundaries we had. They had freedom, and we had rules. If a woman was sexy, she was seen in a negative way. Jewish girls had to be sweet, pretty, and homely. Every Jewish man wanted to date a Muslim girl but marry a Jewish girl.

DIFFERENCES BETWEEN JEWISH AND MUSLIM WOMEN

In fact, many women claimed that one of the major differences between Jewish and Muslim women was that Muslim women focused too much on themselves and not enough on their families. "I had a close Muslim friend," recalled Mehri, "who loved her husband, but he had a stroke, and she would still smoke in front of him, give him food that was high in fat—and he died at a very young age. A Jewish woman, even if she didn't like her husband, at least for the sake of her children, she would take care of him." So while Jewish women complained that they had to be too selfless, they simultaneously judged Muslim women, whom they believed did not share the same altruistic ethos that they did.

Many women also claimed that, unlike Jewish women, Muslim women were quick to get divorced. Mehri stated:

> Muslim women divorced a lot easier than Jewish women. Jewish women wouldn't even think of getting a divorce. We go through a lot in a marriage. Many women married men who were physically and

verbally abusive, yet they still would never get a divorce. A divorce ruins the family forever. It was so rare in the Jewish community. But Muslim women didn't have the same stigma associated with divorce, and it was a lot easier for them to get one. I knew a Muslim woman who had five kids and was pregnant with her sixth; she wasn't happy with her husband, and she left him while she was pregnant. A Jewish woman would never do that.

The second generation of women had the same mentality about divorce as did the first generation. They felt that one should not get a divorce because it affected the whole family and its reputation. It would be difficult for children of divorced parents to find a spouse because no "reputable" family would want their child to marry into a divorced family. If a woman was married but did not have children, then there was less of a stigma attached to her divorce. If, however, she did have children and still got a divorce, she was seen as being selfish or was accused of not caring about her children's future. It was extremely rare for a Jewish woman to get a divorce, especially if she had children. Yet, according to some of these women, it was not rare for a Muslim woman to leave her husband.

However, not all the women agreed that Muslim women had more freedom and rights. Ladan, a forty-eight-year-old Tehrani woman, recalled her experience at boarding school in Geneva. She remembered that there were not many differences between her and Iranian Muslim girls from the same socioeconomic background. Ladan said, "It was the incredibly wealthy Muslim girls, those that came from the shah's family or from families that worked for him, that were the ones who had all the freedom in the world. They were very open about their sexual activities, abortions, dating. All the Muslim girls I went to school with who had a similar background to mine also had to maintain their *najeebness* and were expected to come home after boarding school and get married."

Delaram had only Muslim friends when she attended a secular elementary school, high school, and university. She did not agree with a majority of the women in regard to Muslim women and their lax ways. She believed that because a majority of Jewish women did not have close Muslim friends, they did not have an accurate concept of what a Muslim woman's life was like. "All of my friends were Muslim," said Delaram, "and they too had to be *najeeb* and live a morally strict lifestyle. Muslim women had the same values as Jewish girls. I don't see a difference in values between my Muslim friends and me. I don't think Jewish women had the social interaction with Muslim women to know what their values are."

Delaram does admit that the difference between a Muslim woman and a Jewish woman was a gap in educational and career ambitions. She recalled:

Most of my classmates, if they were Jewish, they were very behind academically. They all got married at a very early age, and if they finished high school, they went into home economic classes. I studied literature, and there were other Jewish girls who were very progressive and took science courses. But usually the Jewish girls, they were trained from the beginning to get married by the age of eighteen; they didn't believe there was a need for them to study or think about a career. I was told numerous times as I was pursuing my academic degree, "What are you doing this for? If you go to university, the men will not marry you."

Delaram recalled that after her divorce, it was her Muslim girlfriends who encouraged her to go back to school to pursue her master's degree. While the Jewish community felt pity for her, it was her Muslim "sisters" who reminded her of her academic ambitions and urged her not to let the divorce stop her from achieving them. Delaram and other women who worked and continue to work in Los Angeles said they were frustrated that the Jewish community did not encourage women to develop their intellect, fearing that men would be threatened by intelligent women and it would hinder women's chances for marriage. They believed that Muslim women valued education and a career more; this, Delaram believed, was the only difference between Muslim and Jewish women.

According to Delaram, Muslim women had more freedom and opportunities because they were not bound by Jewish cultural practices that held that a woman must choose between a family and a career. She said: "The only difference between me and my Muslim friends is that I had less of a chance to meet someone that I could have married because they weren't Jewish, and intermarriage was unacceptable. So as a Jewish woman, I had less exposure to more educated men for myself, and I had to marry with the standards of the Jewish community. I had to downplay my intelligence and settle for a man. I have Muslim friends who were and are still my best friends, and I don't see any difference between them and me."

Nina, a fifty-five-year-old Iranian Muslim woman who converted to Christianity when she moved to Los Angeles, disagreed with the way Muslim women were perceived. Like many Iranian Jewish women, she grew up in a "progressive" family that was not religious. She was sent to a British school where she had many Jewish friends, and like them, her family stressed the importance of being *najeeb* and getting married. She admitted that because the Jewish community was a minority community and very insular, her Jewish girlfriends had to worry more about people gossiping and about maintaining a reputable image. But she did not have any of the sexual freedom and openness that the women earlier in this chapter discussed.

According to Nina, a woman's religious tradition did not determine the amount of freedom she had. She recalled, "I always thought that I was discriminated against because I am a woman. I never looked at it within a religious context but within a gendered one. Boys had more freedom than girls did; I don't think religion made a difference. Even if you came from the most secular Jewish or Muslim family, girls had to follow many restrictions." Nina was also divorced from her husband by the time she was in her midtwenties. Although she had no children, her family did not approve of the divorce and tried to force her to stay in a bad marriage. She said, "It is completely untrue that Muslim women can get a divorce and face no repercussions. I was in a loveless marriage with someone who was not good to me, and everyone treated me like I was crazy for leaving him. My family dealt with the same stigma that a Jewish family would."

TO BE A WESTERNIZED WOMAN

The women in the study discussed the influence Muslim women had on them. Many admitted to wanting to emulate their style and their uninhibited behaviors. For example, it was under the shah's regime that Jewish women began smoking cigarettes in public, an ultimate sign of rebellion. For the first generation, smoking was considered to be an unladylike action; a Jewish woman was never seen smoking in public. Smoking still held the same stigma for second-generation women; however, as society was becoming more assimilated and "Europeanized," many wanted to emulate the European and secular Muslim women in dress, style, and lifestyle. Many women began smoking in their teens; they never smoked in their parents' presence or in front of other adults because they feared the reputation that would follow them. Many said that it was only after they were married and gained more autonomy from their parents that they began smoking in public.

What was the appeal of smoking for this generation? As Iran began to be more Westernized, and as American, European, and Persian pop culture and music infiltrated Iranian cinemas and radios, women saw that lifestyle as being more attractive and worth emulating. Beeta, a sixty-five-year-old Hamadani woman, recalled, "In my generation, the Jewish women who came from a more affluent background were the ones who started smoking, playing cards, drinking, and going to nightclubs and flirting. Of course, their parents didn't know about it; they did it behind their backs, but they were less worried about the repercussions."

Under the shah's regime, a Jewish woman who smoked was seen as being more acculturated and Europeanized. As one woman said, "It almost became a status thing. If you smoked, you were seen as being more progressive and assimilated into secular Persian culture." None of the women in the study who came from lower socioeconomic families smoked. Sheilah, a fifty-two-year-old Tehrani woman, came from a religious family that had recently moved out of the *mahaleh* under the shah. She explained, "I would never smoke; my parents would kill me if I did. Smoking was not a ladylike trait, and no Jewish woman who came from a religious family would think of picking up a cigarette. Besides, I was always with my parents or with my brothers; it was not as if I had the opportunity to do things on my own socially and run off dancing and smoking."

European clothes and home decor also became increasingly popular in the Jewish community. Those who could afford it would buy their clothes from some of the top designers in Europe. Many women discussed going to Europe to purchase clothes or having their husbands and other family members bring back children's and women's clothing for them when they would go on business trips. "Everything European," said Deborah, "was in mode. We were obsessed with European clothes, vacations, going there on our honeymoon. We were convinced that anything coming from Europe was far more superior to our domestic products."

European furniture—particularly eighteenth-century and early nineteenth-century French furniture—was a popular choice among the elite to decorate their homes. Many homes in Iran and Los Angeles were decorated like little Versailles. They had European furniture with gold trim and gold leafing around it. The living rooms all had large crystal chandeliers. This type of furniture was favored by the shah and the Persian elite. Many homes of Iranian Jews in Los Angeles, the San Fernando Valley, and Beverly Hills still have this type of décor. Iranian Jewish architecture and interiors consist of homes built with large columns, even if the plot of land is extremely small. Marble is a popular stone used in homes, and of course, all have the large crystal chandeliers in the entrance way, living room, and dining room.

Most Iranian Jewish homes in which the study interviews were conducted, whether with affluent women or less affluent women, all had beautiful furniture in expensive European fabrics of silk and velvet. The window treatments were draped and designed with trims and many details. The homes were decorated with Italian, English, and French antiques, and the only sign of any traditional Iranian décor was the large Persian rugs on the floor. The appropriation of European antiques and décor is another example of how the Pahlavi regime, and the Jewish community, loved all things European and brought this aesthetic with them to America.

The next chapter discusses the positive and negative experiences of Iranian Jewish women when they immigrated to Los Angeles. For some women, immigration to Los Angeles gave them a new sense of freedom. It increased their access to education and employment and gave them an opportunity to study Judaism. While some women were able to maintain their leisurely lifestyle, many other women felt marginalized and experienced a decline in their own socioeconomic status or that of their husbands. Thus, for the first time, many Jewish women had to work in order to help support their families. For some women, working outside the home provided them with a better self-image, and they gradually gained power within the home. Other women felt embittered that they had to work, and others said that having a career had not given them any equality within the home. The following chapter discusses women's experiences in Los Angeles, looking at topics such as careers, social expectations and hierarchies within the community, women's religiosity, and women's mental health.

FOUR

LIFE IN LOS ANGELES

This chapter explores what life is like for second-generation Iranian Jewish women in Los Angeles, including how immigration forced many women to start working and contributing to the family income. Some of the women reveled in being working women, while others felt a great deal of animosity and embarrassment for having to work. This chapter also examines the qualities these women are expected to possess, such as being active in *dorehs* (social get-togethers), giving and attending parties, and being on top of the social hierarchy. With their immigration to Los Angeles, many women found a new level of Jewish observance. Some became a part of the Reform or Conservative movements, enjoying and supporting the egalitarian roles that these movements give to women. Others found a spiritual home in the Orthodox movement, which not only gave them a newfound religiosity but also allows them to separate themselves from the Iranian Jewish community—a community that, according to many of the Orthodox women, has become too absorbed in wealth and materialism. Finally, the chapter looks at the role of secrecy in these women's lives and how women are pursuing a life outside of the home.

Nayareh wrote that when Iranians immigrated to Los Angeles, there were both costs and benefits for women. Some of the positive experiences included the sense of freedom, new opportunities and options, increased access to education and gainful employment, and a move toward egalitarian conjugal roles in many Iranian families. On the negative side, there was grief over the loss of the homeland and loved ones and the social and emotional support of the kinship network. Many women felt marginalized and experienced a decline in their own socioeconomic status or that of their husbands.[1]

In regard to Iranian Jewish women, some aspects of Tohidi's analysis are applicable, while others are not. For example, even though many Jewish women began to work in Los Angeles, they did not experience egalitarian conjugal roles. Most did experience grief over leaving Iran, but believed that the religious freedom they experienced in Los Angeles would make them never want to return to a country in which they had to hide their Jewish identity. And while many Muslim women left a lot of family behind in Iran, none of the Iranian women interviewed had any family or acquaintances left in Iran. Their family and kin also lived in Los Angeles, often only blocks away.

WOMEN CONTRIBUTING TO THE FAMILY INCOME

Most women who escaped the 1979 Iranian Revolution moved to West Los Angeles, Beverly Hills, or the San Fernando Valley. The women interviewed for this study had full social lives that revolved around their immediate families, in-laws, and friends, along with social and religious gatherings. For some women, their immigration to Los Angeles had allowed them to continue to maintain a leisurely life, while other women and their husbands found themselves having to start all over again economically. Thus, for the first time, many Jewish women had to work in order to help support their families. For some women, working outside the home provided them with a better self-image, and they gradually gained power within the home. Other women felt embittered that they had to work, and others said that having a career had not given them any equality within the home.

Firoozeh, a fifty-six-year-old businesswoman, recalled, "During the first couple of years in Los Angeles, I would get in the car with my husband and kids, drop them off at school, and then we would head off to the garment district of downtown Los Angeles. We came here with nothing, and I had to help my husband build our life. I couldn't just sit around and be a housewife; he needed my help, and I had to meet his expectations." Today, Firoozeh still works with her husband, and they have built a very successful business. She has the luxury to retire, yet she chooses to work, believing that she would be bored if she did not go to work every day. She admitted that even though she works side by side with her husband, she must always make sure that he never feels emasculated or threatened by her.

Moujghan, a fifty-seven-year-old Tehrani woman, also started a business with her husband when they moved to Los Angeles. She described the difficulties of being a working woman in a community where very few women had careers:

> It was very hard to commute to downtown every day and deal with the traffic coming back. I was not able to pick my children up from school on time, and then I would rush home and have to make dinner and tend to the house. We did not have a housekeeper,

so here I was, a working woman during the day and then coming home and having all the responsibilities of a wife and mother. It was incredibly exhausting, and I constantly felt guilty. My children were upset for having an absent mother, especially because very few of the mothers worked. Thus, my kids felt like their mom was the only one not at school events or always picking them up late.

Many of the working women interviewed felt guilty for not spending enough time with their children and not meeting their "feminine" responsibilities adequately.[2]

Heideh, a successful beautician who owns her own salon, believed that because she worked, her husband saw her as his equal and treated her differently then he did in Iran. She remembered: "In Iran, I was like a child. Yes, I was a wife and a mother, but I didn't know how to do anything outside of the house, I didn't even know how to balance a checkbook. My husband saw me as less of his equal because he had to take care of me. And now in Los Angeles, I bring in just as much money as he does, and he sees me in a different way. I am more his equal, his partner, as opposed to a fragile woman who needs to be protected from the world." Not all women were happy with their new roles as career women. One woman described the hostility she felt toward her husband because she had to work: "You know, when you live in a community where working women are rare, you begin to resent the fact that you have to work while other women didn't. I wasn't used to working, I never had to in Iran, and then we moved to America and our lives changed. In order to maintain our lifestyle, I had to join my husband and work in his office. I gave him a very hard time for that."

MARRIAGE CONFLICTING WITH A CAREER

Many working Iranian women found that their marriages conflicted with their roles as career women. There is a conflict between the American idea of marriage and traditional Iranian family roles. Traditionally, the Iranian husband expected his wife to take care of the home and children. Her actions at home and in public were expected to help his and the family's status. The father has the authority in the home, and the mother is there to comfort her children when needed and act as an ambassador between child and father.[3] When Iranian women began to work, they expected the traditional family role to change, but it did not. All the women interviewed who worked, whether by choice or out of necessity, expressed their frustration regarding the lack of help they received from their husbands in the domestic sphere.

The women worked all day and then were responsible for the maintenance and nurturing of the home. Their husbands did not believe in sharing the responsibilities of housework, dinner, laundry, or other chores. In studies of acculturation of Iranians in the United States, Tohidi has found that Iranian women migrants had more egalitarian views of marital roles than did Iranian men.[4] They criticized Iranian men for failing to adjust their attitudes and expectations in the face of new realities. Women criticized men's resistance to egalitarian relationships and their conscious or unconscious adherence to traditional values and patriarchal norms.[5]

One woman said, "Taking care of my children is my responsibility, and it is my pleasure. However, throughout my marriage, no matter how supportive my husband was and still is of my career, it has always been a struggle to get him to accept that fact that he has to help me with the housework. No matter how progressive he thinks he is, he still believes that any work done in the house is solely my responsibility." While the women transgressed their gender roles by day at work, traditional gender roles were still maintained and enacted within the home.

Fariba expressed the same sentiments, saying, "I would come home exhausted and tired, and even if my husband came home from work before me, he would not even consider making dinner or cleaning the house. An Iranian Jewish man believes he has to be served by his wife, even if she works as hard as he does." Almost all of the interviewees discussed the old-fashioned mentality of Jewish men in regards to helping within the home. Many of the women who pursued careers in academia or the social sciences married American men. There is a saying, "An American man appreciates what a Persian man expects," and many women noted this difference between marrying an American man and an Iranian man.

Parvaneh, who credits her American husband with encouraging her to go to graduate school, explained, "Most Iranian Jewish men were threatened by an educated woman. American men are raised by mothers who have been respected at home by their husbands. That's the reason why marriages between Iranian women and American men work. Both sides expect less from each other. An American man doesn't feel inferior or insecure if his wife is educated, even if he is not as educated as she is." Parvaneh and many women expressed how difficult their mothers' lives were and that they were not appreciated or valued for their sacrifices. According to the women, the cultural expectation that a woman should take care of all the domestic needs was passed on to Iranian Jewish men, but American men were raised with more responsibilities in the home and valued an educated woman more. Therefore, many working Iranian women found American Jewish men to be more suitable partners, as they participated more in the upkeep of the domestic sphere.

SOCIAL EXPECTATIONS

In Los Angeles, Iranian Jewish women must meet social expectations as well as domestic expectations. The Iranian Jewish community is known in Los Angeles for its weekly parties, large *bar* and *bat mitzvah* parties, and weddings. It is the responsibility of the wife to put these events together, whether it is a weekly women's gathering (*doreh*), weekly card games, or preparing for a *bar mitzvah* or wedding. The women discussed the rich social life they had in Iran and continue to have in Los Angeles involving their family, in-laws, and friends.

In Iran and now in Los Angeles, the role of a daughter, wife, and daughter-in-law requires that a woman also include extended family members in social gatherings, thus paying respect to her own family and her husband's family. Many women explained that during Shabbat dinners or family events, such as a wedding or engagement, they would have to invite not only their own family and their in-laws, but also their sibling's in-laws and their husband's siblings and their in-laws. Touri, a fifty-seven-year-old Tehrani woman, gave an example of a typical Shabbat dinner she threw in Tehran in the 1960s: "When we moved into our new house in a nice part of town, I threw a large Shabbat dinner. I not only invited my family and my husband's family, I also had to invite my sister's in-laws [meaning parents, siblings, nieces, and nephews] and all of my husband's siblings and their in-laws. Before you know it, you have a hundred people over. That was a lot of cooking and entertaining. But you get used to it; it is like that for all our social gatherings in Iran, and it is still like that in Los Angeles. It is considered highly offensive if you do not include everyone."

Significance of Parties

Inviting people to one's home and to one's parties, such as weddings, engagements, *sheereeni-khorun*,[6] and other occasions, is very important. For example, all the women interviewed who were married in Iran said that anywhere from four hundred to five hundred people attended their weddings. Those who married into very wealthy families had even more guests. Engagement parties were even larger because people who were not invited to the wedding were invited to the engagement party instead. There were numerous parties that took place before the wedding, each of them having hundreds of guests. Iranian Jews place a lot of emphasis on *paziraeeh* (hospitality). It is important within the culture to always act correctly and not offend anyone. People take invitations to weddings and parties very personally; if they are not invited, it is a sign of disrespect to them and their families. Thus, the simple act of inviting someone to a wedding takes on tremendous social significance.

The extensive invitation list includes one's immediate family, aunts, uncles, cousins, great-aunts and -uncles, in-laws, siblings' in-laws and their children, business associates, and then friends. Marjan recalled her wedding in Tehran in 1970:

> We had our wedding at a hotel. There was no such thing as kosher catering; we had a Russian caterer for all the food. Besides the *ketubah* signing, the wedding was very secular. I had 550 people at the wedding, and that was normal at that time; it still is. Who were the people that were invited? Everyone! For example, of course, I would have my brother and his wife, but then I had to invite her parents and all of her siblings along with their spouses. I have four siblings, so you can imagine how many people were there. But [it] wasn't an issue we even thought twice about. It was so common to invite everyone.

There is an unspoken sense of reciprocity involved in invitations. Marjan explained, "When someone invited me and my family to their wedding, my parents had to invite them to mine. They would not only be invited to my wedding but to all the parties before the wedding. It is a sense of giving back." Excluding someone from a wedding meant dealing with the social consequences. "It is almost as if you get blacklisted or something," said Louis. "People would get so offended. They no longer maintain a friendship with you or invite you to their parties. It is seen as an absolute sign of disrespect to that person." Even someone who did not come from an affluent background had to throw an extravagant wedding with numerous guests. "Even if you could not afford it," said Louis, "you still acted like you could. As soon as your child is born, parents saved for their wedding and all the parties and jewelry that go along with it. That's how important it is." Thus, there is an obligation within the community to attend weddings and repay those who invited you by inviting them to your wedding and social functions.

Many of the women interviewed were concerned with social indebtedness and said their community prioritizes reciprocity. Weddings and other parties hold the great significance for Iranian Jews, and there is a social obligation to host a large wedding to display one's financial means. It is a way to let the community and one's in-laws know that a son or daughter is not marrying into a poor family. Weddings and other events are important because they keep the community together through a network of socializing and indebtedness.

Weddings and other social gatherings have become more showy and expensive, with each couple trying to entertain their jaded guests. In discussing her experience living in Iran, Anne H. Betteridge wrote, "When it was one's turn to act as host, the party had to be a very expensive and time-consuming affair to repay everyone else's invitations and gifts."[7] Through the three obligations—giving, receiving, and repaying—people demonstrate their economic strength and repay their social debt while maintaining communal ties and solidarity. People who are unable to repay the community socially feel a sense of indebtedness and inferiority.

Homa Mahmoudi, a clinical psychologist at Cedars-Sinai Hospital, explained the Iranian concern with class and status and how it is manifested in the arena of social function. She believes that wealthy Iranians emulate the European way of living. They are concerned with taking care of the external and putting their best foot forward. This is best demonstrated in regards to entertaining: "The importance of guests in the Iranian community is unbelievable! If you don't have anything to feed your own children, you feed your guests the best! It really is important. That's where people judge you. Because Iranian society and the Iranian community ran on connections, importance, and status rather than on your education or expertise, the external—'how you walked in'—became important. The superficial."[8] Thus, social functions became a way of demonstrating one's status in the community.

All the women interviewed agreed that they had more of a social life in Los Angeles than in Iran. "In Iran," Moujghan said, "you socialize mostly with your family and your husband's family. In Los Angeles, there is now more emphasis placed on seeing friends." Socializing with friends does not come at the expense of seeing family; they are combined. Thus, a typical week for a woman would be attending at least one *doreh* (many women attend more than one), having a card game with other couples, Shabbat dinners with the family, and then a wedding or a *bar* or *bat mitzvah* party on Saturday night. Funerals are also big events within the community. Everyone will come to the synagogue, even if it is the funeral of a friend's distant relative, to give their *tasliyat* (condolences).

Dorehs

Most *dorehs* take place in a woman's home during a weekday afternoon. Each week or every other week, the women rotate hosting duties. It is during this time that women display their best cooking skills, dishware, and clothing. Many women said that their *doreh* groups consist of women they have known from elementary school or high school, mothers of their children's friends, wives of their husband's friends, women from the same charity organizations, or women they have developed a friendship with over time.

The women who attend each other's *dorehs* tend to come from the same socioeconomic background. There are some exceptions; for example, socioeconomic background is not an issue for women who have known each other from childhood and developed a bond stemming back to Iran. Sahar explained, "For the most part, you attend a *doreh* where the women are at the same level of comfort. There are some exceptions, but you see that once a woman's husband becomes wealthy or something, all of a sudden, the wealthier women start inviting her to their *dorehs*." Some women attend numerous *doreh* groups, while most of the working women said they could not take off from work during the day and instead would meet their friends at night in their homes or at cafés or restaurants.

On one Tuesday afternoon, Jalleh, a fifty-five-year-old woman who lived in Beverly Hills, hosted a *doreh*. Jalleh's home was typical of that of most Iranian Jews in Los Angeles, decorated with numerous European antiques and paintings. The furniture and drapes were made out of expensive silk and velvet materials, and each room in the house had a Persian rug on the floor. Among the antiques were pictures of Jalleh's children and grandchildren, and there were numerous Jewish artifacts lying around— Shabbat candles, a menorah, a blessing for the house, and a *mezuzah* at every doorpost. The tables in the living room were filled with antique bowls holding fruits, cucumbers, dates, and nuts. There was a samovar in the kitchen in preparation for the numerous rounds of tea that would be offered by Jalleh's housekeeper.

By one in the afternoon, most of the women had arrived at Jalleh's home. They were all in the same age group as Jalleh, and all the women looked younger than their age. They were dressed in the latest fashions, with expensive jewelry and designer bags and shoes. The women gathered in the living room, where, like young schoolgirls, they sat, talked, and caught up. Conversations revolved around family, school, children, grandchildren, who's marrying whom, who is getting a divorce, and other gossip involving the community.

Lunch was served soon after, and the table was set for what one might think would be a party of a hundred, although only fifteen attended. Numerous salads were served, along with traditional Persian food and the latest recipes the women had acquired. A *doreh* is a time for women to show off their cooking skills with new and exotic dishes they have made. Cooking is an important skill for an Iranian Jewish woman to possess, and the more exotic the dish, the more everyone is impressed. "There is a woman," said Joya, "who is a part of my *doreh* group, and she will not give her recipes out to other women. She doesn't want people emulating her dishes. She doesn't say it straight out, but you never get a decent answer from her when you ask how she prepared certain dishes." Although Joya's experience is rare, it does demonstrate the significance placed on cooking skills.

A woman's cooking skills are not the only thing being demonstrated at the *doreh*; she is also displaying her *paziraeeh*. *Paziraeeh* is translated as "hospitality," and it encompasses all aspects of hosting a party. Everything is examined, from the flower decorations, to the way a woman sets the table, to the overabundance of food and desserts that are offered. There is no such thing as simplicity at Persian parties, whether it is at a *doreh* for fifteen women or a wedding for a thousand. Women invest a lot of time not only in preparing food but also in presenting it. Everything from the décor of the house to the linens has been set out with great care.

At Jalleh's gathering, the dessert table was set up after lunch. (Most *dorehs* have similar desserts: fruit tart, chocolate cake, and numerous bite-size éclairs, tarts, and cakes from the more popular Persian and European bakeries.) A silver platter full of watermelon, honeydew, and cantaloupe was placed on the table, along with a large bowl full of strawberries, raspberries, and blueberries. English tea and Turkish coffee were offered. By late afternoon, the women said their goodbyes, kissing each other on both cheeks, and headed out to their Jaguars, Mercedes, Lexuses, and other luxury cars. The women would most likely see each other again over the weekend at a wedding, at synagogue, or at a *bar* or *bat mitzvah* service and party. And the same *doreh* would take place at another woman's house in a couple of weeks.

The *dorehs* set a tone for the unofficial social hierarchy that exists among the Iranian Jews of Los Angeles, and there are many people in the Los Angeles community who find the enormous displays of wealth to be overwhelming and disheartening. This desire to entertain, host, and display one's wealth is not just a trait common to Iranian Jews but is a trait common to most Iranians, no matter what religious tradition they are from.

For example, Iranian Muslim women in Los Angeles also participate in a religious meeting called *sufreh* (charitable table). The original purpose of *sufreh* was to lay a charitable table for the poor and hungry to thank God for fulfilling a wish. Each of the several different kinds of *sufreh* is dedicated to and named after a female or male figure from an Islamic legend. However, while a *sufreh* is seen as a solemn occasion for spiritual elation and loyalty to God, Neyereh Tohidi wrote that affluent women in Los Angeles use it to display their wealth, generosity, and homemaking skills.[9] Thus, *sufrehs* have turned into *dorehs* for Muslim women; they are social occasions where women can show their wealth and *paziraeeh* skills.

The *dorehs* the women attend serve numerous functions. It is a time for women to socialize with each other and to display their expensive clothing, jewelry, and accessories. It is a time to welcome women into the home and to show off antiques, cooking, and *paziraeeh* skills. While some *dorehs* are very intimate times in which women gather together as close friends, many *dorehs* function in preserving a social hierarchy, with women from the same socioeconomic background socializing. Many women feel it is important to be in the right *doreh* because it makes their family popular and can help their children marry within "good" families. A marriage within the Iranian Jewish community is really a marriage between two families; thus, marrying into the "right" family is very important. The "right" family usually means a family that is well known, highly regarded within the community, and affluent. Many women feel that by being social in *dorehs*, they become popular within the community, and, thus, they and their family become better known.

Touba, a fifty-three-year-old working mother who resided in Beverly Hills, believed that "the Jewish community was very superficial in Iran, and unfortunately, they have kept that superficiality here." Touba and many other women discussed the significance of parents needing to socialize with the "right" people in order to ensure that their children married within reputable families. In regard to young women within the community, she said, "It is the appearance of the girl that is important, what her figure is like, how much money her family has, if they socialize with the right people. No one looks at the intelligence of the girl or her capabilities. Now all the boys are only looking for attractive, skinny girls, and the parents are looking for wealthy families. Unfortunately, the superficiality of the Persian community has stayed the same."

Another woman, Shohreh, discussed *dohrehs* and why she does not attend them:

> I don't understand how women can go to a different *doreh* every day. It is exhausting. Plus, so much of what goes on there is a lot of gossiping. I don't care who lost their job or whose husband is cheating on them. I don't get happy if someone is getting a divorce. I don't envy these women who don't work, and I do. But I envy them because they are creating a better opportunity for their daughters to get married. I feel like it is important to socialize. But I cannot socialize in that circle that other people do. I can't go to parties every night, *dorehs* during the afternoon, and events with my husband on the weekend. But I worry that because I don't socialize as much as other women do, I am not creating opportunities for my daughters, and I feel guilty about that, I worry about that.

For Shohreh and many other women, many *dorehs* are synonymous with gossip and superficial matters, yet Shohreh acknowledged that women make social connections through these gatherings. She feels guilty that she is not fulfilling her maternal duties because she works and does not have time to socialize as much as other women do.

Nilou explained that her social circle in Los Angeles has gotten larger. In Iran, her social life revolved around her family. However, socializing and maintaining friendships with those outside the family has become important in Los Angeles. Therefore, Nilou attends five different *doreh* groups: "The people from my *doreh* are from high school. Then I have a *doreh* group with my children's parents, my husband's business, and then socializing with my family and cousins. I also have my husband's family, my own family, my paternal family, my maternal family. It branches out to a lot of social gatherings!"

Many women agree with Nilou and have said that while they had a rich social life in Iran, it paled in comparison to their social activities in Los Angeles. Many believe that improved economic status, more time and comfort, nostalgia for traditional rituals, and more knowledge of Judaism, along with the security of being in a pluralistic society, enabled Iranian Jews in Los Angeles to indulge in social rituals. Nahid believed that Iranian Jews

> have picked up on social rituals in Los Angeles more than they did in Iran due to economic reasons and having a more comfortable life. In Iran, we didn't have all these parties before we got married. We would have one shower and one *hennah-bandan*.[10] We didn't observe a lot of Jewish celebrations and rituals like having a *bar mitzvah* or a *sukkah*[11] party. Now everyone builds a big *sukkah* in their backyard and has a large party celebrating the holiday. A lot of rituals that have been forgotten in Iran you see a resurgence of in America. People have more comfort, more time, and more of an income. Plus, in Iran, we wanted to blend in with Muslim society, but in America, we want to blend in with the dominant Ashkenazi society.

Parties

One of the most important events for Iranian Jews is their child's *bar* or *bat mitzvah* service and party. Jewish men did not have a *bar mitzvah* service in Iran; instead they had *tefillin bandan*,[12] while Jewish girls were completely left out of any coming-of-age rituals. Under the secular regime of Mohammad Reza Shah, even *tefillin bandan* became obsolete. Thus, for Iranian Jews in Los Angeles, many of whom sent their children to Jewish day schools, it is very important to give their children a *bar* or *bat mitzvah* service. Emulating the dominant Ashkenazi community in Los Angeles, Iranian Jews throw very big parties for their children, and it seems that each year the parties become more extravagant, with no expenses spared.

As one woman said, "You would think this is the child's wedding or something, the parties are so over the top these days." It is now common to invite four hundred to six hundred people. The parties are usually held in expensive hotels, with a party for the adults, while simultaneously, in a connecting room, there is a separate party for the kids. There really is no difference between an Iranian wedding and a *bar* or *bat mitzvah* party, except that weddings usually have more people in attendance. The tables and the banquet hall have expensive flower arrangements, and the best and most popular band is hired, playing a mix of Iranian, Israeli, and American music. The party will start at seven at night and go until the early morning, with the adults dancing more than the kids. One woman told me that her daughter's *bat mitzvah* cost between fifty and sixty thousand dollars. She said that most people in her group of friends spend a comparable amount.

The average amount of money people pay for a wedding ranges from sixty to one hundred thousand dollars, which does not include the numerous parties that take place before the wedding. The typical Iranian Jewish wedding will have anywhere from five hundred to one thousand guests. Many weddings are held in hotels by the LAX airport because they are equipped to accommodate large groups.

Farah, a fifty-two-year-old woman from Brentwood, explained, "My daughter wanted a smaller wedding. She had it at a more intimate hotel, and we could only invite 250 guests. You can imagine. I offended so many people in the community. That was six years ago, and to this day, many people from my family and friends who were not invited are still holding a grudge against me." Farah threw an engagement party for her daughter that by other cultural standards could easily be a wedding. She hired a band, had catered food and expensive flower arrangements, and there were five hundred guests in attendance, many of whom were not invited to the wedding. However, she still offended many of her distant relatives and friends by not inviting them to the actual wedding.

All the women interviewed said weddings in Iran were not as ostentatious as they are in Los Angeles. In Iran, one only had to invite family members, even if they were distant relatives. People did not socialize with friends as much, so there was less of an obligation to have them as guests. However, the social climate changed for Iranian Jews when they moved to Los Angeles, and friends have become more significant in people's everyday lives. Now, a wedding list will include immediate and distant family members, relatives of relatives, and then friends and business associates. Even if people cannot afford to have a large wedding or *bar* or *bat mitzvah* party, they still feel compelled to do so in order to maintain their social status in the community.

Each one of the women interviewed, spanning all socioeconomic backgrounds, was critical of this pressure to be wealthy and maintain one's social status in the community, saying that it could cause much strife. Dora explained, "Not everyone in the community has money, but you have to pretend like you do. Everyone has to maintain a very expensive and high standard of living, and it is a struggle for a lot of people. There is a feeling that you have to always keep up with the Joneses and throw these lavish parties and drive expensive cars and carry expensive handbags. You know, it's not easy for a lot of people, and they really have to stretch themselves."

Many women feel that they must drive the right car, live in the right zip code, and wear expensive clothing, accessories, and jewelry in order to be accepted and respected within the community. The pressure of maintaining a certain lifestyle has put a great deal of pressure on many families. The men in the community feel that they have to make a lot of money, and the women believe they must live up to a certain standard of material possession and beauty.

WOMEN'S LEVEL OF JEWISH OBSERVANCE

Most of the women in the study said they attended synagogue frequently. All but two women light the Shabbat candles weekly. A majority keeps kosher in the home. Every woman interviewed, aside from the Orthodox women, supported the movement toward gender equality and emphasized the importance of their daughters and granddaughters having a *bat mitzvah* service and being able to read from the Torah. Three women had their own *bat mitzvah* services in their midforties. Shahla said, "The reason why I had my own *bat mitzvah* service was because this was something that wasn't offered to women during my time. I wanted to embrace it and feel the delight of reading from the Torah." Many women have taken classes in Hebrew and actively participate in Iranian Jewish charities.

Iranian Jewish women have embraced the opportunities Jewish feminists have fought for since the late 1970s. Religiously committed women began to seek greater participation within the synagogue as well as greater access to positions of religious and communal leadership. Some worked to develop prayers and rituals that would give expression to women's own sense of spirituality, and some began to pursue advanced degrees in Jewish history and thought. All of these efforts reveal the impact of feminism on American Jewish life.[13] While a majority of these women would likely not consider themselves Jewish feminists, they nevertheless participate in an egalitarian form of Judaism that has reformulated a woman's religious and communal role.

There are many reasons that women have become more observant. The Iranian Hostage Crisis occurred shortly after many Iranian Jews moved to America. It was very important for the members of the Iranian Jewish community to separate themselves from the Muslim Iranians; thus, they emphasized their Jewishness. In Iran, people tried to hide their Jewish identity while living in a dominant Muslim society. However, in Los Angeles, especially during a time of hostility toward Iran and within a dominant Ashkenazi community, Iranian Jews openly emphasized their religious affiliation. Not only did they no longer fear hostilities toward them for being Jewish, but they believed that they would be more accepted in American society because they were Jewish. "In Iran," said Nahid, "everyone hid their Jewishness, because even though the shah was accepting, there was still a lot of anti-Semitism. When we came to America, we reinforced our Jewish identity because we didn't want to be associated in any way with the Muslims of the new Islamic Republic and wanted the American Jewish community to know we are just like them."

Many women said they learned about Judaism vicariously through their children. When most families immigrated to Los Angeles, they sent their children to Jewish day schools or after-school programs. Many Iranian families believed that Jewish traditions could only be maintained in Jewish schools.[14] Not only did their children learn how to read and write Hebrew, but they also studied the Torah and learned the rituals and the significance of the Jewish holidays. Heshi explained:

> My daughter would come home and tell us how she learned about all these holidays that we didn't even know existed. Just by being involved with her school and listening to her, I learned so much in regards to how to observe holidays. In Iran, we wouldn't light Shabbat candles, but how could I not light candles in Los Angeles when my daughter expected me to? Now she sends her children to Sinai (a Jewish day school), and they are learning more than all of us. My grandchildren say the Shema[15] before they go to bed, and they lead the prayers at Shabbat. You don't know how happy that makes me, especially to see my granddaughter say the blessings.

Like Heshi, Jillah Binah Rezmanpour got involved with her Conservative synagogue, Sinai Temple, when her two daughters started to attend the day school there. After her daughters had their *bat mitzvah* services at the temple, she also learned how to read Hebrew and had her own *bat mitzvah* service. For the past twenty-seven years, she has been involved with the school and the synagogue; for the past sixteen years, she has been on the temple board; and she became the first Iranian president of the Sisterhood,[16] a job she has held twice. I asked Jillah what the reaction was of the Ashkenazi group of mainly older women who made up the Sisterhood when she first got involved in the 1980s. She said:

> I had a lot of support in the Sisterhood, and I had a lot of resistance when I first got involved. It was not only because I was the first Persian woman to join the Sisterhood, but the Sisterhood was made up of older women, and they weren't open to new ideas and younger people, but gradually things changed. When I became president, I brought some younger Persian women into the Sisterhood, from forty-five to fifty years old. We targeted women that were involved in the schools and scheduled the programs and the speakers at 8:30 in the morning so that when the moms would drop off their kids, they can attend our programs. Out of a total of forty-three women on the board, there are eight Persian women.

Jillah is the only Persian currently involved with the Women's League for Conservative Judaism.[17] She strongly believes in egalitarianism in Jewish movements, and she is trying her best to get more Persian women involved in the Women's League.

Another woman who was very involved in her synagogue was Morgan Hakimi, a PhD in organizational psychology and the department co-chair for the department of psychology at Touro College. Morgan first sat on the board at her Reform synagogue, Stephen S. Wise, where her children attended day school. She was recruited in 2000 to become a board member at Nessah Synagogue,[18] an Iranian synagogue in Beverly Hills. As a board member, Morgan was active in classes and education. She brought speakers as diverse as Dennis Prager (who gave a sermon once a month over a period of three years) to well-known Iranian Muslim writers to speak to the congregation. From 2003 to 2008, Morgan was the president of Nessah Synagogue, where she says most of her energy went into creating therapy sessions, Torah study, meditiation, yoga, and many other classes. The role of women was very important to her. She said: "The community was ready to see female leadership. I brought three members to the board who were educated women; all of them had either a PhD or an MD. To me, those women represented what the community was missing. I thought that . . . bringing in a younger generation of educated working women brought a different flavor to the board."

It was as president of Nessah that Morgan wanted to increase women's roles in this traditional Orthodox synagogue. Through extensive research on the rules and regulations within the Modern Orthodox movement and numerous trips to Israel and New York, Morgan approached Nessah's rabbi, David Shofet, to set up a women's *minyan*.[19] She explained:

> I hired an Iranian Jewish teacher, Parvin Saraf, from New York who created a women's *minyan*. In our *minyan*, we had all the women participate and read from the Torah. The room was full—there were eight hundred to nine hundred women there. We tried to do it once a month, and Parvin would always give the sermon from a feminist perspective. As a result of our women's *minyan*, a new group of younger intellectual Iranian women started to attend our synagogue. We had *bat mitzvah* services where girls read from the *haftorah*. The next issue I wanted to deal with was the *get*.[20] With the help of other Iranian Jewish women, we had many meetings with the rabbinical community, and with the help of the Orthodox community in New York, we had ordained rabbis that came in and talked to the Iranian Rabbinical Council as to the problems that we face and how to resolve them. The Iranian Rabbinical Council was very welcoming of these ideas because this was a huge struggle for them. And during my tenure, what I tried to do was create a stronger bond, a firmer bridge, between American and Iranian Jewry. I thought the best thing that can come out of this is . . . the younger generations' ability to acculturate and translate to American Jewry without any pain and restrictions.

As a board member and president of Nessah, Morgan succeeded in increasing a woman's role in the synagogue; she brought attention to women's issues within the community; and through her classes and guest sermons, she attracted diverse groups of not only Iranian Jews, but also North African, Iraqi, and French Jews who would also attend Nessah's services. Morgan continues to be a board member at Nessah and Stephen S. Wise synagogues.

Finally, many women expressed that they now had the time, the financial capabilities, and the interest to learn more. Women in Los Angeles have opportunities that were never available to them in Iran. Many of the women attended Jewish seminar courses provided by their synagogues and used religious holidays as an excuse to throw large parties. Some have said that although they still love to travel to Europe, it is important for them to go to Israel and support the people and their economy. "When we were growing up," said Parveneh, "no one wanted to go to Israel. It was a third-world country to us. We supported it; however, we didn't want to go and vacation there. Now it is a priority of mine to try to go every summer."

ORTHODOX JUDAISM AMONG IRANIAN WOMEN

Some women felt that the community has gotten too superficial and have chosen to disassociate themselves from it, and instead they embrace a more religious and modest lifestyle. There is a group of Iranian women who have embraced the Orthodox movement and are more religious in Los Angeles than they were in Iran. As mentioned earlier, Iran did not have different religious movements. When Iranians immigrated to America, for the first time, they were introduced to different movements within Judaism and had the chance to choose their degree of religious observance. Most Iranians in Los Angeles are part of the Conservative or Reform movement; however, an increasing number of Iranian families are becoming Orthodox and establishing their own Iranian Orthodox synagogues.

Most Orthodox Iranian Jews live in the Pico/Robertson area, which has a large Ashkenazi Orthodox Jewish community. They attend their own Iranian synagogues, such as Torat Chaim, and also send their children to Orthodox elementary schools and high schools. Many of their sons are sent to Yeshiva University in Jerusalem and then come back to the States to attend college. Three women from the Orthodox community were interviewed for this study. All three are more observant in Los Angeles than they were in Tehran.

In her research on secular women in New York who showed interest in Orthodox Judaism, Lynn Davidman wrote: "It is well known in Jewish circles that Orthodox Judaism delineates a role for women that is largely defined in terms of their duties as wives and mothers in nuclear families. Therefore, Orthodoxy's appeal to young, middle-class, educated women, who would appear to have a wide range of options, and at a time when feminist critiques of women's traditional roles are so widely available, is even more surprising."[21]

Why are Iranian women from less observant families attracted to orthodoxy? Sherri, a thirty-eight-year-old mother of four, who lives on the bottom floor of a duplex in the Pico/Robertson area, agreed to be interviewed for this study. She had her hair covered in a large hat and wore a long black skirt and a long-sleeved shirt. Sherri had grown up in Tehran and attended a secular school. Some of her family members still lived in the *mahaleh* of Tehran, while Sherri grew up in an assimilated neighborhood. Most of her friends in Iran were Muslim; however, Sherri's family was more observant than most of the women interviewed. She explained that she grew up in a household that kept kosher, observed Shabbat, and strictly enforced their daughter's *najeebness*. Her two older brothers were sent to the United States, where they became religious, and then returned to Iran to teach the family what they had learned. Sherri said that her brothers

> became religious in America. The things my brothers learned about in regards to religion they came back and taught us, and we would practice it. My father was very traditional, and really, everything he taught us then, such as not touching a boy, is everything that I understand now that I'm religious. He was basically telling us about being *shomeret negiah*, but he just didn't know the Hebrew word for it. It was coming from a woman having to be *najeeb*—they didn't know the *halakhah*. But now that I've studied, I have learned that the Torah tells us that both men and women need to be *najeeb*, to respect their bodies.

Sherri's brothers decided it was time for her to get married, and they asked their rabbi in Los Angeles to introduce her to a man. Her husband proposed to her after their fourth date, and they married soon after. Sherri had the traditional parties before and after the wedding—the *shereeni-khorun*, *hennah-bandan*, an engagement party, the wedding, and then the *sheva berakhot*.[22] However, the parties were modest in comparison to those hosted by less religious Iranian Jews, and Sherri expressed dissatisfaction about what she viewed as the increasing ostentation and superficiality in the community:

> The Persian community is very judgmental and gossipy. They put me down for being religious and judge me for that—not all of them. Some of them are very nice, but I don't interact with them too much. I have tried to go to their nonreligious *bar mitzvahs*. They don't serve Glatt kosher food, they dance with each other, and they will have a belly dancer at the *bar mitzvah*. They don't know the meaning behind a *bar mitzvah*. It means that this boy is at the right age to do *mitzvah*; he is now obligated to do it. What kind of example are his parents showing him by eating unkosher meat or having a half-naked woman dancing for everyone? They go and spend tens of thousands of dollars for what, so the boy wears his *tefillin* once or twice in his life? Everything is done to out-do other people. I go to these secular parties and come home disgusted. Every time we leave them, I fight with myself and with my children. We lose the *shalom* in our home. So it isn't worth it for me anymore. Everyone is upset with me, and they accuse us of

separating ourselves from the community. But I had given them a chance, and it is not working. I pray that one day everybody will come back to religion.

The Orthodox women interviewed believed that without religious extremism or anti-Semitism, it would be difficult for Iranian Jews to maintain their religiosity. The secular lifestyle of Americans would have a negative effect on their children and grandchildren, and a non-Orthodox lifestyle would cause them to forget about their rich Jewish heritage. This sentiment is also expressed among Orthodox Iranian Jews living in New York. One young writer stated, "A *yeshiva* is the best institution from which children can nourish themselves with Hebrew, Torah, Israel, and morality." Another Orthodox Iranian Jew concurred, saying, "The only answer is religion. It is one of the only things that differentiates us from other people."[23]

According to Iranian journalist Karmel Melamed, the origins of Iranian Jews adopting the religion of ultraorthodox Ashkenazi Jews can be traced back to the Iranian Revolution of 1979, where a number of American Jewish organizations, such as Chabad, helped male Iranian Jews out of Iran. Their families were happy to have their sons leave Iran and be taken care of by fellow Jews in America. Many of these young men were in their impressionable teens and were taken to Ashkenazi yeshivas and schools. Their training in these schools influenced these young Iranians to adopt the ultra-Orthodox lifestyle of Judaism. Thereafter, many joined their community in Los Angeles with a new Jewish identity and formed their own synagogues and schools.[24]

Another woman became more religious when she and her husband began attending a Chabad synagogue when they were living on the East Coast. She said Chabad provided them with a sense of family and community that they missed when they left their family in Iran. She said it was from the wives of the Chabad rabbis that she learned to cover her hair with a wig and follow the correct *halakhot* in regard to women's purity rituals, such as the rules for *niddah*. Although it was through an Ashkenazi Orthodox synagogue and movement that she became religious, she, like Sherri, now lives in the Pico/Robertson area and attends an Iranian Orthodox synagogue near her home.

Before Iranian synagogues developed, many Iranians were attending Ashkenazi synagogues. (Many still do.) But not all Orthodox Iranians were introduced to the movement by the Ashkenazi community. In the past ten to fifteen years, the Iranian Jewish community has begun operating its own synagogues, many of which identify with the Orthodox movement. Now that there are numerous Iranian Orthodox synagogues in Pico/Robertson and the Valley, many Iranians are introduced to Orthodoxy through their attendance at these synagogues, which are led by Iranian rabbis. Thus, there has been an increase in Orthodoxy among Iranians that has been influenced not by Chabad or other Ashkenazi synagogues but by Iranian ones. In the past, many Iranians became interested in the Orthodox movement because they were living away from their families and communities and thus found solace by confiding in and befriending Orthodox rabbis and attending their synagogues. But now, Iranians are inspired and influenced by their own Iranian Orthodox rabbis and have turned to Orthodoxy as a way of escaping the community, which they criticize for having become too materialistic.

The Attraction of Orthodox Judaism

The three Orthodox women interviewed immigrated to Los Angeles in the mid-1980s. A majority of the women interviewed came to the United States right before the revolution in 1978, or they came quite some time before that. When these now-Orthodox women came to Los Angeles, they were overwhelmed and disheartened by what they described as the excessive display of wealth of the Iranian Jewish community. These women came from a more modest and religious background, and they felt that as part of the Iranian Orthodox community, they would not have to participate in the superficiality of the nonreligious Iranian community.

Shahnaz, a thirty-nine-year-old mother of four, described what made her and her husband attracted to the Orthodox way of life. Shahnaz felt that she could not tolerate the materialistic and social pressures placed on women, and, thus, Orthodox Judaism provided a less superficial community that placed its importance on God rather than on materialistic objects. She recalled, "When I first came here from Iran, I was alone, and my parents didn't live here. I was alone for a long time and came to Los Angeles a lot later than most people. I didn't expect that along with feeling homesick, I would experience all these materialistic and social pressures." She described the pressures placed on her by the community to embrace a less religious lifestyle. She remembered:

> When I first moved here and got married, everyone said, "You are in America now, throw away your religiosity." I thought to myself, if I want to live a life like theirs and be nonreligious, I would have stayed in Iran. I came to America to be Jewish. I have the freedom now to enjoy and learn about Judaism, so why would I want to be less religious?
>
> When I first got married, it was too much pressure. You have to look wonderful all the time. Every day it is a new shoe or a new dress. I couldn't compete with the situation, and I saw

that people would look down on me for that. I stopped going out. I stopped associating myself with the nonreligious people. The religious community I am a part of is not like this. They don't care about what you are wearing or how much money you have. There are some people in the nonreligious community that are very nice. But then there are some people who judge me and belittle me.

Shahnaz turned to Orthodox Judaism as a way to escape the materialism and pressures placed upon her by the less religious Iranian community. She also turned to the Orthodox Jewish community because in her view, it does not focus on gossip and hearsay. Gossip, discussed in greater detail in the following chapter, is significant because it brings the Iranian Jewish community together. Gossip plays a vital role in establishing the reputation of families (which is significant for marriage) and serves as a reminder to members of the community that there are consequences to acting inappropriately and disregarding the community's moral standards. By placing themselves outside of the less religious Iranian Jewish community, Shahnaz and other Orthodox Iranian women disengage from the gossip that can surround them and their families. Not engaging in gossip and not being gossiped about places them outside of the community, and, thus, they do not have to worry about competing and maintaining an extravagant lifestyle that they cannot afford and do not approve of.

Like Shahnaz, the secular Jewish women Lynn Davidman studied turned to Orthodox Judaism out of feelings of isolation, rootlessness, and confusion about gender roles.[25] The *ba'alot teshuvah*[26] in Davidman's study became Orthodox because they wanted to find a fulfilling way of life. They felt that Orthodox Judaism had answers to their questions regarding the true nature of femininity, their role as women, and how they could construct a sense of self and place in the world.[27] Iranian culture already defines women's primary roles; therefore, Iranian Jewish women turned to Orthodox Judaism not to define and construct gender identity, but instead, to separate themselves from the nonobservant community that they found too materialistic. Through religion, they were able to escape the pressures placed on Iranian Jewish women.

Like less religious Iranian women, the Orthodox women also attend weekly *dorehs*; however, they said the ones they attend were "holier; we try to make it more *kadosh* (holy)." Shahnaz explained, "We say prayers. We don't play cards, or wear expensive clothes, or participate in *lashon ha-ra*,[28] or gossip about other people. There are about ten women who attend. We meet during the day. We eat; we read from Tehillim (Psalms) and discuss Torah. They say it brings good luck." Shahnaz participates in a cultural tradition that a majority of Iranian women take part in weekly; however, her *dorehs* revolve around Torah study, as opposed to what she regards as "trivial pursuits."

Many less religious Iranians have criticized the Orthodox Iranian community. However, all but two of the women in this study said that they, too, have found comfort and solace in Judaism and have embraced the religion more now that they live in Los Angeles. Ethnographic studies have shown that Iranian Jews have become more observant in America. In the United States, Iranian Jews are exerting a considerable amount of effort in reconciling and restating their Jewishness to the idiom of a democratic, pluralistic, secular society, while retaining some features of their Iranian cultural heritage.[29]

The Iranian Jewish women of Los Angeles have become more religiously observant, yet they have appropriated American culture. However, it is the American "Ashkenazi" Jewish culture—specifically the Reform and Conservative movements—that they are now incorporating into their religious lives. When the Iranian Jewish community members immigrated to Los Angeles in the 1970s, they were proud of both their Iranian and Jewish heritages, and they no longer felt that they must hide their Jewish identity. Many embraced Jewish practices and wanted to learn more about their religion. Iranian Jews witnessed American Jews succeeding in all areas of economic and political life, and they wanted to replicate their success.[30] Iranians realized that many successful business and professional people were observant Jews, and they did not have to hide their religiosity in order to succeed in the United States.[31] Thus, they explored and embraced their Jewish identity, and many parents wanted to give their children the Jewish education they had never received.

All of the women interviewed made a distinction in regard to being more observant but not being "fanatical" about their religion. There is a certain level of religiosity that is accepted, and that is within the Reform and Conservative movements; any more religious than that is considered to be too religious by these women. When living in Iran, the women were busy enjoying the freedoms the shah allowed them; they believed in his modernization of the state, and as many said, "Religion was not something we focused on." However, living in Los Angeles, with its dominant Ashkenazi influence, has granted Iranian women the freedom to embrace Judaism and celebrate holidays they never knew existed. "Religion is in the hands of women," one Iranian Jewish woman said in an interview with Nayereh Tohidi. "It is women's duty to teach, preserve, and safeguard our religion." Tohidi observes that Iranian Jewish women seem to be doing just that, though they adhere to the practices of the faith with varying degrees of strictness.[32] Many women are not content with the religious knowledge they received from their mothers and are now making the effort to learn more about their faith.

Disagreement over Religiosity

There is a schism among Iranian Jews in America over the proper level of religious observance. The Orthodox community and the Reform/Conservative community judge each other. Leah Baer reports that animosity over assimilation and lax religious observance is a new phenomenon. In Iran, observant Jews did not look down on nonobservant Jews who were negligent or inattentive in their observances. Nonobservant Jews never hid their heritage and religion from their children; their children knew they were Jewish and felt an affiliation with their religion.[33] Nonobservant Jews were generally traditional in their beliefs but not necessarily in their actions.[34] However, the non-Orthodox Iranian Jewish community in America has a sense of intolerance toward Jews who have become more observant. Many women talk about Orthodox Iranians as if they have joined a cult. They believe that becoming too religious will steer women away from their families and the community, and anything that threatens the familial and communal bond is viewed negatively. Farnaz recalled:

> In Iran, the Jewish community was more cohesive because religious movements didn't divide everyone. You didn't have kosher or Glatt kosher, Conservative or Orthodox; these differences keep the family apart. My sister and her family keep Glatt kosher, so they don't eat at my house; they won't come over for Shabbat. You see, becoming too religious keeps the family separated. In Iran, everyone kept kosher, and that was it. Over here, two Orthodox Jews will not even eat from the same place. There are so many different opinions, and it is destroying the family solidarity and communal solidarity.

Many Iranian Jews are frightened by any changes in a person's viewpoint and the potential hindrances to traditional family and community involvement. They are alarmed by some of the new influences that encourage a person to "strike out" on one's own and discourage a family-oriented lifestyle as well as unity in the community.[35] Many women see the Orthodox lifestyle as being divisive to traditional family and communal solidarity.

The women in this study said they did not understand why other Iranian Jews would become more religious after moving to the United States. One woman explained:

I think you need to modernize your religion. The Conservative and Reform movement works perfectly because you are able to maintain your Jewish practices while also embracing modern American society. It doesn't make sense, now that we live in America, to practice such an old-fashioned way of living. Plus, this isn't the way we practiced Judaism in Iran. The Orthodox Iranian community has learned from the religious Ashkenazi community. No one was this religious and fanatical in Iran. We didn't have so many degrees of keeping kosher, wearing a wig, wearing [a] long skirt covering your whole body. This isn't even an Iranian tradition but an Ashkenazi tradition.

All the Orthodox women interviewed agreed that they were less religious in Iran. They were grateful to live in Los Angeles with its dominant Ashkenazi community because it taught them the *halakhot* that they never were able to learn in Iran. Fariba, the wife of an Iranian Orthodox rabbi, admitted that she did not know the rules of *niddah*, wearing a wig, and other *halakhot* in regards to women until she moved to Los Angeles and sent her children to Ashkenazi Orthodox elementary schools and high schools. "My family was religious in Tehran," she said. "However, the first time I went into a *mikveh* was in Los Angeles. The first time I covered my hair and actually bought a wig was because my son's teacher told me about the rules I need to follow. I would then hold classes in my house for Iranian women from my husband's congregation."

Sherri admitted that there were "lots of rules to learn about that we didn't know in Iran. When I got engaged, I started taking classes, and that really helped. I took classes in the synagogue. Monday nights were for both men and women. Tuesday mornings were only for women, and then on Wednesday nights, we would meet at the home of the rabbi and learn from his wife. The classes were conducted mostly in Persian." Orthodox Iranian women are thankful to the Ashkenazi community for teaching them the Jewish laws that they were not able to learn in Iran. These women are a part of a community that has emulated the Ashkenazi Orthodox lifestyle yet has made it into their own with Iranian Jewish synagogues, schools, and communities. However, the nonobservant women interviewed did not understand why the Orthodox Iranian Jews chose to live such a traditional lifestyle in Los Angeles, especially when this level of observance took them away from their families and communities. In addition, many of the nonobservant women pointed out that this traditional lifestyle was not what Iranian Jews practiced in the past, but was a result of moving to the United States. "Instead of modernizing," one woman said, "they are living in the past, and it's not even our past."

Iran has always had one Jewish community, though each family had its own religious practices and celebrations, depending on its location and political rule. There were minor differences in how Iranian Jews observed Judaism. Such differences were based on rituals and not on philosophical or ideological matters. Each Jew understood the common rules and regulations and recognized the symbols, signs, omens, and limiting boundaries that marked the space where he or she belonged and that defined his or her identity. Differences among Ashkenazic Jews in the United States are based upon ideological differences, but this was not the case for Jews in Iran. However, once they moved to the United States, the ideological differences among Ashkenazic Jews filtered into Iranian Jewish communities.[36] Iranian Jews in the United States broke into factions, with each faction holding different interpretations and philosophies of religious laws and customs and criticizing the other factions.

THE TOLL OF SECRECY

For the women in this study, living in Los Angeles not only has reconnected them to their religious traditions, but it has also given them the opportunity to spend more time pursuing their own interests. However, cultural taboos and a woman's domestic role are still significant. One aspect of Iranian culture that is still dominant, even in the United States, is secrecy. Women are not supposed to discuss personal family problems or their own issues, out of fear of ruining the family's reputation. The cultural taboo associated with revealing one's innermost thoughts, difficulties, and feelings has caused many women a great deal of stress.

Homa Mahmoudi, a psychologist who works with many Iranian Jewish patients, explains that the unconditional trust and openness we might have in the United States is seldom found in Iranian society. Families and friends keep many secrets from each other. Many women feel depressed, isolated, and disconnected, but there is still a stigma associated with seeking therapy or openly discussing personal matters.[37] One woman said, "Carrying the weight of your family on your shoulders and not being able to really discuss it with anyone has really taken a toll on my life and my psyche. I have no one to turn to or to vent my feelings to." Secrecy is so embedded in the Iranian psyche that many women feared having a candid interview for this study—they needed reassurance that their actual names or identities would never be revealed. One fifty-eight-year-old interviewee explained: "The traditional Iranian Jewish woman is an amazing wife and mother, but that came at the expense of nurturing her own mind and soul. I think deep down a lot of women are depressed and angry. They were not able to follow their own paths; it was forgotten amongst all these traditions they had to follow and all the responsibilities they had. That path is lost now, and now the emphasis is placed on looking good—not about whom you are, your potential, and your role as a human being, but the emphasis was placed solely on being a wife and mother."

LIFE OUTSIDE OF THE HOME

Seeking therapy is so taboo that it could not be discussed for this research. However, when it comes to pursuing a life outside of the home, it appears that many of the women interviewed are now stepping outside of their domestic role. Because of financial comfort and age, most of the women are now grandmothers or have older children and are now able to participate in activities that they find stimulating. For example, many of the women are involved in multiple Iranian Jewish charities, and they attend classes about Iranian poetry, psychology, computers, accounting, real estate, cooking, and, as mentioned earlier, religion and Hebrew language. Many of the women said they go on vacations with their girlfriends, without their husbands and children. Others attend the gym regularly and meet with friends for power-walking sessions, and one woman attends meditation classes.

Iranian Jewish women believe that it is their duty to transmit group values and to preserve the Jewish Iranian heritage. By being involved in cultural and religious ceremonies and by attending monthly and weekly dorehs, they feel that they are safeguarding the cultural integrity and ethnic identity of the Iranian Jewish community.[38] While they all admit that there is a lot of social pressure placed on them to be a "good Iranian wife," many women have broken out of the mold in order to slowly redirect themselves toward the paths that they left behind for motherhood.

The next chapter looks at the daughters of these women, the first generation of Iranian girls who have grown up in the Iranian Jewish community of Los Angeles. For these young women, Iran is a distant country where they were born but that they left at a young age or a country that they have never seen at all. They must deal with the challenges and pressures of maintaining three identities: Iranian, American, and Jewish. Some of these women choose to emulate their mothers' lifestyle and embrace the cultural and social rules of the community, while others find this type of conformity to be suffocating and limiting. The chapter examines some of the pressures they face from the community, the criticism they have of life in the community, and those aspects they cherish, as well as how they define themselves, their womanhood, and their Jewish identity in a pluralistic environment with a dominant Ashkenazi community. Finally, it discusses those rituals that were passed on to them, those they discarded, and those they maintain. All of these topics help us to understand how these women maintain their Iranian Jewish identity while embracing American society.

FIVE

JEWISH AMERICAN *AND* PERSIAN

A large house in Beverly Hills has turned into a nightclub, celebrating a graduation, an anniversary, a birthday, or no specific event at all. There is a large bar serving alcoholic drinks. The bartender is busy serving whiskey, vodka, tequila, and the latest "it" drink—one year it was apple martinis, the next year cosmopolitans were in vogue, now it is mojitos or caparinhas. There is a sushi chef at one corner making all the popular rolls and sashimi, while on the other side beef and chicken kabobs are being grilled and served with numerous rice dishes. The DJ is spinning hip-hop and Persian, Arabic, and Latin music, while young Iranians are dancing and flirting on the dance floor. The majority of guests in attendance are Iranian Jews, with a couple of token "white" people. All the guests have grown up with each other in the same community, and if they have not, then they know each other from the numerous parties similar to this. The girls are all dressed in the latest fashions—tight jeans, expensive jewelry, very high heels, a sexy top—and carrying the latest Gucci, Dior, or Prada bag. They size each other up; they are looking at each other's clothes and accessories and watching who is dancing seductively, who is drunk, and who is secretly dating. If you are a married woman, you are coming to these parties with your husband to dress up, have fun, and get away from the kids. If you are single, this is the place to see and be seen. This is the place to flirt, dance, and socialize in hopes of finding your husband.[1]

The previous paragraph describes a typical party, which takes place almost every weekend somewhere in Beverly Hills, West Los Angeles, or the San Fernando Valley. A large community of Iranian Jews has been living in Los Angeles for more than twenty-five years, and while the community has maintained its insularity, the children of Iranian Jewish immigrants were born or have grown up in Los Angeles. Thus, unlike their parents, a majority of the children have only known life in America, and most only know Iran through the romanticized stories of their parents and elder family members.

113

They do not live in the same physical space or the same sociocultural landscape of their parents' youth, and few of them are able to read and write Persian. Therefore, it would not be correct to say that their identity is characterized by symbolic ethnicity[2] because, unlike their parents, they do not have a nostalgic allegiance to the old country.[3] Yet, the Iranian Jewish culture is a major aspect of their lives. Given these sometimes-competing cultural forces, the first generation Iranian Jews who are growing up in America have learned how to balance having multiple identities—that of being an American, a Jew, and an Iranian.

This chapter explores how young Iranian Jewish women establish and juggle their multiple identities, how notions of womanhood and Judaism, as well as the rules and expectations placed on them by their families and the community, fit into their lives as young Americans. The chapter examines the changing meanings of *najeeb* and how these young women have reclaimed and redefined the word in order to empower their lives. Because a mother holds great significance and influence in a Middle-Eastern household, the chapter examines the relationship of these young women with their mothers and what aspects of their mothers' lives they choose to emulate and what they choose to reinterpret in order to fit into what they see as a more modernized American society. Finally, it discusses how these women have embraced American society without compromising their Iranian Jewish traditions and beliefs.

This chapter explores how demographic change and modernization have affected the first-generation Iranian Jewish women in America in regard to three interrelated topics: being *najeeb*, pressures placed on women, and mother-daughter relationships.

ETHNIC INCORPORATION

Ethnic incorporation into American social life has been historically defined between two modes of thinking. One mode believes that assimilation is inevitable, and cultures will eventually be absorbed into mainstream white society, with ethnic identities eventually fading into a "twilight of ethnicity."[4] The other mode believes that regardless of the level of acculturation or socioeconomic attainment, ethnic groups will resist blending into the majority and instead experience persistently high social distances in intergroup relations and discrimination.[5] Young Iranian Jewish women have not completely assimilated into American society, nor have they socially distanced themselves from it; instead, they have formed a hybrid identity that has allowed them to pick and choose aspects of American society into their life while still maintaining their Iranian Jewish identity. In many instances, they have reclaimed Iranian Jewish cultural beliefs and added their own Western interpretations.

Editors Carles Feixa and Pam Nilan looked at the social construction of identity among local youths in a globalized world through a collection of essays.[6] They found that instead of completely appropriating Western culture, young people form a hybrid identity. They define "hybridity" as the making of something new through the combination of existing things and patterns. Thus, for these globalized youths, ethnic and cultural traits are not set on a fixed tablet of tradition but are instead conceived of as a complex and ongoing negotiation that seeks to authorize cultural hybridities that emerge during historical or, in the case of Iranian Jews, demographic transformation.[7]

Hybridization is a process of cultural interaction between the local and the global cultures; Nilan and Feixa look at the way in which global cultures are assimilated in the locality as well as how non-Western cultures impact the West.[8] Hybridity connotes border-crossing, in-between-ness, mobility, and multiplicity. Hybridity believes that contemporary young people inhabit plural worlds. However, as the authors point out, as far as the youth are concerned, they only inhabit one, highly complex 'world.'"[9]

American culture has shaped young Iranian Jewish women as they negotiate their identity and construct their own cultural world. These women are in the process of a cultural syncretism and mixing that produces a hybrid identity that allows them to live in plural worlds revolving around their Iranian Jewish culture, their American landscape, and their gender. Whether or not they realize it, they are appropriating a more egalitarian lifestyle, while still respecting and paying homage to their parents and culture.

NAJEEB: THIRD GENERATION

The common academic perception of female sexuality in America seems to emphasize personal and social independence, sexual experimentation, and sexual maturity.[10] However, this is not the case for first-generation Iranian American Jewish women who are raised by immigrant parents and a community that does not encourage social independence and sexual experimentation. Iranian Jewish women are raised to be *najeeb*. This word is used specifically for women when discussing virginity or lack of sexual experience. A woman in the Iranian Jewish community is supposed to be a virgin when she gets married. In addition, she is not supposed to have had boyfriends and is only allowed to date with the intent of marriage. *Najeeb* also connotes virginal qualities—those of a woman who is docile, domestic, sweet, and unknowing of the world. The young women interviewed all said their parents raised them to be *najeeb*.

Many of the young women said sexuality was never discussed in their homes; it was simply assumed that Iranian Jewish girls must be *najeeb*. One thirty-four-year-old woman said that her mother never discussed sex with her. She said, "She never said I have to be *najeeb*. It wasn't something I consciously thought about. It was unconscious; it was a given. I accepted this as being a part of who I am and what makes up my identity." Shira, a twenty-seven-year-old lawyer, said that her mother never discussed the concept of being *najeeb*; she learned about it through her Iranian Jewish girlfriends at Beverly Hills High School. She said, "In high school, I had a boyfriend, and all my girlfriends said I have to hide our relationship and act like I am a *najeeb* girl. That was the first time I heard of this word, but it didn't matter if I knew the word or not, my mother and I had an unspoken knowledge of what was the appropriate way for me to act."

Diana, a thirty-two-year-old teacher, said that although her mother never openly discussed the concept of being *najeeb* with her, she was brought up to think that Iranian women had to posses "feminine" traits, meaning being virginal, docile, and shy, in order to convey their *najeebness*:

> I am a very outspoken and aggressive woman, and I was very confident with myself as a young girl. My mother didn't like those traits in me because she thought it would give men the wrong message, and the community would assume my lack of shyness meant that I lack moral values. My mother would tell me that I should never talk to a boy first but that he should come talk to me. I should never make eye contact with men because it sends them the wrong message, that I shouldn't look at him first—I should let him be the aggressive one, and I should be that meek and timid girl. She had all these rules of engagement to interact with boys, and I thought it was so stupid. What did she know of interacting with men? The first man she ever dated was my father. Their courtship lasted a couple of months, and then she got married at a young age.

Sahar felt frustrated that her mother did not acknowledge and commend her for her self-confidence but instead taught her that confidence is a negative trait for a woman to posses because it does not fit into the mold of a *najeeb* woman.

While many of these women's mothers never openly discussed values and beliefs about sexuality with their daughters, all the young women knew what was considered proper behavior through comments their mothers had made. While Iranian Jewish mothers may have never openly discussed sex and sexual taboos with their daughters, through the mothers' opinions of others and their comments about how a proper girl should act, their daughters knew exactly what proper behavior was expected of them.

Research suggests that young women whose parents talk to them frequently about sex adopt their parents' values and beliefs about sexuality are less likely to be sexually active at an early age and have fewer sexual partners.[11] However, open communication with mothers about proper sexual behavior has not made an impact on these young women, most of whom are not virgins, even the ones whose mothers specifically discussed sexual matters with them. Many of these women felt that maintaining their virginity was an outdated belief and, because many young women are getting married at a later age, that remaining a virgin was not only unnecessary but also nearly impossible. While some mothers did not discuss the concept of virginity and *najeebness* with their daughters, other mothers made it a point to discuss these matters and make their daughters aware of their social responsibilities and the consequences of wrong behavior.

Roya, a twenty-eight-year-old teacher, grew up with many American friends. Her mother disapproved of her American friends having boyfriends and would sit Roya down and explain the concept of *najeebness* to her. Roya said, "The concept of virginity is infused in every Iranian girl's upbringing. It mostly started when my girlfriends started getting boyfriends in high school. My mother would tell me that I couldn't date yet; it's not the time. I was always told that I'm different, and I have different things in store for me. My parents told me that I'm the type of girl that boys will not want to fool around with but will want to marry in the future." Roya's parents felt that it was important to remind her that while she does have American friends and does live in an American society, she is different than American girls and has a set of cultural standards she must abide by.

The main reason why mothers told their daughters they must be *najeeb* was fear of their daughters getting a bad reputation in the Iranian Jewish community. Rebecca, a nineteen-year-old student, said that her mother discussed the proper way for her to act. "She told me that I have to be modest because people are watching you in the Persian community, and other people's opinions matter a lot. It matters what they think; you are always in the public eye." In an extremely insular community where everyone knows the details of each other's business and personal lives, it becomes important for parents to make sure their daughters act appropriately and follow the rules and standards of the community. Parents want to ensure that their daughters do not get a bad reputation because it can ruin their chances of marriage and can tarnish the family name.

The belief that a woman's behavior is the measure of the status of the household is promulgated among Iranian Jews in Los Angeles. Thus, her reputation and proper behavior are instrumental in ensuring a reputable status for both her and her family. The idea that a daughter's behavior represents family honor is seen in many cultures.

IRANIAN JEWISH VALUES

The concept of an unmarried woman being *najeeb* is so important for Iranian Jews that traits that are valued in American culture, such as independence, are seen as a threat to her *najeebness*. Core American values include autonomy and individualism; these values operate throughout the life cycle. Typically, American parents teach their children to be self-reliant, and the children grow up and move out, establishing households of their own.[12] In contrast, the traditional Iranian Jewish family is characterized by role prescriptions, family obligations, hierarchal relations, intense emotional expressiveness, and collectivist values. These values contrast sharply with the emphasis on individualism, self-sufficiency, egalitarianism, and self-development in mainstream American culture. Immigrant children tend to quickly adopt American values and standards, which can create great schisms and challenges to parental control and authority.[13]

One trait many of the women appropriated from American culture is the desire for more independence. However, the prevailing belief in the Iranian Jewish community holds that if a woman shows any sign of independence from her family, it is assumed that she is not *najeeb*, and she is immediately stigmatized. For example, Rebecca said that her parents would not let her stay out late at night because they were fearful people would say, "Look whose daughter is out so late." They would tell her, "The community is watching you, so don't step out of line."

Nilou, a thirty-four-year-old stay-at-home mother with four children, explained that, although she was an extremely good student who was accepted to Georgetown University and Harvard, her parents did not let her go away to college: "They thought that the community would think I am not a *najeeb* girl if I lived on my own and away from Los Angeles. My parents said these aren't the rules they agree with, but because they are such a minority in the community, they feared that if they would let me go away to school, people would think of me in a certain way, and it would affect my future. The community is scared to have women explore too many things, to have power, to be their own person, and to live on their own and explore all the knowledge outside of their little bubble."

Nilou attended the University of California, Los Angeles (UCLA), and her parents allowed her to live in a dorm during her freshman year. She admitted that even though she is happy with her life now, she wishes she had had the opportunity to reap the benefits of her good grades and to experience an Ivy League education. Instead, she was forced to conform to the rules and expectations placed on her as a *najeeb* girl.

Similarly, Naomi, a twenty-seven-year-old interior decorator, moved out of her parents' house for the first time and into an apartment a couple of miles away. However, her parents specifically told her to not tell anyone in the community that she has her own apartment; she said they feared people would assume that she is not *najeeb* because she now lives on her own or, alternately, that she comes from a bad family situation and has moved out of her home in order to escape it. Unfortunately, Naomi's parents feel that the community will not commend their daughter for being independent and living on her own but, instead, will gossip about her reputation or assume the family is unstable.

While the idea of a young woman living on her own is new for many immigrant communities, in America, after the Second World War, it became increasingly common for adult children to move out of their parents' home before marriage. The trend continued throughout in the 1960s and 1970s. By the 1980s, this new life course pattern had become normative for young adults. It changed the relationships between parents and children, since premarital residential independence reduces parental influence over the daily lives of their children. It may also have had implications for future family structure and relationships, since young adults who have experienced premarital residential independence become less traditional in their adult family orientations.[14] Whether it is the fear of waning influence on their daughter's life, a fear of community gossip about their daughter's *najeebness*, or a fear that the community will assume there is something wrong with the family that has caused their daughter to move away from them, parents do not encourage or allow their daughters to live on their own before marriage. This has made many of the young women interviewed feel that the rules placed on them are too confining, only further fueling their desire to move away and live on their own.

The same desire for independence is seen among the members of the Muslim community of Los Angeles. In her observations of a 1996 International Islamic Unity conference in Los Angeles, Karen Isaken Leonard described how a young woman speaker talked of giving more equality and independence to women. The speaker was a medical practitioner, the daughter of an immigrant father, and a leader of Islamic women's activities in southern California. According to Leonard, this young woman spoke movingly of two principles that could create and preserve a strong Muslim family: respect and flexibility. She said children should be wanted and should always be listened to and shown respect. When young, they need boundaries; however, later in life, they need to be given loving autonomy, so they can make choices and experience the consequences of those choices as they become adults in the United States.

The young woman also spoke of a more egalitarian relationship in the household, in which women should be encouraged to play a major economic role, and men should be able to accept that and help with domestic chores and childcare.[15] What this young speaker tried to encourage within her community is the desire to hold on to Muslim cultural and religious practices yet embrace a more egalitarian and autonomous role for women. Young Iranian Jewish women echo similar sentiments: they want to gain more independence and live a less restricting life, while still participating in the social and culture norms of their ethnic community.

DOUBLE STANDARDS IN GENDER ROLES

With respect to the role of women within the Iranian Jewish community, many women criticized the double standard and hypocrisy that exist between male and female gender roles. While the teenage girls and unmarried women have to maintain their *najeebness*, unmarried men and teenage boys do not have to follow the same sexual standards. In fact, there is passive encouragement within the community for teenage boys and men to have sexual experiences with non-Iranian Jewish women and then take a *najeeb* woman as their wife. All of the women expressed how unfair they found this double standard.

Sarah, a twenty-five-year-old accountant, explained how her father encouraged her younger brother to be sexually promiscuous. She said, "My brother would come home and tell our father, 'I hooked up with so-and-so,' and they would give each other a high five because that is what he's supposed to do—to go out and have all the sex he wants. And I couldn't even casually date a guy. From a young age, my father would coach my brother on how to go out and get women." Sarah tried to address her frustrations with her father, "but there was no point," she said. "My dad is so hard-headed and fixed in his ways that he didn't even listen to me. My brother never tried to defend my perspective, either. It was just understood that girls and guys are different, and we as women have to uphold all the rules of purity."

All of the women said that they believe most parents do not care if their sons are casually dating or sexually involved with non-Jewish Iranian girls. They believe that it is okay for men to date a woman from another ethnic background for "fun" and then when they are ready to settle down, they will marry an Iranian Jewish girl from a good family. Thus, many Iranian women expressed their disgust with how many Iranian men objectify women from other cultures and then once they had their "fun," they are ready to be with their *najeeb* wife.

Jennifer, a thirty-three-year-old designer with mostly American friends, said that in high school and college, Iranian Jewish boys would approach her to set them up with her American friends. She refused to introduce her girlfriends to them because she knew the only reason they wanted to meet them was for sexual reasons. She said she knew Iranian Jewish boys would never consider a serious relationship or marriage with her American friends. She said, "I found it to be so disrespectful, as if they wanted me to pimp out my girlfriends for their sexual pleasures. They didn't see these girls as respectful women, they didn't want to date them and have a relationship with them, they just assumed that if she is an American girl then she must have loose moral values and will sleep around."

Not only do Iranian Jewish boys and men have more sexual freedom than women, but they also do not have to follow any of the rules that many girls find to be suffocating. For example, Ashley, an eighteen-year-old high school student, said that her older brother "could do what ever he wants." She said, "If he wanted to move out at any age, he could have. My parents are totally okay with what he wants to do. They always encouraged him to date. When it comes to me, they are very strict: they would say, 'You have to wait until you get married, and he has to be Jewish.' When it comes to my brother, they are not strict with him at all." Ashley had numerous discussions with her parents about the discrepancy in the way they have raised her and her brother, and their response to her was, "You are a girl, and you have to live up to your reputation; you can't have a bad reputation because it will affect your future."

Similarly, Victoria, a twenty-year-old college student, explained that at one family Shabbat party, she drank too much, and her parents scolded her, saying, "Why would you do that? Women don't behave this way. It is not proper!" She noted, however, that her older brother drank frequently, and her parents' response to his drinking was different. She said: "My parents get on my brother's case, too, if he drinks, but they say it is because it is bad for his liver, not because it is improper. Smoking hookah is really popular for us now, and they are always telling him not to smoke because it is bad for him. They tell him 'don't do it for your health,' and they tell me not to drink or smoke because of other people's opinion of me." Like most Iranian Jewish families, Ashley and Victoria's parents justify being strict with their daughters for their own self-interest. They believe that they are acting on behalf of their daughter's future, in order to ensure that she will marry a "good" guy.

For her article "How *Najeeb* Are You? Reflections on Persian-American Girlhood," Pegah Hendizadeh Schiffman interviewed three Iranian Jewish women in their early twenties and asked them about the tensions in regard to balancing their Persian identity with their American one. Rachel, a twenty year old from Long Island, discussed the double standard in the way she and her brother were raised. Rachel discussed how her parents raised her to take on "feminine" roles. She explained that the complete double standard in her household commenced when she hit puberty. It was assumed that whomever she dated might be marriage material, while her older brother was able to date whomever he wanted, from any religious or racial background. Because her parents wanted her to marry into a reputable family, Rachel was pressured to wear more formal clothing to the Iranian parties, while her brother wore jeans. And she discussed how it was important for her to know how to be a hostess, how to set the table, how to serve tea, and how to clean the house, while her brother would learn how to sit and watch television.[16]

Rachel said that she resented her culture for making premarital sex taboo for women, while praising men who have it. She resented her culture for making her feel like a second-class citizen and denying the fact that she had the same desires as her brother.[17] This double standard is also seen within the South Asian community, where daughters are the primary concern of parents. One young Indian Muslim woman wrote, "In my culture, it's O.K. for a man to marry outside our Muslim community, go away to college, stay out at night, do whatever he pleases. A girl, on the other hand, must learn to cook, not say what's on her mind, and repress sexual desires."[18]

Thus, though these women each come from different communities, they all deal with the same double standards in their community. All three communities encourage women to take on roles that prepare them to be wives and mothers, while simultaneously raising their daughters with different standards than their sons.

Many Iranian mothers acknowledged the double standards placed on young women within the community and said that, although they do not agree with it and wish things could change for their daughters' sake, they have no choice but to play by the rules of the community. One forty-seven-year-old mother with a teenage daughter said: "Although I think it is really unfair that girls are treated differently from the boys, I had to be more strict with my daughter because I wanted to make sure she does not get judged by others in the community and ruin her chance of marrying someone because of it. She thinks it is so unfair that she has to come home earlier than her brother and can't have boyfriends, and I told her that I agree with her, and she might be angry with me now, but I am doing it for her own sake because I want the best future for her. She might not understand now, but she will be grateful for this later."

The response of many of the young women is that they do not care about living up to a certain reputation, and, unlike their mothers, they are from a generation that is not as concerned with what people think of them and do not believe that pleasing the community should be their life goal. Tania, a twenty-six-year-old accountant explained, "My mother always said, 'Don't do this, and don't do that because what if one day, the parents of the man you want to marry find out about it, and they won't let their son marry you?' What my mom doesn't understand is that I would never marry a man who would judge me in that way, and I would never marry a man who would allow his parents to have so much influence in his life."

GENERATIONAL CONFLICTS

There is a clear disagreement between the two generations on the significance of the community, one's reputation, and the influence of parents. Iranian Jewish mothers were heavily dependent on their reputation and family name in order to marry a husband from a reputable family. Their parents had more of a say in their children's lives than in this generation. Thus, if a man's mother did not approve of his wife, he most likely did not marry her. Many first-generation Iranian American girls refused to allow others to dictate their lives; they believed that if a man is so heavily influenced by his mother and "does not have a mind of his own or a backbone to fight back," he is not worth being with.

The larger issue is how much influence first-generation Iranian-Jewish women want their parents, specifically their mothers, to have in their lives. This is one of the most difficult and sensitive issues within the community. The traditional Iranian Jewish family, like most Middle Eastern families, is extremely tight-knit and parents have ultimate control over the lives of their children, especially their daughters. This is a community where one does not move out of their parents' home until they get married and whom a woman marries is heavily dependent on her parents' approval and sanctioning. However, these parents are raising their children in America, a country that encourages independence. This has caused a lot of strife within the family unit.

Many first-generation women challenge the amount of influence their parents have on their lives. Shari, a twenty-two-year-old college student, explained, "I just want to tell my mother to butt out of my life and to live her own life and not fixate on mine so much." When Shari has said as much to her mother in the midst of an argument, her mother, according to Shari, "got so mad she almost slapped me in the face. She said, 'How dare you speak to me in that way. You are not an American child who disrespects your parents. You were raised with better values.'"

Within the Iranian culture, it is strictly taboo and considered extremely disrespectful for children to tell parents to mind their own business and to not interfere in their lives. In an insular community where everyone's life is everyone's business, it is assumed that the opinion, rules, and regulations of one's parents should not only be appropriated, but also appreciated. The mothers of these young women told me that one of the hardest aspects of raising children in America is the lack of respect and reverence for parents; they fear their children have been influenced by that mentality. Their own parents had complete control over their lives, and they never disrespected, refuted, or questioned any of their rules and opinions. Now, they feel like their own children have been influenced by American culture, and they have less control and influence on their children, and they find that to not only be threatening but also really sad.

Overinvolved Mothers

Many immigrant children write about and experience difficulties with overinvolved mothers. One young South Asian female writer asserts that all second-generation South Asians share one thing: "Parents who are over-involved, over-worried, and over-protective. Parents who have an opinion on every minor life decision, who make demands, impose guilt, withhold approval." She goes on, "We entered the world the axis around which our parents' lives revolved, their source of fulfillment, their contract with the future. So we must become respectable, make money, buy a house, bear children. My parents' love supports me and enfolds me, but sometimes also weighs me down. Still, I carry the burden of their unhappiness."[19] This writer experienced a common upbringing with those whose interviews are the basis of this book—the appreciation for the love and support they get from their parents, specifically their mothers, but also the desire to live a more autonomous life, to make their own decisions, and to fulfill their own dreams, as opposed to the dreams of their parents.

The young women from this generation cannot help but be influenced by the American culture that surrounds them. It is inevitable that some form of acculturation will occur and that parents cannot assume that raising a daughter in Los Angeles in the twenty-first century will be the same as raising a daughter in Tehran in the 1950s and '60s. Many girls feel that their mothers do not understand how difficult it is to be a young woman balancing two cultures in America. Many feel that their mother's advice about their lives is outdated—even ignorant.

"How can my mother assume I will take in her advice in regard to dating, boys, and my own social life?" asked Nasi, a twenty-one-year-old student at UCLA. "My mother cannot possibly understand the social and academic pressures I am dealing with. She doesn't know what it is like to be in your early twenties and living between the Iranian Jewish world and the American world. Whenever she gives me her opinion on something, it goes in one ear and out the other. Maybe when I am older, and I need advice on cooking and other domestic things, I will go to her, but she is so concerned with pleasing everyone else and not offending or challenging anyone in the community that I don't look to her as having solid and insightful advice."

Many young women expressed the same sentiments as Nasi. They adamantly express love for their mothers, saying that they respect them as matriarchs and for uprooting themselves and starting their lives all over again in America, but many said that they do not feel close to their mothers because they come from such different worlds and feel that their mothers are overinvolved and protective. A majority of the women said they do not believe their mothers could understand how difficult it is to be a young woman in two dominating, yet extremely different, cultures. Most admitted to lying to their mothers about their personal life in order to do what they want to do and not get into trouble.

Many of the girls are frustrated by how confining the community is and how strict their parents are. Most of the things parents think are inappropriate for a girl to do are considered to be typical behavior for teenagers, such as staying out late, dating, wanting to go away to college. As Monir, a nineteen-year-old college student, explained, "I'm not going out and shooting heroin and sleeping around with guys. I just want to be able to hang out with my friends, hang out with boys, and have the option of having some type of independence. We're all good kids, and our parents need to trust us more with our capabilities to make good and wise decisions, and they need to care less about what the community would think."

Talia, a thirty-one-year-old mother, explained that when daughters do not open up about their personal lives with their mothers, the relationship between the two of them suffers greatly:

> There is no closeness with your mother when you have to lie to her all the time. Ultimately, you can grow to resent her for forcing you to have to choose between wanting to be a normal teenager and wanting to do normal teenager things or listening to her archaic rules of what a *najeeb* girl should be. The relationship between a mother and daughter in this community is more of a hierarchy of rules than a friendship. That is how it is until the girl gets married and moves out of her parents' house and gets more independence. This explains why so many girls get married at such a young age; it is the only way they can get their independence.

Talia went on to explain the relationship between her and her mother. "I didn't feel like I can turn to my mother and confide in her. Even though I love her to death, I never felt like I could emotionally depend on her and talk to her about the angst I was feeling as a teenager and as an unmarried women in my early twenties who was dealing with identity issues."

Although the girls are closely bonded with their mothers, especially when they are young, once they became teenagers the young women said they felt a rift because that was when their mothers became stricter. Many of the married women said that once they married, they no longer had to lie to their mothers about their social lives and, thus, felt closer to them. As one woman explained:

> An Iranian woman, as a mother, is there physically and emotionally for her kids. I think that when her children are younger, they are very close emotionally to their mother. But as Iranian Jewish girls get older, there is a distance between mothers and daughters because the mothers want to prevent their daughters from dating, integrating into American society, and basically acting like a normal teenager in America. This wasn't allowed or encouraged in the Iranian Jewish culture, and now what we see is that daughters are constantly lying to their mothers in order to do what they want to do.

Arizou, a thirty-four-year-old mother of two young girls, said she always lied to her parents when she was in high school and college. It was not until she got married that she finally told her parents the truth about her very active social life. "I finally told them," she said, "of the boyfriends I used to have and how I would pretend I was sleeping over at a girlfriend's house but would really be with him or how I would sneak out of the house. What do I have to lose at this point? It's not like they could punish me. I wasn't even doing anything bad; I was still a virgin, but my parents were so traditional that even socializing with boys at night was considered unacceptable to them."

The women interviewed with young daughters said that they hope to have a different relationship with their daughters than the relationship they had with their mothers. They want a more open relationship and hope that their daughters will not lie and hide so much of their lives from them the way they did. Arizou said:

> Kids are going to do what they want to do, so either you can accept it, raise your children with good morals, and be more accepting of how things are changing and encourage dialogue with them and guide them, or you can live in a bubble and pretend like your daughter is going to follow all the rules of being *najeeb,* and in reality, she is doing things behind your back. I want to have an open relationship with my daughters, so they don't end up like me. I was the girl who was always lying to my parents in order to do what normal American kids in my high school and college were doing.

Many of the young women desperately wanted to be close to their mothers growing up but felt that, because of the cultural discrepancies, they could not open up to their mothers about personal issues, especially those dealing with the opposite sex. Schiffman's article on Iranian Jewish young women describes how her interviewees felt hurt and resentful of the culture for putting a barrier between them and their mothers. As one twenty-year-old interviewee expressed, "I have lied to my parents so much that I can't even count. I do it not so I hurt them but so I don't hurt them. They don't want to know the truth. Almost all of these lies deal with people of the opposite sex. Other than those issues, I am a really good daughter and have done everything they expect of me. That's why I almost can't wait to get married so that they hopefully will accept everything about me and I won't have to hide anything from them."[20] She sees marriage as the only way she can truly become closer to her parents and no longer lie to them about her personal life.

Another one of Schiffman's Iranian Jewish interviewees, Shadi, a twenty-year-old lesbian, was resentful of the community and her parents for being homophobic and judgmental of girls who are not virgins. She said, "I resent the culture for putting this barrier between us. If they [her parents] saw me as a whole person, our relationship would be better and they would be much prouder of me, if they could move past their Persian cultural socialization. If I told them things like I was not a virgin or that I liked women, they would make me feel dirty. I don't have any shame about what I have done but I know if I told them they would shame me."[21] Shadi, like many of the women in this study, longed for a more open and honest relationship with her parents, specifically her mother. The women believed they are living a double life and that their mothers do not truly know who they are because they have to hide so much of who they are due to a fear of hurting their parents or being judged. Most of the women said that if their mothers knew they were not virgins before they were married, their mothers would be utterly devastated and embarrassed.

LIVING A DOUBLE LIFE

Many of the women interviewed described a sense of living a double life or myriad lives and characters that they appropriate in relationships with different people. They take the persona of a *najeeb* woman in front of their parents and within the community; they are hard-working business women, mothers, and/or students in their personal and professional lives, and for those who feel lucky enough to have friends they are close to, their true personality. One woman who has mostly American friends said,

> When I'm around my parents, family, or the community, I act like I'm that innocent *najeeb* girl. But it is my American friends, those

that I know who won't judge or gossip about me, they really see my true character. With these women, I feel safer. I can be who I want to be—vulnerable, raunchy, a woman who is navigating my personal, sexual, and professional life. Where within the community, I have to act so one-dimensional. However, it is within my family and the community that I sense a real love, a real belief of taking care of each other and watching out for one another. I feel like my non-Iranian Jewish friends and their families do not have that same sense of devotion to each other. So, sometimes I feel like a fish out of water in both communities, taking on different personas in each yet not really feeling completely comfortable in either.

One woman jokingly said, "Persian girls should join the CIA; they are so good at living double lives, lying, and hiding so much of their personal life."

In her research on the autobiographies of children of immigrants, Nedim Karakayali suggests that many immigrant children take on numerous personalities in order to fit into their immigrant community and their North American one. She wrote that almost invariably, autobiographical sources indicate that an immigrant child is likely to develop myriad relationships and participate in many different lives. There is seldom a group of "people" to which immigrant children claim to belong. They seem to exist in different worlds that are fragmented and in flux. Karakayali believes that children of immigrants are not migrants, yet, throughout their lifetime, they migrate between numerous milieu.[22] Children of immigrants often feel that they are caught between two worlds because almost from the day they are born, the distinction between "homeland" and a "new land" permeates their lives.[23]

As Karakayali suggests, young Iranian Jewish women also take on numerous personalities. They are constantly listening to the cultural expectations placed on them, expectations of what a *najeeb* woman should be and the ideal role a woman should play within her family and community, while struggling to make amends with Western expectations to be an independent and sexually free woman. These numerous personalities can be exhausting to keep up, leaving young women to question who they really are and which cultural milieu they identify with most. It has made these women feel frustrated, lonely, and confused.

This cultural disorientation is not found within the earlier generations. Although under the shah's regime there was more assimilation, the Iranian Jewish community still maintained its insularity, and Jewish women rarely left the community. Even though the women from the prior generations claimed there were a lot of differences between Jewish and non-Jewish women, in actuality, there were not. Most Muslim women also had to abide by the rules of *najeebness* and had strict family upbringings. Thus, there was not too much of a discrepancy between the ways women were raised in Iran. The same is not true here in America. America and its culture of independence are completely foreign to the Iranian Jewish community. Thus, this first generation of young Iranian American Jewish women has to deal with a cultural disorientation that the earlier generation of women never had to encounter. While being *najeeb* is expected of young Iranian Jewish women, it is not expected of American women.

SEXUAL BEHAVIOR

Thus, while being *najeeb* is expected, many of the women said that they are not or were not virgins when they got married. All the women in the study who were still in high school were still virgins. The young Orthodox girls were still virgins, but many of the other women were not. Most of the married women in their early thirties lost their virginity to their now-husbands before they were actually married, but many of the single and married women in their twenties and early thirties had had at least one or more sexual partners.

Ashley, an eighteen-year-old high school senior, wanted to maintain her virginity until she got married. She said, "A lot of Iranian Jewish girls in my high school are having sex at fifteen and sixteen years old—not my close friends but a lot of the girls around me. I think the girls who are having sex in our community are so young, they think they are so mature, but they aren't. There is a backlash against being *najeeb*; it's like their mothers told them for so long they have to be a virgin that their way of rebelling is by sleeping around with all these guys. They flaunt their sexuality; you can tell by the way they dress and the way they present themselves. All the tiny shirts and skirts and the way they pop everything out." While Ashley does not know for a fact that other Iranian Jewish girls in her high school are sexually active, she assumes they are because of the gossip she hears and the way the girls dress and present themselves.

The issue of clothing choice and sexual behavior is something that many young women discussed. According to sociologist Joanne Entwistle, "The fashion system's obsession with the sexuality of the body is articulated through particular commodities which are constructed as sexual."[24] Short, tight-fitting, low-cut, revealing dresses and high heels are seen as highly sexualized clothes, widely recognized with (a particular version of) female sexuality.[25] Many of the women explained how from a young age, non-Orthodox Iranian Jewish girls are taught to be put together and dressed in a certain way that shows off their beauty and body, yet still, they are supposed to give off the idea that they are *najeeb*.

Younger Iranian Jewish women are supposed to look beautiful and sexual, but they are not supposed to act upon that sexuality. Sociologist Joanne Eicher wrote that the visibility of the body and flesh is subject to order, surveillance, and regulation, but the exposure of the body is fundamental to femininity and social order.[26] Thus, young women show off their bodies as a fundamental aspect of their female sexuality, while parents regulate women's behavior in order to maintain her virginity. A majority of young Iranian Jewish girls, with the encouragement of their mothers, are waxed, tweezed, manicured, and groomed from a very young age. They are in heels and somewhat revealing clothes from their early teenage years.

Thus, many say they have been raised to go to parties and show themselves, be beautiful and feminine. By the time they are teenagers or in their twenties, young women are attending Iranian Jewish parties, where they exude their femininity. As one woman said, "We dress sexually but classy. We reveal some stuff but not too much." However, no matter how sexy a girl dresses, she is still supposed to give off the belief that she is a virgin. Thus, women (especially adolescent girls) are encouraged to cover up, be modest, and conceal their flesh, and yet at the same time to reveal their bodies through certain styles of clothing.[27] For these young women, the ambiguity of dressing sexy, dancing seductively, and exuding self-confidence at Iranian parties while still supposedly maintaining their *najeeb*ness is integral to their sexual identity and their negotiation of identity.

Iranian Jewish Parties

This particular expression of sexuality is sanctioned only in the space of an Iranian Jewish party where it is seen as a place to meet potential marriage partners. There are rules that young people formulate concerning what is and is not allowed, what they may do, and where they may do it. Thus, there are certain spaces that are viewed as free spaces, where youth can express themselves more freely and not risk being subjected to social control, while other places are more regulated and controlled. The threat of rumors and being labeled by those thought to be the moral majority in a neighborhood may become a dominant factor governing how young people move about in space and charge it with meaning.[28] Despite the alcohol consumption and intimate dancing, the space of an Iranian Jewish social event is where most women feel that it is okay to act out their sexuality while still conveying the belief of their *najeeb*ness.

Unlike their mothers' generation, where women were not supposed to dance provocatively or dress sexually, in order to maintain their *najeeb* image, these young women do not have the same rules. Many interviewees said that their mothers are the ones who encourage them to show off their bodies, albeit tactfully, and be good dancers. Yet, as Julia, a twenty-seven-year-old graduate student, explained, "You go to these Iranian parties, with your mom's approval and, at times, encouragement, wearing the tightest and form-fitting clothes. As a girl, you're supposed to show off your assets but not do it in a tacky way. You go to parties, flirting, dancing, drinking, and socializing with your friends. The girls give off this attitude of sexual freedom, but at the end of the day, we are still supposed to be virgins and *najeeb*."

This is what Julia refers to as the virgin/whore identity: within the enclosed space of an Iranian Jewish party, the girls give off the attitude that they are sexually free, but they, according to the culture, are not supposed to really act upon it. Indeed, many of the women discussed the virgin/whore dichotomy. The virgin/whore dichotomy represents a patriarchal continuum, situated in a framework where women are positioned either as saint-like good girls who wait until marriage to have sex and, even then, only for the purpose of satisfying their husband's desires, or as bad, promiscuous women who sleep with multiple partners, flaunt their sexuality, are not taken as serious relationship partners by men and suffer the scorn of society.[29]

Young Women Who Maintain Their Virginity

Still there are many young women who do follow the rules of the culture and believe it is important to maintain their virginity. Ashley, the eighteen-year-old woman, stressed the importance of maintaining her virginity until she is married. For her, sex is an important act that she only wants to have with her husband. Ashley believes in the values her mother taught her in regards to maintaining her virginity. Rebecca, a nineteen year old who has recently become modern Orthodox, also believes in the significance of maintaining her virginity, but, unlike Ashley, she is not concerned with being *najeeb* for cultural reasons but for religious reasons.

Rebecca is not *shomeret negiah*;[30] however, she says that through her Judaism classes, she has become more aware of the significance of touching. She said:

> I always knew that Persian Jewish girls do have sex. A lot of them do; in fact, a majority of them do; I am in the minority. The reason why I am still a virgin is because of religious and not cultural reasons. Not that sex is bad in Judaism because Judaism embraces sex. Sex is holy, and you should be open with your sexuality, but only with your husband. It is something intimate and should only be done with your husband. Even the whole concept of touching, you can touch and touch and then eventually it leads to sex. I'm not *shomeret negiah*, but I am aware of touching. I have learned about *shomeret negiah*, and I think it is a beautiful concept. It means a lot because when you wait, it means so much.

For Rebecca, abstaining from sex until she is married is a decision she has made because of the religious classes she is attending, which are taught by modern Orthodox women. Her parents are not as religiously observant as she is and while her mother is elated that their daughter is still a virgin, she is worried that Rebecca will become too religious and fears her daughter will become *shomeret negiah*.

According to these women, for their mothers, religion was not a factor in the push to be *najeeb*. Religion, God, and the Jewish understanding of sex were never discussed. Most of the mothers have very little knowledge of Jewish law, and it was never enforced because of their own *najeebness*. Virginity was enforced for cultural reasons: the fear that a man would not marry a woman who was not a virgin. Very few of these women's mothers spoke to them about sex; for the ones who did, their mothers never mentioned the religious significance of being with one's husband or that sex was supposed to be sacred.

Instead, if mothers discussed sex with their daughters, they basically told them to not be sexually active and wait until they were married because of the social stigma attached to a non*najeeb* girl. As one thirty-one-year-old woman said:

> We were never brought up to look at sex as a sacred or beautiful act. The significance of waiting until you get married was never explained in a way that I thought was reputable. My mom didn't say to me, "Wait until you get married because you can share this act with your husband," or something like that, but instead, "A man will never marry a woman who has spoiled herself," or, "If you lose your virginity, you have shamed your dad and me forever." Thus, why am I supposed to be a virgin? Only to appease the old-fashioned and hypocritical view of women that most people in our culture embrace.

All of the women, virgins or not, admitted to finding the views the community has on *najeebness* to be outdated and unfair.

Not Being *Najeeb*

Each of the women in this study was brought up with the values of *najeebness*, especially virginity, yet very few of the nonmarried girls over the age of twenty-five are virgins. As mentioned above, none of the women agree with their mother's version of *najeebness*, and all the women have explained the difficulty of maintaining these traits in America. Shira, a twenty-eight-year-old graduate student, explained why she did not abide by her mother's rules of *najeebness*:

> It is so hard to maintain these archaic rules of purity, especially when you are growing up in America, and you have American friends. You feel like, "Why do I have to maintain these standard[s] when Iranian Jewish guys are not and none of my American friends are either?" When it comes down to rationalizing it and questioning what this is for and whom it is for, you realize how pointless it is and how unfair and hypocritical it is. You just can't assume that girls living in America and influenced by American culture are going to agree and maintain these outdated views on what a woman should be.

Shira is very outspoken with her mother about how much she disagrees with the concept of *najeebness*. To her surprise, her mother agrees with her, yet like most mothers, she feels that if they live within the Iranian Jewish community, they must be conscious of the community's standards and values. Shira said, "I explained to my mom that *najeebness* doesn't need to exist anymore and that there is so much hypocrisy in the community. Guys go and have all their fun and then they want to marry a girl who is a virgin. Meanwhile, girls are supposed to wait all their life for a guy who has slept around and is now ready for marriage. I told my mom how unhealthy that is and how it really hurts a relationship because you're always wondering what you didn't have. And it is unfair to the girls; it shouldn't have to be this way." While Shira's mother agrees with her daughter, she is still a part of the insular Iranian Jewish community and feels that it is difficult to change people's mentalities.

Sexual Anxiety

Many young women admitted that because sex and sexuality was such a taboo subject in their home, they grew up having a lot of anxiety associated with sex—and that anxiety continues today. Some said they do not feel comfortable with their sexuality, while others have admitted that even though they are married, they still have a hard time being sexual, because for so many years, they have had to repress their sexuality in order to fit into the archetype of a *najeeb* girl. Jessica, a thirty-year-old entrepreneur, discussed the negative associations she has with sex. "Every Iranian Jewish woman I talk to, including myself, has issues with sex. We have had these issues when we were single and still have them now that we are married. I think it is the culture. If our parents explained to us that sex isn't bad, and we should not listen to the judgment of our culture, I feel like Iranian Jewish women would not be so anxious about it."

Shireen Oberman, a licensed clinical social worker at Jewish Family Service of Los Angeles, counsels many young Iranian Jewish women. Oberman discussed how many of her clients associate sex and sexuality with guilt. "I see it more with clients who are in their late twenties and early thirties. They have this concept of guilt and that there is a guilt associated with wanting sex, enjoying sex, and wanting that to be a part of an adult, relationship-developing process. This is specifically with women outside of marriage. I see a lot of women who are reluctant to acknowledge that they have had sex and who are reluctant to acknowledge that they have had intimate relationships."

Women who are in their late twenties and early thirties tend to have a more negative association with sex, as opposed to the younger generation of girls, because they are the first generation of children raised in Los Angeles and have struggled with more traditional immigrant parents. They had to delicately balance their Iranian culture at home while trying to appropriate the American culture in public. Many of the women have said that as immigrants, their parents were very fearful of the American world outside their home. Thus, one way parents tried to maintain cultural standards was to instill fear in their children, and for women, sex was associated with fear and guilt. Young women twenty-five years old and younger have fewer negative associations with sex. Their parents moved to America at a much younger age and tend to be a bit more assimilated. Thus, while virginity is still stressed, very few of the younger women (ages eighteen to twenty-five) said that they have negative associations with sex.

Oberman believes that because sex is taboo and is not discussed within the community, the lack of discussion about the importance of sexual compatibility can seriously affect relationships and marriages. She said: "It seems that a lot of women in the community have an altered vision of what they are looking for in a romantic relationship because they are taught that sex is such a nonissue in a relationship. There is not a lot of paying attention to being sexually compatible. What we see is that what goes on in the bedroom is reflective of what goes on in a relationship, so there is a whole degree of intimacy that is not being encouraged or acknowledged and is not being taught to develop." The idea of a woman being sexually satisfied in her marriage is completely foreign to the Iranian Jewish culture. A woman's sexual needs and compatibility is never addressed; therefore, many women find themselves in marriages where they are sexually unhappy and taught to believe that sexual fulfillment should not be a significant aspect of their marriage.

Oberman believes that women should address their sexual needs because sexual incompatibility tends to manifest itself in other parts of the marriage. This generation of women is different than the prior generations because many young women are not looking for a financial supporter, but, more importantly, a life partner. But Oberman believes that Iranian Jewish women are not taught or encouraged to find a compatible partner; instead, they are encouraged to marry someone from a wealthy and "good" family. "There is very little education in regards to dating in this society and in this day and age, it is no longer just about 'Can he can take care of me financially, and does he come from a good family?' It is a transition between marriages for economic security as opposed to marrying someone who is a compatible life partner. When you look at marriage for a partnership, sex does become a big deal because you're not only having sex for the sake of procreation but because you enjoy it." Many of the single young women agree with Oberman and want to marry someone to whom they refer as their soul-mate, as opposed to someone who seems like a "good" match in their parents' eyes.

Pressured into Marrying

Mariam, another licensed clinical social worker at Jewish Family Services of Los Angeles, discussed the pressures placed on her patients to marry men their families would approve of and how many young women do not feel like they have the option to be anything else but a wife. She said, "I see a lot of women who feel like they have to fit into a mold and just kill themselves to fit in. They place these cultural expectations on themselves to fit into what the culture wants them to be, and, thus, they come to me feeling depressed, having low self-esteem, and feeling bad about themselves. And these girls end up making poor decisions for themselves."

One of the poor decisions Mariam sees her patients making is marrying someone because their parents want them to, because they fear their daughters are "too old," even if they are in their early twenties, or because the parents fear the woman will not have other options in the future. She said, "There are a lot of marital issues with my patients because a lot of times they are not looking at the person, but instead they are looking for the package, and once they get married, they realize they are living with the person, and there is a lot of disappointment in their marriage. Most of our phone calls are from young girls who are confused in their marriage. I see a lot of girls who are married to a certain guy because they think they have to marry him; they are not aware of having options in their lives." There is such an emphasis placed on marriage and so much pressure for women to marry at a young age and to marry someone that their families will approve of that once these women do get married, many find themselves dissatisfied and disappointed in their lives and in their spouses.

Parents have "requirements" for their sons-in-law, and many young women feel that if they find a man who fits into those requirements, then they should quickly marry him, whether or not they are truly compatible with him. Thus, parental expectations have a lot to do with whom a daughter marries. The Iranian Jewish women Schiffman interviewed also discuss the requirements their parents have for a son-in-law. All three women said that their parents expect a future son-in-law to be between four and six years older than their daughter, but not more than eight years. He has to be well established, family oriented, educated, and a professional, preferably a doctor—someone who can put a down payment on a house when they get married.[31] He should be from a good family—one that is well off and has no history of divorce. With all these incredibly difficult criteria, it is no wonder that daughters feel so much pressure to find a suitable husband, and the men in the community feel a lot of pressure to make money and be able to provide immediately for their wives.

However, many of the women interviewed for this study refuse to allow parental or societal pressures to force them to get married to someone who will not make them happy. These women are frustrated that the matriarchs in their lives do not respect or understand their desire to marry someone they are attracted to and compatible with. As one woman said, "All anyone cares about is if he has money and comes from a good family. My mom doesn't get it when I say that I'm not attracted to so and so guy or that we have nothing in common. 'Who cares,' she said, 'that's not important; you will learn to be attracted to him.' But that's not the way I want to live my life. I see a lot of girls marry for money or because they think they should marry young, but I wouldn't be happy with that. I wouldn't be happy being this simple-minded *najeeb* girl."

Reclaiming the Meaning of *Najeeb*

While most of my interviewees have an issue with the traditional meaning of the word *najeeb*; there is a group of women who have reclaimed this word and have assigned a new and more culturally appropriate meaning to it. Neda, a thirty-four-year-old realtor, explained what it meant to be *najeeb* when she was growing up. "A *najeeb* girl didn't pay attention to guys or go out with guys, even if they would call. She wouldn't do anything physical with them, let alone sleep with them. She wouldn't date guys, and if a girl had a boyfriend, she was seen as 'one of those girls.' There was definitely a stigma attached to her." But Neda explained that as she has gotten older, she has reinterpreted the concept of being *najeeb*. She believes this word "does not have to connote a woman who is a virgin and timid but instead, a woman who is *najeeb* has self-respect. It doesn't necessarily mean that she denies herself life experiences and doesn't date or have intimate relationships with men, but instead, it means that she respects herself as a woman; she knows where to draw the line, and how to demand that men respect her."

Shirley, a thirty-two-year-old dental hygienist, also reclaimed this word to connote an empowered woman as opposed to the traditional understanding of *najeeb* that characterizes a woman as weak and ignorant. Shirley said:

> The traditional Iranian Jewish understanding of a *najeeb* woman is this young virginal wide-eyed girl who is waiting for her prince/ husband to come and show her the world. It is as if she is ignorant and unexposed to everything until he comes around and shows her the way. In our mothers' generation, an unmarried woman was either *najeeb* or a slut. They didn't understand that you could be intimate with someone and still maintain your self-respect. That is what a *najeeb* woman is to me. It is a new definition that fits into the culture that we are living in. A *najeeb* woman is a woman who is comfortable with her body and herself and knows how to make men respect her. I want to take all the negative association out of this word and use it to empower women as opposed to demoting them.

Some of the more religiously observant women define *najeeb* within a religious context and believe it should not only be used for women, but the new definition should also describe a man's character. For example, Rebecca believes that a *najeeb* woman should be a good wife and mother. She should build a strong Jewish foundation in the home, follow the rules of *niddah* (rules pertaining to menstruation), and observe all the *halakhot* (Jewish laws) that pertain to her. However, Rebecca points out that "both men and women should be humble and respectful to themselves, their bodies, and to each other. It shouldn't just be the woman who is humble, selfless, and respectful of her body, but he should be, too. I think there should be more equality between men and women in our community, and a guy should be *najeeb* along with his wife." While Shirley and Neda's new definition of *najeeb* allows a woman to be sexually active yet empowered within her own body, Rebecca's definition still requires a woman to be a virgin, yet she has a more egalitarian and religious approach to the new meaning of *najeeb*, believing that both men and women should possess these traits. There is no Persian translation for the word "feminist,"[32] but what these young women are doing is reinterpreting the concept of *najeeb* in order to fit into a more modern and American concept of womanhood while maintaining the Iranian Jewish standard of self-respect and moral integrity.

PRESSURES PLACED ON WOMEN

Many of the young women said that along with the pressures of dealing with dual identities and struggling with wanting to embrace American culture while feeling held back by their immigrant parents, some of the most difficult aspects of being a young woman are the physical and material pressures placed on them by the community. The Iranian Jewish community in Los Angeles places significance on one's appearance and financial wealth. This is a community where the area code one lives in, the car one drives, and the purse one totes carry a lot of weight. While these values can extend to the larger culture of Los Angeles, not all communities in Los Angeles place so much significance on wealth and beauty. As one woman said, "Everything in this community goes back to the emphasis placed on image. It is all about your image in the society. It's all about your physical appearance, your social status appearance, and how you portray yourself and your wealth in our society."

There are many reasons why physical appearance and monetary and social status are so significant. The Jewish community in Iran did not prosper financially until the reign of Mohammad Reza Shah, whose regime was characterized by European imperialism and his taste for all things beautiful, expensive, and, some might say, gaudy. As discussed in prior chapters, the Jewish community was heavily influenced by the shah's aesthetics, and everything European and non-Middle Eastern was embraced. Thus, expensive European clothing and accessories became popular within this nouveau riche community, and Western standards of beauty were appropriated. Furthermore, in a community where most parents want their daughters to marry into the most reputable and financially secure family, there is a lot of competition between women to look their best. Thus, the culture of competition only furthers the significance placed on one's looks and wealth.

Lilian, a thirty-four-year-old single woman, explained the social pressures placed on women. She said, "Physically, you have to look good. You get accepted by certain groups of people if you carry a certain purse and shoes, and if you are well put together. The community does not stress working out and being fit, but you do have to be skinny. You always have to get your nails done, your hair done, and carrying a certain bag is really important. It is all about the purse, shoes, clothes, and car. There is a lot of talk about purses." Each one of the interviewees discussed the significance of carrying the "right" purse—meaning anything coming from a high fashion house such as Gucci, Christian Dior, Prada, Louis Vuitton, or Chanel.

The impact these social pressures place on women is that it makes them feel that they must strive to look perfect and have a lot of material wealth in order to be socially accepted in the community. According to these women, it makes a lot of young women feel like they have to live beyond their financial means and pretend to have money even if they do not. The women also discussed how it could create emotional and physical insecurities, making women hyperaware of dieting and exercising. Also, because of the emphasis on material wealth, many women said it has led to a lot of girls marrying a man not because she loves him but because of his wealth and what he can provide for her. The focus on beauty and material wealth is seen even among young teenage Iranian girls.

Significance of Designer Clothes and Accessories

It is not uncommon to see girls as young as sixteen carrying purses that range in price from hundreds to thousands of dollars. Many women in their early thirties and midtwenties stated their disapproval of this phenomenon. One woman said, "The materialism in our community has only gotten worse and more out of hand. When you see a sixteen-year-old Beverly[33] girl carrying an expensive Gucci purse, you know it has gotten out of hand. If she is sixteen and already has this, what is she going to expect to get when she gets older? Did she work for that purse? Chances are, her parents bought it for her, and what values does that teach her?"

An expensive purse is the easiest way for a woman to show her social status in the community. The label is easily identifiable, and, thus, a woman "in the know" can determine what one's financial situation is through the purse a woman carries. Of course, there are always knock-offs of expensive purses, as well as women who will pay a lot of money for a purse even if they cannot afford it, proving the lengths women in the community will go to in order to dress in the latest fashions. While there is no doubt that these women buy these purses for their own aesthetic desires, there is no denying the significance the purses have in determining one's social status in the community.

In her essay, "Jamming Girl Culture: Young Women and Consumer Citizenship," Anita Harris describes how young people find a place in contemporary social life primarily as consumer and that it is young women who exercise the most consumer power.[34] She wrote that because community spaces have become either nonexistent or sites of surveillance, for young people, the shopping mall has almost entirely replaced public spaces, such as the streets or parks.[35] It is within this consumer atmosphere that young people find a site for community, and according to Harris, the confidence and success of young women is measured by their purchasing power.[36]

Harris refers to this as the "Girl Power" market, in which advertisers try to imply that strong and empowered girls are those who have and spend money. Harris wrote that for many young women, this conflation of power with consumption is experienced as being deeply problematic. These women do not see female consumption as representing feminist success.[37] Similarly, many of the women in this study expressed concern about the excessive consumption that takes place within the community, especially among younger girls. They believe that parents, no matter how wealthy they are, should not purchase expensive purses and accessories for their daughters because it only promotes a preoccupation with material, rather than intellectual or spiritual, things, and it further promotes a social hierarchy within the community that is dependent on money and consumption.

Significance of Beauty

Having the right accessories is considered important, but of more significance is a woman's beauty. The first thing discussed when describing a young woman is her physical appearance. When one finds out about a couple's engagement, the bride is always described not by her personality but by her looks. Women who are lighter-skinned and have less "Semitic" but more Anglicized features are traditionally considered to be the most attractive. The ideal bride/daughter-in-law is described as *zagh o boor*, meaning she has light eyes and light hair. One woman said that the women who have classical Iranian features, such as olive skin and dark eyes and hair, are considered to be attractive, but there is an exoticism to a lighter-skinned woman because she is seen as more European. Thus, many Iranian women will play up their exotic features while simultaneously Anglicizing themselves through rhinoplasty, blonde highlights, and permanently straightening their hair.

Sepideh, a thirty-one-year-old accountant, described the pressures her family and the community put on her to get a nose job and to have her dark curly hair permanently straightened. She believes the community is "progressing toward such an American white ideal." Sepideh said:

> My whole family has approached me at one point or another to get a nose job, and frankly, I like my nose. If I turn to one side I can see my grandmother, and if I turn to another side, I can see my grandfather. This was a huge thing for me when I was growing up because I looked so different than my American friends—it was really painful. But when I look in the mirror as I have matured and grown up, I feel that I look different and that I have uniqueness. I feel like the community is washing away our uniqueness through surgery, dying our hair, etc. Look at all the older Persian women: the

older they get, the blonder they get. Everyone takes their beautiful jet-black hair and puts these gold and blond steaks in it. So many women from my mother's generation had nose jobs and convince their daughters to do the same.

The pressure among young women to get rhinoplasty is not only seen in the Iranian Jewish community, but as Lisa Jervis wrote in her essay, "My Jewish Nose," among the Ashkenazi community, too. Jervis wrote that many of her Jewish girlfriends were coerced and shamed into getting a nose job, usually by an older Jewish female relative, such as a mother, grandmother, or aunt. According to Jervis, the desire for the "button nose" is the desire for a "pretty" femininity more than for any specific deethnicizing. However, while these women might not consciously acknowledge it, the true motivation stems from their desire to expunge their ethnicity from their looks as much as possible in order to get a prettier, more "white," or "more Gentile" version of themselves.[38] Like Sepideh, Jarvis observed, while at a leftist charity event in Manhattan attended only by Jewish women, that all of the women had "WASP noses and had nose jobs." She wrote that the pressure Jewish women feel to get nose jobs might stem from the desire to break the mold of the stereotypical Jewish woman as being loud and pushy—qualities that girls, according to Jervis, are really not supposed to have. Jervis questions if a nose job not only ushers in physical femininity but also a psychological, traditional femininity, as well. By altering one's nose, a woman becomes feminine in both mind and body.[39]

The women in Sepideh's family not only pressured her to change her nose but also to straighten her long curly hair. She said, "Curly hair is unpredictable; it makes you look free, wild, and sexy. My mother wants me to straighten my hair because she said it makes me look more presentable." Sepideh refused to let her family or the community persuade her to change her looks in order to mold into a "whiter" version of herself. She believed that her nose, her dark hair, and the texture of her hair made her unique and connected her to her Iranian roots.

The Iranian Jewish community has appropriated and accepted that straight hair and other dominant features of white beauty are coveted and emulated. The pressure for Anglicized features comes from within the Iranian Jewish community, with women—mainly mothers—permeating the idea among the younger generation that women with Anglicized features are more attractive and presentable within the community. Yet at the same time, traditional Iranian features, such as almond-shape eyes, thick but nicely defined and groomed eyebrows and hair, and long, dark eyelashes are believed to be attractive physical traits. Therefore, Iranian women attempt to negotiate two standards of beauty—Iranian-Jewish and contemporary

Western beauty. In this process, a new definition of beauty has emerged, where the standards mold both traditional Middle-Eastern traits with Westernized traits, creating an anglicized Middle-Eastern beauty—where one is not too ethnic looking but yet not too white.

While the women interviewed acknowledged that, in today's society, it is impossible not to focus on one's looks, many expressed frustration that physical appearance is considered more important than one's education, job, and other accomplishments. Azadeh, a twenty-eight-year-old graduate student, said,

> What really saddens me is not the emphasis on education but the emphasis on outer appearance and how you present yourself. I see a lot of girls who are either thinking about or doing plastic surgery, and they don't have to. There is so much emphasis placed on beauty because the belief is that if you want to marry a rich Iranian Jewish guy, you have to look a certain way. And it is repulsive because there is not a lot of pressure on guys to be presentable for the girls; he only has to be wealthy. But there is nothing that says a girl has to have substance behind her. It doesn't matter if she is not educated or has never worked a day in her life; what matters is how beautiful she is.

Many professional, unmarried women, like Azadeh, find it frustrating that the community places so much emphasis on one's outer appearance and marital status and less on their accomplishments. Many women have said that they feel their mothers and the community want them to focus less on their jobs or education and more on getting married.

MARRIAGE

For many women in the community, marriage offers an opportunity to finally live life outside of parental constraints. When a woman is in her father's home, she must act like a proper Iranian Jewish girl in order to find a good husband. When she marries, she is then free to travel, go out late at night, and do all the things that are considered improper for a *najeeb* girl to do. Once she is married, the family does not have to worry about her reputation, and she has the freedom to do what she wants because it is assumed that she is now under the guidance and watchful eye of her husband. Every Iranian Jewish girl has been raised hearing her parents say, "You can do this and that once you are married," or, "You can do that in your husband's house." Many women admitted that it was not until they were married that they were able to travel around the world or see the world outside of their insular community.

A woman's life experience and freedom are validated through marriage and childbirth. Shereen, a graduate student, explained how, at every holiday family gathering, people would say, "Hopefully next year when you come, you will come with your husband." Once a woman is married, they say, "Hopefully next year when you come, it will be with your baby." Women are validated through their husbands, his family name, and his job. It is rare to see girls raised with self-sufficiency and independence. Michelle, who recently married at the age of thirty, said, "I feel so much more accepted and validated in the community now that I am married. People would look at me before as if there is something wrong with me; now women accept me more as one of their own because I have a husband." It is no wonder that many Iranian Jewish girls get married at such a young age. It is the only way to legitimize their freedom, move out of their parents' home, be with a man in public, and feel like they really belong in the community.

Being married allows women to pursue careers that normally would be considered inappropriate for an Iranian Jewish woman. For example, acting is considered a taboo field of pursuit. There is a stigma against a woman entering a profession that is unstable and where she can come into contact with so many people outside of the insular community. However, one woman who is a successful actress admitted that she thinks the community is more accepting of her career choice because she is married. She said, "The community and my family have been unbelievably supportive and proud of my acting career, a career that is out of the norm for an Iranian Jewish woman. I think being married makes it easier for them to support me because there isn't that fear that I would run off with a random director or make unwise decisions. In the community's mind, once you get married, your husband calls the shots, so he decides if he needs to worry about me or not." Thus, because this woman is married, the community believes it is okay for her to pursue a profession that might otherwise seem improper for an Iranian Jewish woman.

Tannoz Bahremand-Foruzanfar, a thirty-four year old who was born in Iran and raised in Los Angeles, attended cantorial school at the Academy for Jewish Religion in Los Angeles. She is the first cantor in the Iranian Jewish community. She recalled how her extended family was opposed to her becoming a cantor because they feared a Persian man would not marry a cantor. She said:

> My parents were really excited for me to go to cantorial school, but other family members and people in the community thought that doing this would be a mistake for me. They were telling my parents, "Don't let her do this, she's not going to get married if she becomes a cantor. No Persian guy is going to want to marry

a cantor." Being on the *bimah* [stage] and singing was so different for them. What ever is unfamiliar they think is not appropriate. In a sad way they are right. Most Persian men would be intimidated by someone who is educated or on stage. They just can't handle it. The funny part is that ultimately, I met my husband, who is Persian, through my job. He was a temple member and he would come to my services, so he had been seeing me. He and his family are very supportive and proud of me.

While at first family members and some members of the community felt trepidation about Tannoz pursuing a cantorial career, once she started singing at Sinai Temple and currently at Stephen S. Wise, they were incredibly proud of her and now take great pride in hearing her. She is so popular that she gets a lot of requests to sing at Persian weddings, and many Persian girls ask for her to be the cantor at their *bat miztvahs*. Tannoz says: "They feel a special connection with me where they might not at all with a man. I mentor these girls for their *bat mitzvah*; it is a seven-month process, and they specifically ask for me to be their cantor on that day. It is a nice time we spend together. I watch them grow, and we create a nice bond. I think it is important for them to see a Persian woman as a role model."

Marriage before a Career

Julia, a single twenty-seven-year-old entrepreneur, discussed how many women within the community and her family members neither understood nor supported her decision to start her own business. She said that, while her mother was more supportive than other women in her family, her mother did say, "Instead of starting your own business right now, maybe you should focus on your social life." When Julia's grandmother asked her why she works so hard, Julia told her grandmother, "I have a lot of creative energy that I want to put out there," to which her grandmother replied, "Well, you can marry someone and put that creative energy into your home." While Julia knows her family is extremely proud of her business accomplishments, she feels, as do all of the other women, that they will be most proud and content when she gets married.

Marriage is considered to be the most important accomplishment in a woman's life. The moment a girl is born into the community, she is greeted with the phrase *ishalah aroos beshi* (God willing, you will be a bride). Girls are raised to be wives and mothers, and it is assumed that family and motherhood is where they will draw their happiness. Azadeh explained: "From a young age they [parents] prepare you; they want you to look presentable and create a good reputation and name, so when we do go out in public, there are people there who see you and want you for their sons. Being a wife is considered to be the end-all and be-all of everything. To me, there is something wrong with that. They are not saying, "I hope you are happy and successful or you are fulfilled in your life." They say, "I hope you become a wife." As if that is the ultimate happiness a woman can strive for."

Nora, a twenty-four-year-old dental student, said, "You definitely get more accolades for being beautiful and marrying young than if you were a doctor or something. Having a postbachelor degree only counts if you are married, because if you aren't married, it means that you have sacrificed everything in your life for your career, which is seen as negative."

Julia agrees with Nora, believing the community gives more merit to a woman who marries young and into a "good" family than to a woman who pursues an education or career. She said, "I swear, the way women talk about someone getting married as if she is achieving the biggest accomplishment of her life, as if she is doing brain surgery or getting her doctorate." While all the women interviewed who were single do want to get married and look forward to meeting the right person, they want their families and the community to value achievements that do not revolve around a man and marriage.

Schiffman's Iranian Jewish interviewees discussed how their parents want them to pursue a graduate degree, but, ultimately, their sole responsibility is to stay home and take care of the kids. All of the women said that is it assumed that once the children are older, it is okay to have a career. One of Schiffman's interviewees explained, "My parents don't encourage me to be a doctor like I want to be. They want me to be educated, but they expect my husband to provide for me and for me to provide the primary care for my children."[40] Even if a married woman does pursue a career, she is still expected to make her family her top priority. It is expected that her husband will provide for her, and she can have a career so long as it does not interfere with marital duties at home.

BURDEN OF SECRECY AND COMPETIVENESS

Because of the emphasis placed on marriage and social status, many women said that girls are raised from a young age to be secretive and competitive with each other. This, according to these women, makes it difficult for many women to have a true and honest friendship. Natasha, a twenty-seven-year-old graduate student, said that even though she grew up in Beverly Hills and was friendly with many of the Iranian Jewish girls in her school, she purposely chose to have American friends, with whom she felt closer and more honest. She said, "When I was younger, I had a lot of Iranian Jewish friends, but when I became a bit more mature, I felt like I couldn't relate to them anymore. There was more of an easiness and honesty with American girls. I had all my Iranian female cousins that I was close to, but I felt like there was too much competition and jealousy between Iranian Jewish girls."

Sahar agreed. "There is a lot of *cheshm ham cheshmi* [competition] and talking behind each other's backs. I didn't feel this with my very close friends, but with my acquaintances it was like that. There is also a lot of family gossiping about your family, and it doesn't make me feel comfortable." Many of the women said that the Iranian Jewish women they are close to and trust tend to be family members—sisters and cousins who are within their age range—but in front of other women, they feel as though there are façades. Even though they grew up with these women and have participated in the same social scene, they refer to other women in the community as acquaintances rather than friends. The distinction highlights the fact that there is very little honesty and openness in those relationships.

According to these women, people within the Iranian Jewish community tend to be very secretive and private about their personal lives. A subject that would seem trivial in another culture, such as whom someone is dating, is not openly discussed within the Iranian Jewish community. These women said there are many reasons why people are so closed off and private. One of the main reasons is that the community tends to be gossipy—so much so that people go to great lengths to keep their private lives to themselves. If someone is seen with the opposite sex, people tend to gossip and assume they are dating or engaged. In many instances, if a woman is dating a man, and it does not result in marriage, her reputation can be defiled in the wider community through local gossip.

GOSSIP

In his book *Synagogue Life*, Samuel C. Heilman wrote about the significance of gossip within insular communities. He asserted that gossip functions as a way for people to exhibit, both to themselves and to others, their status as members and insiders of a community.[41] Gossip is also useful in the exercise of sociability. It is a means of passing time; it offers a means of recreation and tends to solidify group members' identification. Individuals engage in gossip not only as a way of socializing with each other but also as a way of coming together as a community.[42] Through gossip, the community members reaffirm their beliefs of what they see as collective truths and correct behavior. It brings the community together because the realization that control over the facts about oneself is limited by the presence of gossip creates a sort of universal hegemonic weakness that cannot help but foster communal independency.[43]

Gossip not only provides social significance, but it also provides benefits exclusively for individuals. Gossip locates the self in society. It helps place one inside or outside the group, enhances one's status as an insider, allows for characterization that is prestigious and potentially powerful, and generally supports the social position of the gossiper.[44] Finally, gossip also offers the individual an outlet for aggression. Moreover, it does so without forcing an individual into an overt and disruptive show of force. It does so because the community allows individuals to find a way of living within the collectivity, to let off steam, while minimally threatening the stability and security of the group. Gossip can avoid the kind of divisive outburst of anger that often leads to collective disintegration. Members of the community maintain friendly relationships while in private they gossip actively and intensely.[45]

Gossip brings the Iranian Jewish community together. The nature of the gossip tends to revolve around family, divorce, relationships, and so on; thus, it is a way of knowing what is going on within the community. Gossip helps establish a family's reputation, which is then taken into consideration when individuals within that family are dating for marriage. Basically, when a couple starts dating, the parents find out about the reputation of the other family members by inquiring about them, mainly trying to find out any gossip that is associated with them. If the gossip about a family is bad, then that family establishes a negative reputation that can hurt them when it is time for their children to marry. Similarly, if a family's reputation is good within the community, the families will easily support the relationship. Thus, gossip plays a vital role in deciding whether families will be accepting of their future sons- or daughters-in-law.

Gossip within the Iranian Jewish community also helps to establish what the community considers appropriate conduct. Women gossip among each other and relay the gossip back to their daughters as a way of reinforcing correct behavior in the community and also showing their daughters the consequences of acting inappropriately. Basically, gossip displays to the young women in the community what they have in store for them if they too act in some way that can tarnish their and their family's reputation.

Iranian Jewish women tend to be secretive not just because of gossip, but also because of the competitive element to dating and marriage. Many of the women said that they do not openly discuss whom they are dating, out of fear of competition and, as some have said, getting "the evil eye" from a jealous person.

COMPETITION AMONG WOMEN

Ruth, a thirty-three-year-old schoolteacher, explained how mothers teach their daughters to be competitive in order to marry the right man. She believes young women are taught to have an aggressive and competitive stance toward each other, thus, making it difficult for women to maintain friendships with other women in the community. Ruth explained: "I've been warned by my mother and aunts that girls will screw you over to get a man. There is a lot of competition to get married. I have heard mothers tell daughters, 'Don't let her get married before you.' I have also heard that friendship does not matter if the right man is involved. Mothers teach their daughters how to play games; it is infused in the culture, and it makes it very difficult to have honest and intimate relationships with many women in the community."

While Ruth's close girlfriends are Iranian Jews, she believes that the emphasis placed on marriage encourages competition between young women and discourages any type of openness in the community. Thus, when other women are closed off and secretive about their lives, it is hard to develop real friendships. "I go to these Iranian parties and really have nothing to say to these girls," said Sahar. "They don't tell you what's really going on in their lives, if they are dating anyone, etc., so you end up having such a trivial conversation with them which revolves around clothes, shoes, etc. It is hard to be close to someone and share with them if they are not doing the same with you."

Rita, a thirty-three-year-old mother of two, agrees with Sahar but says that not every Iranian woman is like that. Rita said, "Yes, there are a lot of women in the community who are competitive, even after they get married, and secretive, but my relationship with my Iranian friends is not like that. You find the women you can relate to, and we have no problems opening up to each other and using each other as therapists and confidants." Thus, although there is a very private and closed-off environment within the Iranian community, there are many women who do not abide by that ethos and feel comfortable openly discussing their private lives without the fear of gossip or being judged.

INDEPENDENCE

Along with physical and material pressures, one of the most difficult pressures placed on young Iranian Jewish women is the belief that they must live their lives for their family and the community. Girls are not raised to be independent; it is not a trait that is encouraged or valued within the community. There is a belief that parents live for their children, and children live for their parents. Thus, going away to college, living on your own, and exploring the world outside of the insular Iranian Jewish community is not an option for most girls. Getting married at a young age and providing grandchildren is considered more culturally appropriate. Ruth explained: "If you are an independent woman and want to explore the world and want to find yourself and find out who you are, it doesn't lend itself to being a wife and a mother in your early twenties. Women are not raised with a sense of agency and autonomy in their life. There is a fear that if you go see the world outside of our little bubble, you will never come back and be satisfied living in an insular community and playing the role of a wife and mother. Independence is not encouraged, but what you get instead is this promotion of a sense of community that I haven't seen anywhere else."

While Ruth acknowledges the downfalls of raising children to be dependent on the family, she also stresses that there are some positive aspects that come from a lack of independence. She believes that the reason the Iranian Jews have such an incredibly strong sense of community, family values, and respect for the culture and religion stems from having an insular community. While a majority of the women agree with Ruth and appreciate the strong sense of family and love the community offers, most have expressed that one of the many negative aspects of raising daughters with a lack of independence is that careers and autonomy are not encouraged, making women even more dependent on men for money and their livelihood. This can have detrimental consequences, especially if a young woman finds herself unable to leave a bad marriage because she has never been self-reliant.

Natalie, a thirty-year-old writer, discussed how she has seen many girls her age in bad marriages, for whom divorce is not an option:

> I see a lot of girls who have gotten married at a really young age, right out of college, and have never worked and never did anything on their own. Now a lot of these girls are older, and some have found themselves with husbands that they are no longer compatible with. But divorce is not even a reality for them. What are they going to do? Yes, he can still financially support her after the divorce, but she has never been on her own; for a lot of women, the thought of being self-reliant is debilitating. This is the problem with raising girls to get married at a young age and not encouraging them to stand on their own two feet. It makes women feel like they don't have options and must depend on their husbands for everything.

Many of the mothers discussed in chapter 3 said they themselves felt or knew women from their generation who felt the same lack of choice or the sense that they could not be on their own. However, even though many of these women felt trapped in bad marriages, they still encouraged their daughters to marry young and do not foster their individuality and autonomy. Thus, many daughters are emulating their mothers—getting married at a young age without a career to fall back on or any financial independence. Like their mothers, they, too, find themselves married to a man they no longer feel compatible with, yet feeling that they have no choice but to remain in the marriage due to a lack of options in their lives.

However, not all mothers encourage their daughters to marry young and discourage the pursuit of a career or education. Many have learned from their own lives or from the lives of their friends and want to make sure their daughters do not follow in their footsteps. Charlene, a twenty-one-year-old college student, explained that her mother always placed a lot of emphasis on education and career, in order to make sure her daughter will be self-sufficient. She said, "My mom always made sure I did well in school and wants me to have a legitimate career, so I never have to depend on a man for anything. She also does not want me to date and marry someone who is a lot older than me, even if he has a lot of money, because she feels that I will regret it in the future when the age difference catches up with me. She definitely sees how unhappy a lot of her friends are and doesn't want my sister and me to have that life." While Charlene's mother wants her daughters to marry into reputable families, she wants to make sure that they never feel trapped in their marriages and that, if necessary, they feel confident to be on their own.

Most mothers are not like Charlene's and do not encourage their daughters to be independent, but that has not stopped many of these women from living the life that they want, despite their parents' disapproval. Although a majority of Iranian Jewish women stay in Los Angeles for college, it is becoming increasingly common for young girls to attend out-of-state schools. Many of the young women went to graduate school with their parents' encouragement (as long as they still focus on getting married), and more and more families are comfortable letting their daughters pursue graduate degrees out-of-state. Two women traveled on their own through South East Asia, and those less adventurous traveled abroad, mainly to Europe and to Israel.

Many of the younger women (interviewees between the ages of eighteen and twenty-five) said that they choose to get jobs because it allows them more freedom. One nineteen year old said, "My parents will financially support me, but I choose to work because if I have my own money, they have less of a say in what I do and how I spend it. It makes me feel good to buy something and know I worked hard for it. Plus, there are times when I tell them that I am at work and instead, I am out with my boyfriend. So not only does being financially independent give me more freedom, but it also gives me a lot of excuses to spend time with my boyfriend." Thus, many young Iranian Jewish women question and challenge cultural norms by going away to college, attaining a higher education, traveling, and becoming financially self-supporting. Through these experiences, they become less dependent on others and learn more about themselves.

BA'ALOT TESHUVAH (WOMEN WHO RETURN)

Through this process of self-exploration, many girls in the community have become more religious than their parents, and many have said that this has caused a lot of discord within the family. Four of the women became religiously observant. While one, Rebecca, has the support of her parents because they, too, have become more observant, the other young women said that their parents disapprove of their religiosity.

Four of the women became religiously observant when they traveled to Israel with a religious group. While these young women did not discuss wanting to repent for their ways, they expressed feeling more fulfilled in their lives by following Jewish *halakhah* (law). Leora, a twenty-two-year-old college student, said that through becoming *shomeret Shabbat* (observing of the Sabbath) and keeping kosher, she feels calmer and more directed in her life.

As Rebecca's father became more religiously observant, he slowly made the family follow his path. Of all her siblings, Rebecca became the most devout. While her mother approves of her new-found religiosity, she still worries that Rebecca will become too religious, making it difficult for her to live with her family and to find a good husband within the community. Meanwhile, Leora's parents do not support her religious observance and feel that it will destabilize their family. While Leora has forced her parents to purchase kosher meat, she said, "My mom's biggest fear is that I won't eat at their house or come over for Shabbat because their house isn't strictly kosher. She worries that I will marry a 'black-hat'[46] and that her grandchildren will never eat or come over to their grandparents' house for dinner. Our biggest fights occur over driving on Shabbat. If relatives live too far away, I can't walk to their house, so I don't go. 'See,' my mother says, 'that is how your religiosity is disturbing family unity.' In order to compromise with her, I will sit in a car, but I won't be the person driving. She thinks I have become too fanatical."

Research conducted in the United States and in Israel suggests that when young adults become religious, their relationship with their family may destabilize. A study of 150 newly Orthodox women in five American urban areas found that *ba'alot teshuvah* (literally, "women who return") often are estranged from their families.[47] Similarly, Janet Aviad showed that a child's intensified Jewish observance produces strain in relations between parents and children.[48] Adult children who distance themselves from their parents by moving into a religious neighborhood or refusing to eat at their parents' home challenge the family's sense of cohesion and impede family celebrations, which usually involve food.[49]

Iranian Jewish parents feel that adult children who will not eat at their house due to dietary restrictions[50] and will not drive to attend Shabbat dinners are distancing themselves from the family. The disruption of family unity and cohesion is a fear within the culture. Parents fear that their daughters will marry a religious man and raise children who will disapprove of their grandparents' lack of observance, or that their daughter will not bring the grandchildren around the nonreligious family. For Persian parents, the thought of losing a daughter and grandchildren due to religious observance is heartbreaking, and the thought that a rabbi or a religious scholar might have more of an influence on their adult child's life is incredibly threatening. Thus, the slightest sense of increased observance within adult children has parents fearing that their child will be "fanatical" and separated from them.

Leora said that her mother began to worry when she started dressing more modestly. She said, "My mom started freaking out when I started wearing more modest clothes. She feared that I would end up wearing a *shaitel* [wig] or covering my hair with scarves. I told her I will never end up being that girl in the long jean skirt and long-sleeve blouse, but that I care about the way I dress and don't want to attract negative attention. I swear, sometimes I think she would be happier if I wore slutty clothes like some of these Iranian girls, with my skirt up to my thighs and my boobs popping out." Leora has found that the only way she can assuage her mother's fear is through compromising with her; she follows the Jewish laws as long as it does not hinder family cohesion and closeness. However, Leora and the other three observant women said that they wished their mothers would support their decisions to become more devout and would take the time to understand them, as opposed to finding their new religious practices to be threatening.

Because *ba'alot teshuvah* are such a new phenomenon within the Iranian Jewish community, only time will tell how these young women's new religiosity will affect family cohesion and if Iranian Jewish mothers will embrace and accept their daughters' Orthodox practices or if they will reject them.

MOTHER-DAUGHTER RELATIONSHIPS

The bond between mothers and daughters tends to be the strongest and most enduring of family ties and women tend to have the most consistent, direct contact with other generations. The mother-daughter relationship tends to go through a lot of tension and intimacy, where mothers tend to have a closer relationship with their daughters than they do with their sons, but also a higher degree of conflict with their daughters, as well. The psychological reasons for the greater intensity of the mother-daughter bond stems from the development of personality and identity. The ties between mother and daughter in childhood and adolescence shape the daughter's sense of identity. As mothers and daughters age, the bond may change form, becoming more complex as their relationship goes through stages of interconnectedness, independence, autonomy, closeness, and distance. In many instances, this causes mothers and daughters to have both positive and negative feelings toward the other, potentially leading to feelings of ambivalence about the relationship.[51]

The relationship between mothers and daughters within the Iranian Jewish community is ostensibly one of reverence and love. All the mothers interviewed in chapter 3 said they live for their children and, ultimately, for their happiness. Mothers believe it is their duty to not only love and provide for their children, but also to ensure a good future for their daughters and teach them how to be "domestic goddesses." While the young women interviewed expressed a deep feeling of love, respect, and admiration for their mothers, very few admitted to being close to their mothers in regard to personal issues.

Most of the younger women interviewed have ambivalent attitudes toward their mothers and have expressed desires to have, at times, more autonomy and independence. Because many nonmarried women still live with their parents and because familial life and communal life tends to be incredibly dependent and insular, many girls feel that their relationship with their mothers is too claustrophobic, and they need to separate from them in order to establish their own identity. Research suggests that interdependence can create not only positive feelings of solidarity, but also negative feelings of conflict and dissatisfaction. Frequent contact with family members, facilitated by coresidence or close proximity, can foster emotional intensity. Those who live close to one another have more opportunities for both affectionate and distressing relationships.[52] Most of the young women expressed ambivalence about their relationship with their mothers—they simultaneously love their mothers and are incredibly affectionate toward them, yet they also want more independence from them and feel that they cannot confide in them.

However, many of them said that through marriage and motherhood, they have developed a closer relationship with their own mothers. Within the Iranian Jewish culture, it is the mother who plans the numerous parties for her daughter's wedding. She teaches her daughter how to cook traditional Persian meals, how to prepare for a Sabbath dinner that brings the family together, and how to maintain the home. Many of the young mothers depend heavily on their own mothers to help raise their children. In that sense, there are very close bonds among mother, daughter, and grandchildren.

Thus, it is within the domestic realm that daughters, especially those who are married, feel like they can bond with their mothers.

Appreciating Mothers

For many of these women, becoming a wife and a mother made them appreciate their own mothers, especially the opinions and advice they give in regard to maintaining the domestic realm. Joya, who has been married for two years and recently became a mother, explained,

> It wasn't until I got married and more recently, since I became a new mom, that I really became close to my mom. All of the things she is good at—keeping a beautiful home, cooking, and maintaining the family structure—became important to me when I became a wife and now a mother. And now that I have a newborn, I depend on her more than ever. Just having her around with my child is comforting. I would not go to my mom for advice on marriage and how to interact with my husband, she comes from a very different generation in regards to things like that, but I really appreciate her input when it comes to keeping the rituals within the home and helping me with my child.

While many young women might take for granted having their mothers so heavily involved in their lives, Sherri, whose father is Iranian and mother is American, felt the pangs of not having an Iranian mother to help her plan her wedding parties and to teach her how to maintain an Iranian Jewish home. Sherri described how she had to learn many customs from her aunts or create them herself: "I had to create my own rituals in my house because I didn't have anyone to learn from. I learned from watching my cousins' moms and other mothers around me. I didn't have a mother who could teach me all these things. It wasn't done in my home, so I really had to learn how to do these things on my own. I didn't know how to cook Persian food or how to set up my house for a party or for Shabbat. My father planned everything, even my wedding party. He took up a lot of the domestic roles within the house because my mother didn't." While as a teenager Sherri had a lot more freedom than other Iranian girls her age because her mother, as an American, was less strict, when Sherri became a mother and a wife, she wished she had a mother who would pass down the recipes and rituals that characterized an Iranian Jewish home.

Not only do mothers play a significant role in teaching their daughters domestic rituals, but they also help raise grandchildren. Because most interviewees live close to their parents—often down the street or only a few miles away—and because women within the community marry at a young age, it is common to see grandmothers actively raising their grandchildren. Although many of the married women have at least one, and sometimes two, housekeepers, all of them said that their mothers play an integral part in their children's lives, taking them to and from school and spending hours with them during the day or babysitting at night. Children spend so much time with their grandparents that it is not uncommon to hear toddlers speak English with a Persian accent, picking up on their grandparents' way of speaking. Grandmothers believe that taking care of their daughter's children is an extension of their maternal duties, and they do it very willingly. Many attend parenting classes, such as the one offered at Nessah, an Iranian synagogue located in Beverly Hills, in order to learn how to better discipline and relate to their grandchildren.

Mastaneh, a licensed clinical social worker who teaches parenting classes at Nessah Synagogue, said, "Many grandmothers are attending our parenting classes because parenting has become so different over the years, and grandmothers are so heavily involved in raising their grandchildren. When you're talking about the way parents were parented when they were younger in Iran, it is a lot more different than the way their kids are being raised here in America." Thus, the role of grandmother and caretaker is so important to these women that they see it as their job to take care of their grandchildren.

There is a deep sense of camaraderie with respect to the task of raising a child in the Iranian Jewish community. Often, young women not only depend on their mothers but also other women in their family, such as sisters, aunts, great-aunts, great-grandmothers, and cousins. Lena, a thirty-two-year-old working mother, often feels guilty leaving her daughter in order to work, but she takes comfort in knowing that her daughter is being watched over by her mother, aunts, sister, and cousins. She said, "Although I have a full-time nanny, she doesn't really help raise my daughter. She is there more to do the back-bending work such as changing her diaper, feeding her, etc.—things that are more difficult for my mom to do as she is getting older. But when I am off at work, my mother and her sisters are the ones who really take care of my child. My own sister is also heavily involved in spending time with her, and even my female cousins do a lot of babysitting for me. At different times, every one of them has taken her to her numerous toddler classes when I cannot attend. It really does take a village to raise a child, and I am blessed to have so many women around me who help raise her." All the young mothers interviewed expressed the same sense of gratitude.

In his research on multigenerational families and their bond, Vern L. Bengston describes how the involvement of grandparents and other family members provide stability and continuity for families and their children.

The increase in multigenerational kin provides support and well-being for younger family members. The increased longevity of parents, grandparents, great-grandparents, and other family members in recent decades represents a resource of kin available for help and support that can be, and frequently is, activated in times of need.[53] Research has shown how children and mothers benefit from grandparents' involvement in their lives. Grandparents provide many unacknowledged functions in contemporary families. They serve as important role models in the socialization of grandchildren. They provide economic resources to younger family members. They contribute to cross-generational solidarity and family continuity over time.[54] In this study, the deep involvement of grandmothers helps provide the younger generations with a link to their cultural past, teaching them about the Iranian Jewish culture and the Persian language.

Sociologist Lucy Fischer studied symbolic and interactional dimensions of the mother-daughter relationship as young adult daughters move from single life to marriage and motherhood. Throughout Fischer's analysis, she found that both the daughter's marriage and her pregnancy caused mothers and daughters to feel closer to one another; her data demonstrated that marriage and motherhood seemed to increase the daughter's desire for closeness and continuity with her mother.[55]

Unmarried Women and Their Mothers

While many of the married women said that they felt closer to their mothers once they became wives and mothers, almost all of the unmarried women, ranging in age from eighteen to thirty-five, said they found it difficult to confide in their mothers or to talk about personal issues with them. The women felt a generational and cultural gap, making it very difficult for mothers and daughters to understand and relate to each other. Many of the issues these single women are dealing with, such as college or graduate school, jobs, and dating, were not issues their mothers were confronted with while living in Iran. Thus, many young women said that they feel like their mothers' advice pertaining to many aspects of their lives is not applicable.

Many girls expressed frustration with their mothers for being self-sacrificing and for allowing themselves to be taken advantage of by others. They feel that their mothers neglect their own emotional and psychological needs in order to take care of everyone else. They feel that the self-sacrificing and *najeeb* qualities that their mothers were taught to poses hinder a woman's personal growth and emotional expression. Thus, many girls say that because they have seen how their mothers have suffered through their self-sacrificing behavior, they feel that they must protect their mothers. And as members of the younger generation have learned to stand up for themselves, many girls feel that they must share their strength with their mothers, putting themselves in a maternal role. This maternal role makes the daughter the protector of the mother, while simultaneously making her feel that she cannot depend on her mother for her own emotional problems, thus, causing a distance.[56]

One woman discussed this role reversal. She said:

> I really feel like my mother is a child, and I am the mother. I watch the way she emotionally handles certain issues, and it is as if she stopped maturing at the age of twenty-one, which is the age she got married. The way she handles fights with my dad or how quickly she gets offended by her friends or in-laws and doesn't say anything to them or doesn't defend herself—instead, she just holds it in and deals with it like a child. I just sit there and want to say, "Come on, Mom, deal with this like a mature woman." But in a lot of ways, I don't think she is an emotionally mature woman. Yes, she is an altruistic and selfless wife and mother, and I really commend her for keeping our family and home together, but when it comes to dealing with emotional issues and everyday life events, she really acts like a little girl. I am the one who has to coach her on what to say, to tell her to defend herself.

Mother's Keeper

A majority of these women said that they, as daughters, were the ones who had to deal with their mother's emotional unhappiness and discontent. All of the women expressed resentment toward their mothers for burdening them, often times at a young age, with being their therapist and confidant. Because seeking mental therapy is taboo for Iranian Jewish women and because there is a deep sense of secrecy within households, when a mother had problems with her husband or in-laws, or was battling with some type of mental issue, she would confide and often complain, scream, and cry to her daughter, instead of confiding in her girlfriends, sisters, or a therapist.

Sandy, a twenty-year-old college student, expressed what it was like growing up as her mother's confidant and therapist:

> I was the person who had to be there to listen to my mother complain and talk about people who hurt her. She would vent to me and cry. She was brought up to be a *najeeb* girl, which meant that she wasn't brought up to talk back to anyone or to speak her mind. She always had to be nice and proper. Thus, when she got

hurt or sad, she would take it out on us. When her in-laws would speak disrespectfully to her or when she would get into a fight with my dad, she would come to me and tell me about it. She still does that. It is very stressful to me, and it doesn't help me move on from my own stress and problems. She thinks I should be her best friend and should take on all the burdens of her unhappiness, and that is a lot of pressure placed on me.

Sandy finds it hard to manage the issues a normal twenty-year-old girl deals with while also feeling pressure to make her mother's life better. She believes she is not emotionally equipped to handle her mother's mental and emotional unhappiness. Because she is caught in the middle of her parents fighting and her mother's complaining, she chooses to spend less time at home in order to not be involved in family problems.

Marital problems comprise the bulk of the mothers' complaints and unhappiness. A majority of the young women said that from a very young age, their mothers would turn to them to discuss their unhappiness with their husbands. Although many of the young women have older brothers, their mothers never once complained to or burdened their brothers, but instead chose to confide and vent to their daughters. All the girls said that this instilled in them a lot of anxiety from a very young age. Monica, a twenty-seven year old, said:

I resent my mother for making me her therapist and confidant. I think that is the one major fault she had in raising me. From the time I was five years old, my mother would complain to me about my father and their relationship, and she didn't do it to my brother but to me. And even though she has two sisters and a mother that she was very close to, she would never tell them about her problems with my father because she didn't want to upset them. But yet it was okay to upset your five-year-old daughter. It caused a lot of anxiety for me when I was growing up. I was always worried about their fighting and getting in between them to mediate between them, as early as the age of five.

For some young women, living in the middle of a dysfunctional marriage and feeling obligated to make the mother's life better has caused so much angst and trauma that, despite the social stigma attached to a divorce within the community, they have begged their parents to separate in order free themselves of the constant fighting and unhappiness in their home. Dalia, a twenty-nine-year-old mother, begged her mother to seek divorce. She said:

My mother would always cry to me and vent to me about how unhappy she was with my father. I told my mother by the time I was ten that she needed to get a divorce. When I was fifteen they were fighting so much that I said that I couldn't deal with it anymore, and they had to divorce. She told me she needed to wait until my brother and I were married and settled so she wouldn't ruin our chances of marrying into a good family. They finally got a divorce a couple of years ago, and I resent them for not doing it earlier. There was so much pressure on me, never on my brother. I felt like I lost my childhood because there was never a time that I was not worrying about them. I was never carefree; I always had a pit in my stomach because she put so much hardship on me when I was young. I felt like I had to fix their dysfunctional relationship and fix all the sadness and regrets in her life.

Anna, a twenty-two-year-old college student, said her parents' fighting and her mother's unhappiness had become so bad that she insisted numerous times that they see a therapist or get a divorce. She, too, from a young age, remembers her mother complaining and crying to her and her older sisters over her marriage and in-laws. Anna does not feel she can handle her mother's mental breakdowns, nor is she equipped to give her advice. It has become so overbearing for her that she spends less time at home and says she wants to get married only to leave her parents' house. She said:

> I told my mom, "Look, I am twenty-four years old, and I'm not going to cry if you get a divorce. Don't stay with Dad for me. I don't want to hear about your problems any more; if you have a problem with each other, go see a therapist or talk to each other, don't complain about it to me." It has really affected me, and it affects my relationship with men. I feel guilty because I know that she loves me so much, so the least I can do for her is to be there and listen to all her sadness and unhappiness, but it is too much for me to handle. There needs to be boundaries between mother and daughter. That is why I want to get married, so I can get out of the house and not have to deal with this any more.

Many women have begged their mothers to seek counseling and asked their parents to see a marriage counselor. All said that their parents as a couple and their mothers individually scoffed at the idea of going to a therapist. Instead, mothers choose to act as though they have a perfect marriage in front of the community while, behind closed doors, many are extremely unhappy and choose to turn their daughters into their therapist, from adolescence into adulthood. The mothers are not aware of the pressure they have placed on their daughters, or the anxiety they feel, and while all of the mothers say they love their daughters and would do anything for their happiness, they do not realize that part of that happiness entails *their own* happiness and mental well-being. Many of the women interviewed are not only struggling to find their identity while living in two worlds, American and Iranian, but also with the belief that they are responsible for their mother's emotional health.

Mothers Living Vicariously through Their Daughters

Much of an Iranian Jewish mother's happiness is derived from her children's lives. Many mothers look to their daughters, specifically, to live a life that they were not able to have. Each of the third-generation women said that her mother, in many ways, lives vicariously through her, and each discussed the pressure she feels to live their own life while still making her mother happy. A mother's influence and opinion can be so overwhelming that many women discussed how women within the community marry men not for love but because their mothers would consider the man to be a good and suitable husband. Beth, a twenty-three-year-old teaching assistant, whose mother always complained about how little money her father would bring home, said:

> My mom looks to me to find the husband she never had, the house, the car, and the wealthy social group she never had. My mother wishes that I would be more involved in the Iranian Jewish social scene, so I can find a husband to provide the wealth she never had. She always said, "Find somebody that will be a good husband." Not a good partner or a soul mate, but really someone who will be able to provide for you. Surprisingly, what she also means is, find someone you can control and lets you be the head of the household while he is the financial provider.

While Beth's mother wants her daughter to marry a wealthy man, so he can give her the material possessions that her father never provided for the family, other mothers recognize that, because they married at such a young age, had a short courtship, and, most likely, married a man because their family approved of him, their daughters should marry a man she loves and knows well, as opposed to someone with financial resources and good family name.

Mimi, a twenty-eight-year-old graduate student, said that because her mother has seen so many women from her generation marry men that they did not love simply because they would be good providers, she always advised her daughters to marry for love. Mimi said:

> She has seen how so many of her friends are unhappy with the men they married and how they did not know them at all when they got married; she tells me it is important to marry someone that you love than to marry them for their money. Her friends think she is crazy to give my sisters and me that advice because it is so much more common for Iranian Jewish mothers to stress the significance of financial wealth. She also told me to marry a man who doesn't come from money but instead made it himself so he is not spoiled and knows the value of a dollar. My dad comes from a very wealthy family who lost all of their wealth when they immigrated to Los Angeles, and my father was never able to really create his own business and make money on his own. So for my mom, her life lessons have taught her to teach us to marry for love and not for money.

Although most of these women said their mothers would rather see them married than pursuing a career, a few young women said that their mothers are proud and encouraging of their higher education and career. Because few Iranian Jewish women dated or pursued higher education or a career when they lived in Iran, instead becoming wives and mothers at a young age, many mothers are excited to have their daughters date (for marriage) and are very proud of their daughter's education and professions. Helen, a twenty-nine-year-old elementary school teacher, said: "It's interesting because now it is up to me to teach my mom what the outside world is like. She is definitely living through me: She is excited about my dating and my social life, she is excited about my job. Every time I come home from a date she is like a little girl; she wants to know where he took me, what was he like, etc. I think she has some resentment and feelings of sadness that she never lived a life that she wanted. She was really smart, and instead of doing something with her good grades, she had to get married at a young age and be a stay home mom. It makes me sad for her."

Many women expressed similar sentiments. They feel that their mothers turn to them to live the lives they were never able to have, due to social and gender restrictions. Like Helen, they are their mothers' link to the outside world. And like Helen, the women recognize in their mothers a sense of melancholy or resentment for not being supported and encouraged to pursue a life outside of being a young wife and mother.

Many of these women said that their mothers stressed their education because they felt that an education leads to financial independence and makes a woman less reliant on a man for her livelihood. Shauna, a twenty-year-old college student, explained that her mother stresses her college education and wants her to have a good job because she doesn't want Shauna to feel like she needs to marry someone for his money. Shauna's mother does not want her to be dependent on a man or stay with him if she is unhappy because he financially supports her. Shauna said, "My mom has seen so many women stay in bad marriages because they are so afraid to be on their own and have never had a job and made money on their own. She never wants my sister and me to be dependent on a man in that way. She believes that once a man controls the money in the house, he can easily control your life." Numerous women's mothers have expressed similar sentiments: they want to ensure their daughter's happiness and lack of dependence on a man.

However, while many mothers encourage their daughters to pursue an education and a career and to be financially independent, they are simultaneously enforcing traditional gender roles and encouraging them to get married soon. Many of the women said that there are contradictions in their mothers' support for their own interests and self-empowerment. They said that their mothers encourage independence, but not *too much* independence, because they fear that too much independence will lead to marriage at a later age. Mothers also want their daughters to have a successful career, but they do not want that career to interfere with their domestic and maternal duties. Thus, Iranian Jewish daughters are raised with contradictory attitudes toward marriage, motherhood, careers, and independence.

Iranian Jewish mothers do not encourage their daughters to get married later in life but, instead, encourage them to get married while simultaneously getting an education and having a career. However, the mothers do not want that career to interfere with the traditional domestic and maternal duties that are expected of Iranian Jewish women.

Raising Their Own Daughters

The women in this study said that because they had such a difficult time negotiating between two cultures, wanting to respect their parents and their culture yet trying to be normal American teenagers, they hope and want a different future for their own daughters. Many said that they want to raise their daughters with all the love they have been given by their own mothers and an appreciation for the Iranian Jewish culture, yet with more freedom and independence. They do not want to pass on the pressure to be *najeeb*, feeling this is an unrealistic expectation forced on young women and that it will only lead to lying and dishonesty within the home.

Many said that they regret having a distant relationship with their mothers, especially in regard to their personal lives, but felt that they had no choice but to constantly lie to their mothers in order to live like other American teenagers and young adults. As Pouran, a thirty-three-year-old mother of two daughters, said, "I want my girls to be brought up exploring the world, to be independent, and smart. I know my husband and I are raising them in a loving family and teaching them good values; thus I hope they will always make good decisions in their life, and I can trust them to see the world but not participate in the negative aspects of it." In regard to sexuality, Pouran believes, "Our daughters will not have the same expectations that we did. It is ridiculous to assume they won't be sexually active, so instead, I will teach them to respect their bodies and hope that I will create a space that they will feel comfortable talking to me about it, as opposed to sneaking around like I had to."

Iranian Jewish mothers feel that they have to raise their daughters within the ideology of the community, thus condoning and propagating the patriarchy and double standards that exist within it. The mothers might not agree with the rules and expectations they have placed on their daughters, but feel that if they did not go along with them, they risk having the family and daughter's reputation tarnished, thus ruining her, and possibly her siblings', chance of marrying into a "good" family. Few mothers have the support or the strength to stand up to the community and raise their daughters outside of its cultural norms. However, the young women believe that it is time to completely change the rules and expectations placed on women within the community. They want to see a more egalitarian community where men and women are held to the same rules and standards. Unlike their immigrant parents' generation, they do not fear the American culture around them; they believe it is possible to bring the best of both cultures into their lives. Thus, they are able to maintain the love, respect, and closeness of the Iranian Jewish community while also promoting a more self-reliant environment for young women to explore their identity and options outside and within the domestic sphere.

A NEW GENERATION

Young Iranian Jewish women are challenging the strict hierarchical arrangements within the family structure through role reversal and challenging the gendered hierarchy within the community by defining their own sexuality and instigating female independence. They prove that young

Iranian Jewish women do not abide by a rigid interpretation of what is expected of them; instead, they are prone to shift, change, and appropriate aspects of Iranian Jewish and American cultures in order to develop and define their hybrid identity. These women have developed a hybrid identity that allows them to live in multiple landscapes that revolve around their Iranian Jewish culture, their American surroundings, and their gender.

A majority of the women were brought up with the value of being *najeeb*—meaning not only virginal, but also docile and unknowing of the world. However, a shift has occurred in which a group of women have reclaimed the word and assigned it a new and more culturally appropriate meaning. For some women, the new definition connotes a sexually comfortable woman who demands respect from men; a woman who is comfortable with herself, independent, and empowered, yet still respects the values and morals of the community.

For the religiously observant women, the word *najeeb* has a new definition placed within a religious and egalitarian context. For these young women, a *najeeb* girl is still a virgin who observes all the *halakhot* that pertain to her. But, according to these young women, both women and men should be *najeeb*. Women and men are obligated to be mindful and respectful not only of themselves and their own bodies, but more importantly, of each other. Thus, while both groups of women have a different reinterpretation of *najeeb*, they are redefining the word in order to fit into a more modern and American concept of womanhood, while still upholding their community's standards of self-respect and moral integrity.

Beauty is another concept that has been reinterpreted by young Iranian Jewish women. A woman's appearance has always been important to the Iranian Jewish community, and many women said that the community places many physical and material pressures on young women. Iranian women attempt to negotiate two standards of beauty: a contemporary Westernized beauty, in which Anglicized features such as straight hair (often highlighted and bleached) and a less Semitic nose have become the norm, and traditional Iranian standards of beauty. While some young women resist pressure from their families to change their physical appearance, most of the young women complained about the focus on beauty and the ostentation of the community, yet they simultaneously took part in it. Thus, this Anglicized Middle Eastern concept of beauty is now seen as the norm.

The stress on being *najeeb* and acting in a culturally appropriate way, while simultaneously struggling to make amends with Western expectations to be independent and true to themselves, has forced many women to develop myriad relationships and participate in many different lives. Leading double lives has caused a great deal of cultural disorientation and has forced young women within this insular community to be secretive, hiding things from their mothers and, fearing gossip, from the community.

Although gossip is seen as a negative consequence of being a part of an insular community, the positive social contribution of gossip is that it solidifies group members' identification and reaffirms their belief in correct behavior. Gossip establishes, for better or worse, a family's reputation and serves as a reminder to members of the community that there are consequences to acting inappropriately and disregarding the community's moral standards.

It is a mother's fear of gossip and the tarnishing of the family name that has forced many young women to lie to their mothers about their personal lives, creating a feeling of distance in the relationship. Many young women expressed a desire for their mothers to be more accepting of their careers, their dreams, their religiosity, and their lives. They wish their mothers would foster and support their independence and focus less on marriage and abiding by the cultural expectations placed on women. Because a majority of these young women do not abide by the traditional beliefs of *najeebness*, they do not believe that their mothers should be as altruistic and self-sacrificing as they are. Living in America has brought about a role reversal for these women, in which they feel that they must protect their mothers, stand up for them, emotionally and psychologically strengthen them, and put themselves in a maternal role. It is through marriage and child rearing that my interviewees feel that they can bond with their mothers again and share a more open and honest relationship.

These young women are instigating and engaging in social change in their communities as part of intergenerational relationships. They are reclaiming and redefining cultural understandings of sexuality, their bodies, education, careers, the home space, and mother-daughter relationships to bring about social change and cultural transformation, as Iranian Jews continue to live and grow as a community in Los Angeles.

SIX

CONCLUSION

This book has woven together women's stories in order to tell a larger story of the collective history and experience of three generations of Iranian Jewish women.

Through an ethnographic portrait of what life was like for Iranian Jewish women living in Iran and later in the United States, the book has explored the political and social changes that affected them and looked at the parallels and differences among three generations in regard to gender and religion and education and employment opportunities; the role nationalism plays in religiosity; and the development of a hybrid identity. It has also examined the role that sex and being *najeeb* plays in Iranian Jewish identity, mothers' roles within the community, and the significance of finding the right mate and how that fosters secrecy and competitiveness within the community. Finally, it has looked at the relationship between sexual modesty and religion in forming an Iranian Jewish woman's identity.

GENDER AND RELIGION

Gender shapes Iranian Jewish identity, especially in relationships with others outside of the community. No matter how much religious knowledge these women had or lacked, what really marked their Iranian Jewish identity was not their religiosity, but what they—as women—did and did not do in comparison to their Muslim and American neighbors. For the first generation of women, the laborious ritual practices were performed not only for religious reasons but also as a way for Jewish women to distinguish themselves from Muslim women. Women's obsessive cleaning during the Passover holiday and the pride they took in their maternal altruism and piety enabled them to counteract the Shi'i belief that Jews were *najes*; it also confirmed their belief that they were more devoted wives and mothers than Muslim women. Very few of the Jewish women interviewed actually had Muslim female friends

167

with whom they could compare themselves, yet discussing how different they were from Muslim women served to justify their obsessive practices of cleanliness and maternal devotion while providing an identity for them as Jews.

Unlike the women from the first generation, the second generation of women did not practice these extensive religious rituals, nor did they sacralize the domestic sphere. This generation was raised under the shah's secularization policies, which, through attempts to modernize and Westernize Iran, cast religion as backward and negative. Thus, what marked a second-generation woman's Jewishness was not how pious she was within the domestic sphere, but her modesty and *najeebness*. This was how Iranian Jewish women were able to separate themselves from their secular Muslim counterparts. In order to maintain her family's name and honor, a Jewish woman had to show that she was *najeeb* as well as educated and cultured; she had to be a good wife, mother, daughter, and daughter in-law and place everyone in her family before herself.

In a time of assimilation and acculturation, this type of altruism was a distinguishing marker for Jewish women. Because religious rituals were no longer practiced the way they were in their mothers' generation, these women believed that the "Jewish" traits of *najeebness* and selflessness were what separated them from their Muslim counterparts. Another distinguishing factor the women discussed was their unwillingness—no matter how awful the circumstances—to get a divorce. If a mother got a divorce, she was seen as being selfish and careless because she sullied the reputation of her family and ruined her children's chances of marrying into desirable families. A majority of the women interviewed said that Muslim women were quick to get divorces without concern for the consequences.

The Jewish women in this study said that Muslim women were less concerned with their families' happiness than with their own. However, a majority of these women did not recall having Muslim female friends, and those who did lacked close relationships with them. Thus, their conceptions of the differences between Muslim and Jewish women were never truly validated; instead, they were based on ideas they had about other women rather than actual knowledge of them. The three Jewish women who did have very close relationships with Muslim women completely disagreed with the other Jewish women, saying that their Muslim friends also had to be *najeeb* as young women, as well as selfless wives and mothers.

This demonstrates that even during the secular and assimilated period of the shah, Jews and other religious communities had very little interaction with each other. Iranian Jewish women participated in the Persian nationalism and secularism that the shah promoted, and because religion was no longer a distinguishing marker of Jewish identity, Iranian

Jewish women would distinguish themselves from Muslim women through sexual modesty and altruism.

The identity of third-generation women is much more difficult to place. Like the second generation that was between two worlds under the shah—the secular/Western Iranian world and the Jewish one—these third-generation women also have hybrid identities. However, their hybridity is more complicated because it includes numerous identities: American, Jewish, Iranian, and female. Religion plays a major role in the lives of third-generation women because it is used as a medium to empower women. These young women have embraced the religious pluralism offered in America and have consciously joined egalitarian Jewish movements because they want to have more of a role in Judaism. They have *bat mitzvah* services and attend synagogues where female rabbis and cantors lead the services. There is also a group of women who have embraced Orthodox Judaism because they have found their identity through observing Jewish *halakhot* (such as rules of *niddah* or becoming *shomeret negiah*), which has enabled them to rebel against the traditional Iranian Jewish culture, which, according to these Orthodox women, has become too focused on materialism and physical appearance. Thus, the role of religion varies among all three generations, with the third generation having a better understanding and practice of Judaism than the prior generations. Along with a shift in religious identity, there has been a shift in education and employment prospects among the three generations of women.

EDUCATION AND EMPLOYMENT

Throughout the three generations, there has been a shift in education and employment for women, from none (the first generation), to education without employment (second generation), to education and employment (the third generation). While the community's attitudes about educating women have changed, what has not changed is the significance of marriage over education and employment opportunities. The first generation of women barely received a high school education. Most attended elementary school and were pulled out of school on Thursdays in order to help their mothers prepare for Shabbat and other Jewish holidays. Those who did attend high school only attended until they were married and then dropped out. Because most women were married off between the ages of fifteen and eighteen, they did not have the opportunity to attend school and continue their education.

Thus, although most women were educated, and some worked, the general consensus in Iran was that if a woman worked, she should not take a man's job. Most people believed that women should be encouraged to have families, and married women should return from their offices to tend to their domestic responsibilities.[1] The Jewish women raised under the shah's regime reflected the type of femininity that the shah promoted. He wanted women to be beautiful, educated, and secular, but also maternal, selfless, and feminine. While the overall proportion of educated and employed women increased under his reign, he still believed that a woman's place was in the home. The Jewish community appropriated the shah's belief that a woman's place was in the home while simultaneously applauding the Westernized policies implemented during the Great Civilization campaign.

Many of the women complained bitterly that women were not encouraged or expected to have jobs once they got married. It was considered to be emasculating to a woman's husband, and there was a belief that only unattractive women went on to receive higher education or have careers because they were not able to find men to marry. Therefore, second-generation women were being educated, but their education was not being used to start a career or achieve financial independence. Instead, women were being educated in order to be wives and mothers, demonstrating that women's most important task was to manage the domestic sphere and the responsibilities of being a wife and mother.

A shift in economic prospects for women occurred in the third generation. While the second generation had education without employment, the third generation has education *and* employment. However, marriage is still highly regarded and seen as the most important accomplishment for a woman. This generation of women is the product of some of the best private and public schools in Los Angeles. Every young woman is expected to not only go to college, but to have a career after college. Many young women start working while they are in high school in order to supplement their income, and as the interviewees explained, having jobs while in high school or college not only gives them financial independence, but also provides a good alibi while spending time with young men.

Third-generation Iranian Jewish women have attended and are attending some of the best public and private universities in Los Angeles, and many have pursued careers within the medical and psychological fields, science, dentistry, real estate, academia, and design (just to name a few). However, as many of these highly accomplished women have stated, no matter how well they have done in school or how accomplished they are in their careers, the community still judges them on their marital status. Thus, a woman can be one of the top female doctors in Los Angeles, but she is seen as being a more accomplished woman if she *marries* a top doctor in Los Angeles. If a woman goes on to pursue a career or get her PhD or MD, the community is proud of her—but if she is not married yet, she is not considered truly accomplished in life. Thus, just like the generation prior to them, third-generation women are ultimately judged by their marital status rather than by their educational and career accomplishments.

In the younger generation (women in their early twenties), many Iranian Jewish women are getting married at a much younger age compared to the previous generation (women in their late twenties and early thirties). These young girls are getting married right after they finish college, which is a trend similar to their mothers' generation. Asked why they think this trend is occurring in the younger generation, while women of the previous generation pursued higher education and careers and many remain unmarried, most of the older generation's responses were the same. Many women from that generation feel that because there are so many of them who are not married yet and are very accomplished academically or in their careers, they are seen as a cautionary tale for the younger generation. Maybe their mothers or even they feel that they have given up their social lives and their chances of marriage in order to pursue a career (although none of the successful women interviewed feel that they have given up one for the other; they simply believe that they have not found the right man and do not want to settle in their choice of men). There is a Persian saying that if a woman waits too long to get married, she will go sour. Maybe these younger generation women feel that they should get married at a young age before they "go sour." In any case, it is a fascinating new trend of women emulating their mothers' generation and getting married at a very young age.

NATIONALISM AND RELIGION

Among the three generations, nationalism displays itself in different ways. For the first generation of women, nationalism was never really displayed. These women did not show an allegiance to an Iranian identity, but to an Iranian Jewish one. For them, Judaism was a marker of their identity, and in a time when they were stigmatized by their Muslim neighbors as being impure, they did not feel devotion to Iran as a country but to their religion as an identity. But this changed for both the first and second generations of women when Mohammed Reza Shah came into power and propagated his secular ideals, in which religious identity was not aligned with nationalistic identity. Thus, as many of the women stated, no one—Jew, Muslim, or Christian—wanted to be characterized by his or her religion; people wanted to be identified as just being Iranian. While maintaining their Iranian Jewish identity was important to women, religion was practiced in the home and was not carried around with them in the public sphere.

Many of the women discussed how they privatized religion and how religious Jews were seen as being backward or old-fashioned, while the secular and more Westernized Jews were considered to be *roshan-fekr*. It wasn't that Iranian Jews became antireligion; Judaism maintained their identities, and even though the shah condemned anti-Semitism, prejudice was still etched into the hearts and minds of many Muslim Iranians. Thus, even if the Jews saw themselves as assimilated and acculturated Iranians, they were still viewed by others as being Jews, and many still dealt with discrimination. And while they had an intense proshah nationalistic fervor, they were also staunch Zionists: Even the most secular Iranian Jew still supported the state of Israel and felt that it was a part of her Jewish identity in Iran. Nevertheless, religion was something practiced in the home, and Iranian Jewish women from both generations wanted to became the epitome of what the shah promoted: Western, secular, and nationalistic.

The third generation of women has embraced the religious pluralism found in America, and not only does the younger generation appreciate the egalitarianism found in the Conservative and Reform movements, but the women from the two prior generations do, as well. Immigration to Los Angeles and living among Ashkenazi Jews has invigorated Jewish practices among Iranian women of all three generations. Thus, Iranian Jewish women have gone from privatizing their Jewish identity in Iran to publicly taking pride in it in Los Angeles. In any Reform or Conservative synagogue in Los Angeles, one will see that a large group of the congregants are Iranian, and many of them are Iranian women, from great-grandmothers to their great-granddaughters.

In Iran, women would only go to synagogue during the High Holy Days; in Los Angeles, many attend weekly Saturday services, take pride in watching young women attend Jewish schools and have *bat mitzvah* services, and have even enrolled in Hebrew language classes and Torah studies. While very few of these women would identify with the feminist movement, all three generations can be seen as having a feminist mentality in regards to Judaism. These women expressed an appreciation for the Jewish movements in America that enable women to have *bat mitzvah* services, to be cantors or rabbis, and to be actively involved in the synagogue community. Thus, for a majority of Iranian women, their Jewish identity in America is enmeshed with either the Reform or the Conservative movement. They might not know the history behind these movements, but they know that this level of religiosity and practice is comfortable for them and fits in with their lifestyle in America.

Many women in the community have also embraced the Orthodox movement that was introduced to them and their husbands, either through the Ashkenazi community or through Iranian rabbis who studied under Ashkenazi ones. Embracing an Orthodox Jewish lifestyle has not only enabled these women to heighten their spiritual awareness, but it has also given them an opportunity to reject an Iranian Jewish culture that they see as being too materialistic and not religious enough. Because the Iranian

Orthodox community separates itself from other Iranian Jews, there is a big fear within the non-Orthodox community that daughters will become too religious. Orthodox Judaism is seen as a threat to the community because family members believe that it can disrupt family solidarity and create tension between family members. As one twenty-two-year-old woman said, "My mother is afraid of letting me go to Israel with some of the more religious groups because she thinks I will come back Orthodox, and she will lose me forever." While that might sound a bit dramatic, there is no doubt that the Orthodox community intentionally separates itself from other Iranian Jews, so the fear that her mother expressed is not so far-fetched.

Thus, the first generation of Iranian Jewish women embraced religious rituals in order to distinguish themselves from their Muslim neighbors. Juxtaposed with that generation, the women who lived under Mohammed Reza Shah privatized and almost hid their religious identity in order avoid being seen as any different from their Muslim neighbors. Finally, with their emigration to Los Angeles, where there is a dominant Ashkenazi community, Iranian Jews have embraced the city's many Jewish movements, synagogues, and rabbis, and have constructed their own Jewish identities, of which they are very proud.

HYBRID IDENTITY

Iranian Jews have always had a hybrid identity, appropriating and reinterpreting aspects of dominant society into their Iranian Jewish world. The first generation of women picked up certain aspects of Shi'i and Zoroastrian ritual traditions and incorporated them into their Jewish ritual life. For example, Jewish women, like Shi'i women, would frequently visit saints' tombs in Iran. One of the most well-known sites was the Esther-Mordechai tomb in Hamadan. Just as Muslim women would go and ask for the saints to intercede on their behalf, Jewish women would visit the tomb, donate some money for charity, and ask Esther and Mordechai to bless their loved ones; then a female leader guided the women in prayers and lessons from the Torah.

Another Shi'i ritual that was appropriated by Jewish women in Iran was the wearing of a *chador* (veil). For centuries under Muslim law, Jewish women had to wear veils. The shah banned the *chador* in 1936, but many women had a hard time taking it off, believing that it was part of Jewish tradition. Although Orthodox Judaism does require women to cover their hair, the veil is specifically Muslim. Even when the shah banned wearing a *chador* and when it was explained to women that it was not part of Jewish practice to wear a veil, Jewish women from the first generation felt that it was still a part of Jewish rules about modesty.

The Jewish women also appropriated rituals from the Zoroastrian religious tradition, such as celebrating *Nowruz* and lighting *esphan*. Because *Nowruz* is a non-Jewish holiday, many women take aspects of the holiday and make them their own. For example, they put the Bible on the *sofreh-ye-haft-sinn*. One of the older Tehrani women said, "We are welcoming Spring, and by placing the Torah on our table, we are saying, 'Yes, we are celebrating an Iranian holiday, but emphasizing our Jewish identity.' "

Another important ritual appropriated from the Zoroastrian religious tradition is the lighting of *esphan*, which became—and remains—one of the most important duties of the matriarch of the house. Belief in the evil eye is so real and present in Iranian culture that it transcends religious boundaries. All of the women said warding off the evil eye was and still is one of the most important tasks a woman can perform, ensuring the safety and happiness of their loved ones. Thus, the first generation of women appropriated aspects of Shi'i and Zoroastrian ritual life and reinterpreted them within a Jewish context. In that way, they were maintaining their Jewish identity and their Iranian one.

The second generation also had a hybrid identity. Unlike the women from the first generation, the women who grew up under the shah and moved to Los Angeles did not prioritize religion or practice religious rituals. They were raised in an Iran that wanted to modernize and separate itself from its religious past, and these women wanted to embrace that modernization. They cherished and protected their Jewish heritage and identity but believed it should be separated from their public lives; they did not want their Jewish identity to separate them from other Iranians. While the prior generation incorporated other religions ritual practices, this generation incorporated the nonreligious ideology of the shah and secular Muslims.

Hybrid identity is apparent in the way women dressed. The first generation wore *chadors*, while for the second generation, nose jobs, bleached hair, and European clothing became popular. Basically, the women in the first generation were forced to emulate Muslim women and wear the veil, while the women of the second generation looked at the women in the shah's family—his wife, daughters, and sisters, with their custom-designed European dresses, extravagant jewelry, and secular attitudes—and chose to emulate them. Parvin Paidar wrote that Queen Farah represented the paradigm of the emancipated Iranian woman, and most Iranian Jewish women embraced her concept of femininity.[2] Thus, the veil made Jewish women look Muslim, while emulating Farah made them look Europeanized and Western. Either way, neither generation of women looked Jewish.

The women in this study described taking advantage of all the Westernized social activities that became popular under the shah, such as going to discos, coffee houses, and movie theaters, and taking vacations abroad. Many started smoking cigarettes in hopes of emulating the American film actresses they were watching on the big screen. While their families made sure that these women socialized within the Jewish community and maintained their *najeebness* in order to maintain their Jewish identity, the second generation of women developed a hybrid Iranian identity, which in public made them undistinguishable from their Muslim neighbors.

Immigration to Los Angeles introduced these women to the Ashkenazi Reform and Conservative movements. Whereas in Iran these women barely practiced Judaism outside of having a family Shabbat together, in America they attend synagogue weekly and are highly involved in religious Jewish life. They sent their children to Reform and Conservative day schools and Hebrew schools and have learned Judaism vicariously through their children. Many say they feel the most comfortable with the Reform and Conservative movements because they create a perfect balance of religion and secular life. Plus, all of the women said they liked the egalitarian movements, and because women were rarely allowed to participate in synagogue services in Iran, they wanted to take advantage of all the opportunities provided to them at egalitarian synagogues.

Other Iranian Jewish women have been influenced by Ashkenazi Orthodox rabbis or Iranian Orthodox rabbis who studied under them and have now embraced a more religious life than they did in Iran, joining the Orthodox Jewish community and living in the Pico/Robertson area, which borders Beverly Hills. This Orthodox Judaism not only provides the women with a more spiritual path, but it enables them to live completely outside the bounds of what they believe has become a shallow Iranian Jewish community that is more concerned with wealth than spiritual growth. These women will never feel a sense of indebtedness or inferiority to others because they feel they are beyond the trivial bonds that link the community together. A majority of the women who have embraced Orthodox Judaism are more recent immigrants from Iran and from a lower socioeconomic background; thus, in many ways, their religiosity allows them to escape from a community that they would never be able to compete in and would feel judged by.

Many women within the community criticize the newly emerging Orthodox Iranians, believing that their religious lifestyle is divisive to traditional family and communal solidarity. They do not understand why women would choose to be more religious than they were in Iran, now that they live in a pluralistic country like the United States and have the opportunity to become members of the Reform or Conservative movements. In response, Orthodox women believe that they are taking advantage of the multiple Jewish movements that thrive in America by learning about Jewish *halakhah* from Orthodox Ashkenazi and Iranian rabbis. They do not see the egalitarian movements as being a legitimate way of practicing Judaism.

The women of the third generation are in the process of picking and choosing aspects of American culture to integrate into their lives, while still maintaining their Iranian Jewish identity. These women define their identity by appropriating certain aspects of the American lifestyle, while holding onto the Iranian Jewish culture in which they were raised and which remains highly significant. These women are not fully Americanizing themselves; instead, they are delicately balancing and negotiating many identities— that of a woman, a Jew, an Iranian, and an American. While the first generation of women appropriated Shi'i and Zoroastrian religious rituals, and the second generation adopted the shah's secularization mentality and had very few religious practices in Iran, the women of the third generation have adopted and embraced the different Ashkenazi religious movements found in Los Angeles.

Many young Iranian Jewish women attend the numerous Reform and Conservative synagogues in West Los Angeles and the San Fernando Valley. They were raised in many of these Ashkenazi Jewish day schools and Hebrew schools; thus, they feel the most comfortable at a service where they can participate equally with men. Egalitarian worship is a subject for which these women feel great passion. Many women have said that they go to Ashkenazi Conservative and Reform synagogues because they believe that women should be called to read from the Torah and be cantors and rabbis. When asked why they attend the Ashkenazi synagogue Sinai Temple as opposed to Nessah Synagogue—an Orthodox Iranian synagogue in Beverly Hills led by Rabbi David Shofet, an important religious figure in the Iranian Jewish community—one respondent said, "Nessah is too Persian and too religious for me. I feel more comfortable at Sinai." Many other women shared her sentiments. The fact that an Iranian Jewish synagogue is "too Persian" for many Iranian women and that is it "too religious" says a lot about how much Ashkenazi egalitarian movements have influenced the Iranian community.

Not all of these women embrace the Reform and Conservative movements. Many young women are becoming more religiously observant than their families and have become ba'alot teshuvah. Like the generation before them, these young women find the Modern Orthodox lifestyle to be more complementary to their lives, and this form of Ashkenazi Judaism offers an alternative lifestyle to the one provided by the Iranian Jewish community, which they feel has become too secular and materialistic.

These young women find themselves navigating between two worlds: the Modern Orthodox one, which is influenced by the Ashkenazi community, and their Iranian Jewish world. Most of these young women do not come from Orthodox families, and thus, many of their parents fear that their daughters will become too religious, which would cause a lot of family division and strife. They are raised to be najeeb, but if they dress too modestly or are *shomrot negiah*,[3] their parents disapprove and are critical of their level of religiosity. These young women feel as if they can never gain approval in their families' eyes. As one woman put it, "Our mothers complain that either our skirts are too short or too long—nothing will ever be perfect for them." The young women said that they were not trying to make the rest of their family become more observant; they simply wished that their mothers would take the time to understand more about their Orthodox lifestyle and not judge them for making choices that were outside the norm of the Iranian Jewish community.

NAJEEB AND THE IRANIAN JEWISH COMMUNITY

Sexual modesty is an important attribute for Iranian women to possess, but as these women explained, it is even more important in the Iranian Jewish community. As social restrictions declined under the shah's reign and as women immigrated to Los Angeles, being *najeeb* became one of the main ways in which Iranian Jewish women could distinguish themselves from secular Muslims (in Iran) and non-Iranian Jewish women (in Los Angeles). The first and second generations of women unanimously agreed that they had to follow very strict modesty rules in order to maintain and uphold their family name. They claimed that while Muslim women were taught to be seductive and sexually active, Iranian Jewish women were raised to be *najeeb* (a claim that Muslim women refute). They were told that what sets an Iranian Jewish woman apart from a secular Muslim woman is her modesty and respect for her body. In a time when Iranians were appropriating all things Western and European, Jewish ritual practices were waning, and Jewish women dressed in Western clothes like all other Iranian women—rendering them indistinguishable from Muslims—sexuality became the distinguishing marker of a Jewish woman.

A woman not only had to be a virgin, but she also had to act like a virgin; it was considered inappropriate for women to associate and spend time with men outside their immediate family. However, as many women explained, there was some tolerance for women interacting with men outside their family if these men were Jewish—particularly, classmates from their Jewish day schools. And it was these Jewish men with whom women went on *chasteghar* dates, married, and had sex. It was extremely rare for Jewish women to date and marry non-Jewish men—of course it is a different story for Jewish men who dated Muslim women—and if she did marry a Muslim, a Jewish woman was "considered dead to her family." Through endogamy and sexual modesty, Jewish women distinguished themselves from others. Thus, a Jewish woman's body carries her identity. Sex becomes the sacred core of Iranian Jewish identity; it is seen as being holy and must be protected.

INTERGENERATIONAL COMPARISONS

The second generation of women used their sexuality in the same way the first generation used their homes: as a space to mark themselves as Iranian Jews. A ritually clean home for the first generation and, in a time of assimilation and secularization, sexually modest for the second, was a way to demonstrate the purity and sacrality of the Jewish community and to establish Jewish identity.

Immigration to America and raising daughters in Los Angeles have not made families in the Iranian Jewish community any more lax about their daughters' sexuality. Just as sexual modesty was used to distinguish their mothers' generation from secular Muslims, sexual modesty is also used to distinguish this generation of young women from other communities in Los Angeles. In many instances, some of the mothers who were raised under the shah—the ones who smoked cigarettes, went out dancing, and were sent abroad to Europe for an education—tend to be more strict with their daughters who are being raised in Los Angeles than their mothers were with them in Iran.

While the first generation of women were concerned about their daughters intermingling with non-Jewish men during the shah's time, fearing they would appropriate some of their lax social relations, they were still living in their own country and did not feel as threatened by the shah's modernization; after all, they were modernizing with their daughters! Plus, their daughters—the women of the second generation—listened to their mothers in regard to sexual modesty and did not question why they should uphold these values. They bought into it, listened to it, and followed it. If they felt that the expectations for young women in the community or the way in which they were treated were outdated, unfair, or hypocritical, they would never express it. They listened to their parents, never spoke back to them, and accepted the social norms.

Thus, while the second generation was more liberated under the shah than their mothers' generation, sexually, they had to maintain the same purity codes and modesty. Under the shah, both generations appropriated Western culture, privatized religion, and became a bit more accepting of socializing between men and women, yet when it came to sex, they maintained their very strict rules and beliefs. Neither of the two generations questioned it or dared to go against it. As one second-generation woman said, "We would never dare question our mothers, talk back to them, or disagree with them. This was the way our culture was, and we respected it. My daughter's generation is different here in America. They have learned from American kids to be more independent from us, to not listen to us, to talk back to us. American culture has more influence on my daughter than I do, and this is what scares me."

However, it is different for the women of the third generation because their parents are immigrants in a new country; these parents are resistant to change and want to uphold the same morals and lifestyle that they had in Iran. These are two very different generations raised in two very different times with very different cultural beliefs. What was considered taboo in Iran is given not as significant in American society. So while the first generation of women were modernizing along with their daughters in Iran, the second generation, who are now mothers in Los Angeles, are not. Much to the dismay of their daughters Iranian Jewish mothers fear American culture and truly believe it promotes sexual freedom and too much independence. They are afraid that American culture will have too much influence on their daughters, and thus, from the time an Iranian Jewish girl is young, she is raised to know that even though she is living in America and has American friends, she is not like them. She must be sexually modest in order to uphold her reputation and avoid sullying her family name.

Unlike the prior generations, many of the young women in Los Angeles are not easily accepting of the double standards placed on them and are questioning why they must be *najeeb* while an Iranian man is not required to be. Many said they openly discuss this with their mothers and with their friends. Other women said that they would not talk about this with their mothers "because it is a pointless conversation"—according to a twenty-two-year old participant—but instead, they just live their lives the way they want—meaning, they don't follow their mothers' rules about being *najeeb*. It is the concept of being *najeeb* and the significance of virginity in the community that really got these women talking. However, many felt ambivalent discussing sexuality in the course of the study because it is such a taboo subject within the community. On one hand, the young women had a lot to say and were happy to be able to voice their opinions about how restricted they feel. Yet they also worried that they might be revealing too much information that would imply that they were sexually active or that they were not virgins before they wed. Either way, just the mere utterance of the word *najeeb* invoked many different reactions. Many women would roll their eyes when the subject of *najeeb* was brought up, expressing how archaic this notion was, while others— mostly the younger and Modern Orthodox women—still found value in the belief in maintaining their virginity and innocence. In regard to young women and their sexuality, Nayereh Tohidi wrote: "Adolescent girls and young women, especially those who immigrated with their families, must decide how to "become American" without losing their own cultural heritage . . . Conflicts between female adolescents and their parents frequently focus on appropriate sexual behavior."[4]

Shideh Hanassab's study of dating and sexual attitudes among younger Iranian immigrants showed that the women were torn between two norms: behavior acceptable to American peers and their parents' expectations and their own obligation to maintain their *najeebness*.[5] However, this study has found that the young women are not concerned with what their American peers find acceptable; their concerns are based purely on what they see as age-appropriate relationships and their parents' outdated beliefs about chastity.

One of the main reasons that so many of the women in this study disagreed with the idea of Jewish women having to be *najeeb* was that it not only restricted them sexually, but they felt it devalued women who wanted to be independent and strong. Instead, they argued, the community encourages young girls to be meek and solely dependent on men—specifically, on a husband. They feel that their independence is stifled in many ways, such as not being able to move out of their parents' home until they get married, not being able to go away to college, not being encouraged to have significant careers, and being stigmatized for being a "black sheep" in the community. Besides maintaining one's virginity, *najeeb* also connotes this sense of innocence and naïveté about the world. Many of the young women feel that this is the antithesis of what a woman should be in the twenty-first century. They criticize the community for not encouraging a sense of empowerment and autonomy, traits that these women feel are integral for women in the United States to possess.

Furthermore, all the women discussed the double standard between Iranian women and men when it comes to sexual morality. Hanassab wrote:

> There is a gender-based double standard for sexual morality among Iranians, as there is in many other cultures. Traditional Iranian culture distinguishes between a "good" woman, who will be protected as a virgin until marriage and then as a wife and mother, and the "bad" woman, who is available for a man's enjoyment. Although Iranians are extremely protective of their young women, they give much more freedom to their young men. Iranian parents willing to let their sons date freely do not grant the same latitude to their daughters. A young man is expected, and in some cases encouraged, to have sexual experiences before marriage. The myth that males have uncontrollable sexual needs that must be satisfied is still reinforced in most families.[6]

This double standard infuriates these women; it makes them lose respect for their brothers and other young men in the community who remain mute about the gender-based double standard, and it makes them lose respect for their community that perpetuates this patriarchal dichotomy of a woman having to remain chaste and *najeeb*.

Many young women are influenced by female liberation in the United States and are reinterpreting what it means to be a *najeeb* woman in order to fit their Iranian Jewish and American identity. They do not believe their Jewish identity needs to be carried by their bodies, but instead that Judaism comes from learning and studying Judaism, attending synagogue, participating in the liturgical cycle, and being a practicing Jew. Many of the women have said that what sets their Iranian female identity apart from Ashkenazi Jews and other American women is not their sexual modesty, but the closeness they have with their immediate and extended families and the respect they have for their parents, culture, and traditions. All of these women expressed that even though they have issues with aspects of the community, especially when it comes to gender, they are all very grateful and appreciative of it. They believe that these are the important distinguishing markers of their Jewish and Iranian identities and that a woman's body and especially her sex life (or lack of) are not.

Another difference among the three generations is the selection of mates. The first generation of women had arranged marriages and had very little say in regard to who they married. The second generation had *chastaghars*; thus, they had chaperoned courtships, and while they were free to choose their husbands, they were only allowed to meet men that their families approved of. Not only did parents have to approve of the man their daughter married, but they had to approve of a man and his family who just wanted to *meet* their daughter. Women from this generation only dated for marriage and had very short courtships; they did not date numerous men because that would ruin their reputation. And, as many women said, they did not marry for love; they married men whom their families approved of and who met all the requirements for providing a good livelihood.

The third generation has more freedom in regard to their selection of mates. None of the young married women interviewed met their husbands through a traditional *chasteghar*; instead, they either met their husbands in school, through friends, or at social parties. Even if a young man's mother calls a girl's mother to ask permission for her son to call her daughter, a mother knows better than to give out her daughter's number without checking with her first. Thus, parents have more respect for their daughters' decisions, but they still believe that it is their parental duty to guide their daughters' relationships and whom they date.

Mothers believe that one of their maternal roles is to socialize and befriend the right people, so their daughters will be raised socializing with men who come from "good families"; thus, a mother is helping her daughter find the "right" suitor. Therefore, parents—especially mothers—have a lot of influence over whom their daughters will date for marriage. (Just like their mothers' generation, this generation of women is only supposed to date for marriage, not "for fun"; whether women follow this rule is another story.)

Some married and single women said that their parents did not want them to date a man because of the city in Iran that his family was originally from or because of his family's history. Many women did not listen to their parents and thought their opinions were archaic, while others agreed with and listened to their parents' advice. All of the women said that, unlike many women from their mothers' generation, they wanted to marry for love and considered compatibility to be very important. Thus, couples are dating for longer periods of time and are getting to know each other better; "perfect on paper" is not enough for many of these women. Many of the young women had strong opinions about other girls in the community, claiming they were marrying for money, for family name, and so on, but none believed that they fell into that category.

One aspect of the Iranian Jewish community that has not changed is its emphasis on a woman's physical traits and on materialism. The first generation of women was more concerned about fulfilling their duties as mothers and wives; many said that vanity and self-image were not even part of their psyches. However, the emphasis on beauty became incredibly important for the second generation of women through exposure to European magazines, Western entertainment, and traveling abroad to Europe and America. Under the shah, arranged marriages became obsolete, and women were dependent on *chasteghars* to get married; thus, beauty, fashion, and style (along with a family's reputation) became very important in the Jewish community and were required for a woman to marry into a good family. Like the generation before them, these women had to be altruistic and focus on their roles as wives and mothers, but they also had to tend to their physical appearance, too. As mentioned earlier, Jewish women—emulating Queen Farah—Westernized themselves by undergoing rhinoplasty, bleaching, tweezing, and dressing in the latest fashionable clothes.

The emphasis on beauty and appearance was imported to America with immigration. Many women said that moving to Los Angeles, becoming financially successful, and living in an insular community made the community even more materialistic and beauty-obsessed. Everyone is trying to outdo each other with weddings, *bar* or *bat mitzvah* parties, homes, cars, clothes, and diamonds. While there is a competitive factor to it, a lot more people spend lavishly on material possessions for themselves and their children because they truly love to entertain, they appreciate beautiful things, and they want to provide the best for their families.

This is a community that once was relegated to living in ghettos, and when they experienced financial opportunities and equality under the shah, they took advantage of it and became very successful. While some Jews were able to bring their wealth with them from Iran, most did not. Many families had to start all over again when they immigrated to America, and as a community, Iranian Jews have done very well for themselves and have prospered financially beyond anyone's expectations. They have a right to enjoy the fruits of their labor. Nevertheless, there are some in the community, such as the newly emerging Orthodox Iranian women, who believe that the community has become too materialistic and that parents are not teaching the correct values to their children.

Just as beauty and looking presentable were important for the second generation, it is important for their daughters' generation, as well. It is even more difficult for this generation of women because they feel pressured by the community, and on top of that, they also feel pressure from American society and media. The pressures placed on young women are not only present in the realm of sexuality but also in regard to their physical appearance and financial wealth. As the home of Hollywood starlets and a bounty of affluent people, Los Angeles is generally associated with superficiality and accused of maintaining an unrealistic portrayal of physical appearance and wealth. Nowhere is this more visible than in the Iranian Jewish community.

Many women expressed their frustrations that intellectual and spiritual growth is valued less than material possessions and physical beauty. Carrying the right purse, driving the right car, having the correct zip code, socializing with the right people—all of these can help determine who they will marry and what social group they will be a part of. Many young women, like their mothers before them, have undergone rhinoplasty in order to have a less Semitic nose. Most color or highlight their beautiful deep brown or jet black hair to make it more blonde, and many girls said that a curvaceous body is no longer considered attractive: they feel pressure to slim down in order fit into a Westernized standard of physical beauty.

A majority of the women said that their mothers were the ones who were the most critical of them and of other women and were guilty of perpetuating this superficial standard. While some young women refuse to get nose jobs or straighten and highlight their hair and want to embrace a more natural beauty, a majority admit to buying into the superficiality of the community, even as they complain about it. As one woman said, "Being put together is a part of our culture." Indeed it is. From the time she is young, an Iranian Jewish girl is dragged not only to Persian markets with her mother, but also to Neiman Marcus. Thus, being well dressed and well groomed is one of the most valuable lessons a mother passes on to her daughter. All of these women said that the Iranian Jewish community has become more obsessed with material objects in Los Angeles than when they were in Iran. Thus, a pilgrimage to the Gucci boutique has replaced the pilgrimage to Esther's tomb.

A Mother's Role

An Iranian Jewish woman's maternal responsibilities extend beyond the domestic sphere to the social sphere. Whether it is the weekly *dorehs*, weddings, *bar* or *bat mitzvah* parties, or religious gatherings, it is the responsibility of the mother of the house to put these events together and maintain the relationships between families and other members in the community. She is the social glue for her husband and children. She believes that the more social and active she is with the "right" people within the community, the better her children's chances of marrying into a "good" family. She also plays the contradictory role of teaching her daughter to be sexually modest while tactfully sexualizing her in order to find a suitable spouse.

Instead of arranging the marriage, which was the norm in Iran, families (specifically the mother) now find suitors for their children. Iranian parents play an instrumental role by arranging formal introductions to potential spouses.[7] Of great importance is the significance of marriage for women. Marriage can influence the composition of social classes, the social mobility of a kinship network, and the political power hierarchy within a community.[8] No one knows this better than a mother; thus, she takes her maternal role of finding a suitable spouse for her daughter very seriously, understanding that this will cement her role in the community.

Therefore, tremendous pressure is placed on mothers to socialize, give parties, and attend parties. Inviting members of the community to social functions, and reciprocating by attending their social functions, demonstrates one's economic strength and repays a social debt while binding the community together. The Iranian Jewish mother plays a contradictory role in her daughter's life; while young women are expected to be *najeeb*, in a culture that fosters competition for suitable husbands, they are encouraged by their mothers to dress tactfully yet provocatively at social events. There is a mixed message given to young women: look beautiful and sexy, but do not act upon your sexuality. The virgin/whore dichotomy is a patriarchal belief situated within the Iranian Jewish community and perpetuated by the ideologies of mothers who require their daughters to remain virgins, yet encourage them to dress provocatively enough to attract a suitor's interest. Thus, mothers play this double role of eroticizing their daughters, within tactful limits, while still enforcing the beliefs of sexual modesty.

It is very rare to find a close relationship between women from this generation and their mothers. For many women, an appreciation for their mothers and a close bond developed when they, too, became wives and mothers. Since grandmothers play such an integral role in helping to raise their grandchildren, the relationship between mother and daughter is further strengthened when grandchildren are involved.

Meanwhile, single women expressed ambivalence toward their relationship with their mothers. Each one expressed numerous times how much she loved and respected her mother, yet at the same time, she also desired more autonomy from her mother and regretted not having a more intimate relationship based on a friendship rather than a hierarchical mother-daughter relationship. The hierarchical relationship is very descriptive of the parent-child relationships among Iranian Jewish families in the past. The second generation of women said that they loved and respected their mothers and saw their role as a mother and not as a confidant.

However, the unmarried women want to have closer relationships with their mothers and feel they cannot because of a perceived generational and cultural gap, making it very difficult for mothers and daughters to understand and relate to each other. This cultural gap did not occur between the first and second generation of women because they were being raised in the same country. As mentioned before, the first generation of women was adapting to a secular Iranian culture along with their daughters; thus, this cultural friction did not exist in Iran the way it exists in Los Angeles. It was rare to see second-generation women question the authority and the social expectations of the community the way third-generation women are doing now.

Many women also expressed frustration with their mothers for being self-sacrificing and neglecting their own emotional and psychological needs. They felt that this was due to the *najeeb* traits their mothers were raised with, teaching them to put everyone's needs before their own. The young women said that they witnessed how much their mothers suffered in order to be altruistic, and now their mothers expect their daughters to take on the maternal, protective role. This role makes daughters feel as if they cannot burden their mothers with their own emotional problems, and this causes distance in the relationship.[9] The role reversal also leads to intergenerational conflicts and threatens familial hierarchy. Tohidi wrote:

> Immigrant parents tend to be distressed by the rapid pace of their children's acculturation . . . Whereas parental authority in the traditional Iranian family is based on the parents passing on to their children their own knowledge of life, children in immigrant families cannot readily apply their parents' knowledge to their own new lives. Instead, roles become somewhat reversed. The children are the ones passing on important information to their parents, correcting their English, and helping them in their daily interactions

with Americans. Such role reversals threaten traditional relations in the family and create tension.[10]

These young women have been raised in American society and find themselves in a role reversal with their mothers, intensifying intergenerational conflicts and alienation. The second generation did not experience the same type of conflict and alienation because they were being raised in the same country as their mothers. As mentioned before, they were more likely to listen to the rules and regulations their mothers established; it was also easier for these women because their mothers were modernizing with them, unlike the experience of the third generation.

This distance is further deepened by the feeling that mothers depend on their daughters for emotional support, and in many ways, they want their daughters' lives to make up for what is missing in their own, especially in regard to marriage, finding a husband, and being financially independent. Many of my interviewees said that their mothers believe that most of their marital unhappiness stems from their husbands not being able to provide the lifestyle they want or that is expected of them within the Iranian Jewish community; thus, they encourage their daughters to marry wealthy men, thinking this is the key to marital bliss. Other mothers realize how financially trapped they or their friends feel in their marriages; therefore, they encourage their daughters to work and be self-sufficient to avoid being financially dependent on a man.

Yet there are contradictions in a mother's support for her daughter's career and self-empowerment. Mothers encourage their daughters to be financially independent and have a career, but the fear among women is that too much independence can lead to marriage at a later age. Mothers want their daughters to have a successful career, but they do not want that career to interfere with their domestic and maternal duties. Thus, Iranian Jewish daughters are raised negotiating contradictory attitudes toward marriage, motherhood, careers, and independence.

Not only do daughters feel that they must live their lives for their mothers, but because seeking psychological counseling or talking to others about problems is considered taboo within the Iranian Jewish community, a majority of these women said that they, as daughters, were the ones who had to deal with their mothers' emotional unhappiness and discontent, especially in regard to marital problems and dealing with depression. All of the women expressed resentment toward their mothers for burdening them, often at a young age, with being a therapist and confidant, feeling that it caused them a lot of unnecessary anxiety as young girls. Thus, many felt that their adolescence and their lives had been filled not only with the struggle to find their own identity within different worlds, but also with pressure to take care of their mothers' emotional and psychological well-being.

The young women discussed how they want things to change for their daughters. They do not want to place unrealistic sexual expectations on their daughters because they feel this would only lead to dishonesty, and they hope to have more open relationships with their daughters than they had with their mothers. They also want to raise their daughters with more autonomy and encourage self-sufficiency. They recognize that in order for the next generation of women to be raised in this way, the Iranian Jewish culture as a whole needs to be less constricted by patriarchal beliefs and double standards. Ironically, it is the women themselves who enforce these patriarchal rules in order to protect their daughters from gossip and rumors and to ensure a good future for them.

Secrecy and Competition

One aspect of the Iranian Jewish community that has not changed among the three generations is the secrecy and competitiveness within it. Although the community is very intimate, it is also very insular; thus, throughout the generations, secrecy and competitiveness are linked to the sacrality of sex and the competition for the appropriate mate, both in the past in Iran and today in Los Angeles.

Because being *najeeb* is incredibly important in the Iranian community, and because of the tremendous amount of gossip that takes place in the community, many young women said that much to their dismay, they had to lie constantly to their parents and to the community in order to be able to live the lives they wanted. This has caused a lot of alienation among women, making them feel that they cannot have close relationships with their mothers and other women in the community. Iranian psychologist Homa Mahmoudi explains, "Iranian culture is a very secretive culture. And it's a very individually isolated culture. Among Iranians, intimacy does not necessarily go along the same lines as in Western culture. The unconditional trust and openness we might have [in the United States] is very seldom found in Iranian society."[11] Because many women feel they must be secretive in the Iranian Jewish community, they have expressed how much more comfortable they feel befriending non-Iranians, knowing that they will not judge them or gossip about them.

The desire to marry the most eligible bachelor and to maintain a good reputation has made many of the young women in the community very secretive, competitive, and fake. One's personal life is so private that it is common for a woman to not divulge whom she is dating until she is engaged—surprising not only the community, but also those who considered her to be a close friend. Thus, while so many of these women grow up together and see each other weekly at social gatherings, many claim that they do not feel close to other women in the community, going so far as to refer to them as acquaintances rather than friends. These women believe that as young girls they were taught by their mothers to keep their personal lives secret in order to avoid getting the evil eye or becoming the subject of gossip. Yet, although they complain about the shroud of secrecy that defines the community, many young women said that they do have close Iranian girlfriends whom they can trust and with whom they don't feel they must compete. It seems that many women do not feel comfortable keeping their personal lives secret from their close girlfriends. In a community in which women keep so much from their parents, it is understandable that they would turn to girlfriends to confide in.

Sex and Religion

A major theme throughout is the sacrality of sex and how a woman's modesty and body carry Iranian Jewish identity. Yet while sex is considered to be sacred, very few women, especially within the third generation, said that they grew up with it as being sacred within religious terms. Only the Orthodox women referred to sex and sexual modesty in that way. Thus, sex is the sacred, and religion is the carrier for that sacrality, rather than its source.

All three generations believed that other women outside of their community were more sexually free. The first and second generations looked at Muslim women as having more sexual freedom, and the third generation believes that American women are more sexually active. Unlike the third generation of women, who have more interaction with non-Iranian Jewish women in America, the first generation barely interacted with Muslim women. While the second generation had much more social interaction with non-Jews than their mothers did, sex was such a taboo subject that few, if any, of these Jewish women discussed with their Muslim friends whether they were sexually active. Thus, while these women said that Muslim women were more sexually active as if it were a factual truth, in reality, they probably had absolutely no idea if it was.

Another difference among the generations is that the first two generations followed the rules of being *najeeb*, while many of the third generation women have rebelled against the idea of sexual modesty. Some women are still virgins (mostly the younger ones), and most are not, but all the non-Orthodox third-generation women said that the ideas behind *najeebness* were outdated and hypocritical. However, it does not appear that being raised with ideas of sexual modesty make young Iranian Jewish women less promiscuous than their peers. Very few American girls are brought up with the same stringent rules of sexual modesty as Iranian Jewish women (except religious and immigrant women); however, many of these Iranian Jewish women are just as sexually active as their non-Jewish peers. Still, just like the prior generations, third-generation women assume that other women are more uninhibited and promiscuous and that only Iranian Jewish women have had to deal with expectations of sexual modesty.

Thus, one of the many questions that arise from this study is whether sexual modesty is a way to be Persian or a way to be Jewish. Does religion mediate sexuality, or does sexuality mediate religion? All three generations of women believe that the emphasis on Iranian Jewish women being *najeeb* is what differentiates them from other women. However, it is difficult to imagine that Iranian Muslim women were any different in Iran and American women are any different in Los Angeles in regard to "purity." The emphasis on *najeebness* is a way in which the insular Iranian Jewish community has attempted to maintain its identity during a time when Iranian Jews were accused of being impure, and during a time of assimilation under the shah and in America. Whether they are being delusional about other women's sexuality and the realities of their daughters having sex does not matter as long as they believe it and see it as a marker of the community's identity and wholesomeness.

While the Iranian Jewish community has benefited from assimilation, there is also a fear of losing its identity. But preventing assimilation and the appropriation of other cultures and beliefs is nearly impossible, as seen with the first generation picking up Shi'i and Zoroastrian elements; it was also evident with both the first and second generations adopting the shah's beliefs of religious laxity and modernity; it is definitely apparent now with the third generation adopting Ashkenazi elements into their religiosity and American elements in regard to their sexuality and concepts of womanhood. Thus, the ultimate question that arises for minorities, immigrants, and children of immigrants is: am I assimilating into mainstream society or assimilating mainstream society into myself? The author Bernard Malamud asserts that the answer is both: assimilation, after all, works both ways.[12]

NOTES

<hr>

CHAPTER ONE

1. Mehdi Bozorgmehr, "Internal Ethnicity: Armenian, Bahai, Jewish, and Muslim Iranians in Los Angeles" (PhD diss., University of California, Los Angeles, 1992).

2. David Menashri, "The Pahlavi Monarchy and the Islamic Revolution," in *Esther's Children*, ed. Houman Sarshar (Beverly Hills: Center for Iranian Jewish Oral History, Beverly Hills, 2002), 399.

3. Ibid., 395.

4. Mehdi Bozorgmehr and Pyong Gap Min, "Immigrant Entrepreneurship and Business Patterns: A Comparison of Koreans and Iranians in Los Angeles," *International Migration Review* 34, no. 3 (Autumn 2000): 715.

5. Ibid.

6. U.S. Department of Homeland Security, Office of Immigration Statistics, *Yearbook of Immigration Statistics*, 1970–2004.

7. Quicklists. http://www.thearda.com/QuickLists/QuickList_189.asp.

8. Ibid., 718.

9. Bozorgmehr and Pyong, 11.

10. Ibid.

11. Ibid., 22.

12. Herbert J. Gans, "Symbolic Ethnicity: The Future of Ethnic Groups and Cultures in America," in *On the Making of Americas: Essays in Honor of David Reisman*, ed. Herbert J. Gans, Nathan Glazer, Joseph R. Gusfield, and Christopher Jencks (Pennsylvania: University of Pennsylvania Press, 1979), 193–220.

13. Ibid.

14. Persia and Iran are the same country. In 1935, Reza Shah Pahlavi changed the name of the country from Persia to Iran, meaning, "land of the Aryans." In this volume, "Persian" and "Iranian" will be used interchangeably.

15. Rudolph Otto, *The Idea of the Holy* (Oxford: Oxford University Press, 1917).

16. Saba Soomekh, "Between Religion and Culture: Three Generations of Iranian Jewish Women from the Shahs to Los Angeles" (PhD diss., University of California, Santa Barbara, 2009).

17. *Mikveh* is the ritual bath that a woman immerses herself in seven days after she stops menstruating.

18. The discussions have always revolved around the community as a whole or on individual men. Iranian Jewish women are not described in this discourse.

19. Habib Levi, *Comprehensive History of the Jews of Iran: The Outset of the Diaspora* (Costa Mesa: Mazda, 1999), 474.

20. Ibid., 493.

21. Ibid., 478.

22. Ibid., 544.

23. Ibid., 547.

24. Ibid., 550.

25. Menashri, 395.

26. According to Jewish law, when Jewish children, reaching the age of thirteen years for boys and twelve for girls, become responsible for their actions, they become a *bar* or *bat mitzvah*.

27. *Aliya* is the term for when one is called up to read from the Torah in synagogue.

28. Pam Nilan and Carles Feixa, *Global Youth? Hybrid Identities, Plural Worlds*, ed. Pam Nilan and Carles Feixa (New York: Routledge, 2006).

29. Homi Bhabha, *The Location of Culture* (London: Routledge, 1994), 2.

30. Catherine Bell, *Ritual Theory, Ritual Practice* (New York: Oxford University Press, 1992), 14.

31. Ibid.

32. Otto; William James, *The Varieties of Religious Experience* (New York: Macmillan, 1961).

33. James.

34. Ibid.

35. Ibid., 114–15.

36. Jonathan Z. Smith, *Imagining Religion* (Chicago: University of Chicago Press, 1982), 54.

37. Ibid., 56.

38. Emile Durkheim, *The Elementary Forms of Religious Life*, trans. Karen E. Fields (New York: Free, 1995), 34.

39. Ibid., 422.

40. Marcel Mauss, *The Gift*, trans. Ian Cunnison (London: Cohen and West, 1954).

41. Bell, 15.

42. Rachel Simon, *Change within Tradition among Jewish Women in Libya* (Seattle: University of Washington Press, 1992), 21.

43. Calvin Goldscheider, "Demographic Transitions, Modernization, and the Transformation of Judaism," in *Events and Movements in Modern Judaism*, ed. Raphael Patai and Emanuel S. Goldsmith (New York: Paragon House, 1995), 60.

44. Susan Starr Sered, *Women as Ritual Experts* (New York: Oxford University Press, 1992), 92.

45. Ibid., 4–5.

46. Goldscheider, 51.

47. It is referred to as Shooshan in Megilat Esther (the Book of Esther). This book provides the story of the origin of the Jewish holiday of Purim. The Book of Esther tells the story of how a Jewish queen in Persia, Esther, and her Uncle Mordechai thwart a genocide against the Jews by the king's prime minister, Haman.

48. Although Hamadanian Jews did experience anti-Semitism, persecutions, and forced conversions, they were still more integrated in the community than other Jews in other Iranian cities.

CHAPTER TWO

1. This is a typical Saturday morning Shabbat service that the author has observed as a member of Sinai Temple in Los Angeles.

2. This is known as Shooshan in Megilat Esther.

3. Although Hamadanian Jews did experience hostility, persecutions, and forced conversions, they were still more integrated in the community than were Jews in other Iranian cities.

4. Faryar Nikbakht, "As with Moses in Egypt: Alliance Israélite Universelle Schools in Iran," in *Esther's Children: A Portrait of Iranian Jews*, ed. Houman Sarshar (Beverly Hills: Center for Iranian Jewish History, 2002), 199.

5. Ibid.

6. Susan Star Sered, *Women as Ritual Experts* (New York: Oxford University Press, 1992).

7. *Mitzvah* (pl. *mitzvot*), literally translated, means "commandment." It also carries the connotation of a "good deed" or "doing something pleasing in the eyes of God."

8. Rachel Biale, *Women and Jewish Law* (New York: Schocken Books, 1984), 13.

9. Ibid.

10. Parvin Paidar, *Women and the Political Process in Twentieth-Century Iran* (Cambridge: Cambridge University Press, 1995), 3.

11. Ibid., 10.

12. Ibid.

13. Raphael Patai, *Jadid Al-Islam: The Jewish "New Muslims" of Meshhad* (Detroit: Wayne State University Press, 1997), 221.

14. Ibid.

15. Sered 1992, 102.

16. Marital separation when a woman is menstruating.

17. Iranian New Year.

18. Wild rue, considered a sacred herb.

19. Karmel Melamed, "Iranian Community Mourns Its Anchor," *The Jewish Journal of Greater Los Angeles*, September 23, 2005.

20. *Shabbat* is the Hebrew word for Sabbath.

21. Rabbi David Shofet, interview by author, Beverly Hills, California, July 11, 2005.

22. Sered 1992, 30–31.

23. A *samovar* is a heated metal container traditionally used to brew tea in and around Russia, as well as in other Slavic nations, Iran, and Turkey.

24. Isaac Klein, *A Guide to Jewish Religious Practice* (New York: Jewish Theological Seminary of America, 1979), 90.

25. Jacob Katz, *The "Shabbes Goy"* (Philadelphia: Jewish Publication Society, 1989), 139–40.

26. Moshe Shokeid, *The Predicament of Homecoming: Cultural and Social Life of North African Immigrants in Israel* (Ithaca: Cornell University Press, 1974), 89.

27. *Ghondi* and *ob-ghoosh* are traditional foods Persian Jews eat on the Sabbath.

28. Susan Star Sered, "Food and Holiness: Cooking as a Sacred Act among Middle-Eastern Jewish Women," *Anthropological Quarterly* 61, no. 3 (July 1988): 132.

29. Sered 1992, 93.

30. Lynn Harbottle, *Food for Health, Food for Wealth: The Performance of Ethnic and Gender Identities by Iranian Settlers in Britain* (New York: Berghahn Books, 2004), 41.

31. Sered 1992, 88.

32. *Kashrut* is a term for being kosher, following Jewish dietary laws.

33. The Talmud is a central text of mainstream Judaism, in the form of a record of rabbinic discussions pertaining to Jewish law, ethics, philosophy, customs, and history.

34. Shulhan Arukh a codification, or written manual, of *halakhah* (Jewish law), composed by Rabbi Yosef Karo in the sixteenth century. The Shulhan Arukh consists of four parts: Orach Chayim—daily, Sabbath, and holiday laws. Yoreh De'ah—laws about food, relations to non-Jews, menstruation and immersion; vows and oaths; honoring parents and scholars; women's issues; death, burial, and mourning. Even Ha-Ezer—laws of procreation, marriage, and divorce. And Choshen Mishpat—laws about judges and witnesses; loans and claims; theft, damage, robbery, and injury.

35. Mircea Eliade, *Cosmos and History* (Princeton: Princeton University Press, 1954), 28.

36. Ibid., 30.

37. Sered 1992, 89.

38. These and all other biblical quotations are from the King James version of the Bible; Klein, 361.

39. Klein, 368.

40. The only exception was Rabbi David Shofet's wife who told the author that her parents kept separate dishes in the home.

41. *Najes* in Persian means impure.

42. Passover takes place during the Jewish month of Nissan.

43. *Hames* is the Persian term for impure.

44. Klein, 113.

45. Sered 1992, 81.

46. Tumeric.

47. *Charoset* is the traditional Passover food that has a symbolic role in the ceremonial Seder meal.

48. Sered 1992, 108.

49. Impure.

50. Houshang Ebtami, "The Impure Jew," in *Esther's Children: A Portrait of Iranian Jews*, ed. Houman Sarshar (Beverly Hills: Center for Iranian Jewish History, 2002), 101.

51. Rosh Hashanah is the Jewish New Year.

52. Yom Kippur is the Jewish Day of Atonement.

53. Synagogue.

54. Jewish law exempts women from communal prayer that requires a minimum of ten adult Jewish males and that follows a set liturgy. However, women are not exempt from the commandment of prayer. They may pray spontaneously, in any language, at any time.

55. Leah Baer, "Life's Events: Births, Bar Mitzvah, Weddings, and Burial Customs," in *Esther's Children: A Portrait of Iranian Jews*, ed. Houman Sarshar (Beverly Hills: Center for Iranian Jewish History, 2002), 319.

56. *Chastegaree* is the Persian term for when a male suitor and his family pursue a woman in hopes of marriage.

57. Male suitors for marriage.

58. Farideh Goldin, *Wedding Song: Memoirs of an Iranian Jewish Woman* (Hanover: Brandeis University Press, 2003), 155.

59. This will be discussed in later chapters.

60. Arlene Dallalfar, "Worlds Apart: Mothers, Daughters, and Family Life," in *Esther's Children: A Portrait of Iranian Jews*, ed. Houman Sarshar (Beverly Hills: Center for Iranian Jewish History, 2002), 405.

61. The laws of *niddah* are based on Leviticus 15:19–33, 18:19, and 20:18.

62. Klein, 514.

63. Ibid.

64. *Halakhically* means that which is required by Jewish law.

65. The rules of a *mikveh* are very intricate. The *mikveh* pool must contain a minimum of two hundred gallons of rainwater that was gathered and siphoned in accordance with a highly specific set of regulations.

66. *Tefillah* (pl. *tefillot*) means "prayer/ prayers" in Hebrew.

67. Patai, 257.

68. Simon, 60.

69. Baer 2002, 330.

70. Arlene Dallalfar, "Iranian Immigrant Women in Los Angeles: The Reconstruction of Work, Ethnicity, and Community" (PhD diss., University of California, Los Angeles, 1989), 241.

71. The Persian word *abe* is translated as something bad, wrong, or negative.

72. *Yas* is the Persian word for the flower jasmine.

73. No extensive archeological or historical research has been conducted to prove that the grave within the shrine is that of Esther.

74. Elias Yassi Gabbay, "Esther's Tomb," in *Esther's Children: A Portrait of Iranian Jews*, ed. Houman Sarshar (Philadelphia: Jewish Publication Society, 2002), 19.

75. Laurence D. Loeb, *Outcast: Jewish Life in Southern Iran* (New York: Gordon and Breach, 1977), 224.

76. While the Ester-Mordechai tomb was popular for Hamadani Jews, the most important Jewish pilgrimage site in Iran is the shrine of Serah bat Asher, located near Isfahan. It is believed that this is the place that Serah, the daughter of Asher the patriarch, made her appearance in Iran in order save the Jews from persecution at the hands of the Savafid Shah Abbas II. Pilgrims light candles and offer prayers of thanksgiving and petition.

77. Smith, 109.

78. Fatima Mernissi, *Woman, Saints and Sanctuaries* (Lahore: Simorgh, 1987), 7–8.

79. Sered 1992, 120.

80. *Tefillah* (pl. *tefillot*) means "prayer/prayers" in Hebrew.

81. Paidar, 109.

82. *Esphan* is the word for wild rue, a sacred herb.

83. Najimieh Khalili Batmanglij, *New Food of Life: Ancient Persian and Modern Iranian Cooking and Ceremonies* (Los Angeles: Mage, 1998), 384–89.

84. The traditional table setting of Nowruz.

85. *Tzedakah* is the Hebrew word for "charity": giving aid, assistance, and money to the poor and needy or to other worthy causes.

86. Paidar, 356–58.

87. *Najes* refers to anything that is considered to be impure for Shi'i Muslims. Dogs, pigs, Christians, and Jews were put under this category.

88. Calling someone "Juhud" is a derogatory way of calling someone a Jew in Persian.

89. Faryar Nikbacht, "As with Moses in Egypt: Alliance Israelite Universelle Schools in Iran," in *Esther's Children: A Portrait of Iranian Jews*, ed. Houman Sarshar (Beverly Hills: Center for Iranian Jewish History, 2002), 207.

90. Ibid., 207.

91. Nessah Synagogue is an Iranian synagogue; therefore, Rabbi Shofet's sermons are given in Persian.

92. Rabbi David Wolpe is the head rabbi at Sinai Temple, in Los Angeles.

93. Harvey Lutske, *The Book of Jewish Customs* (Northvale: Aronson, 1986), 262.

94. The Conservative movement seeks to "conserve" Jewish traditions while living within the modern world. The Conservative Jew tries to balance the demands of modern times with a commitment to Jewish observance. Conservative Judaism embraces the critical study of Jewish and secular texts along with traditional methods of study. Conservative Jews stress that Judaism has evolved historically to meet the changing needs of the Jewish people in various eras and circumstances. They believe that Jewish Law should continue to evolve in the present and in the future. Nevertheless, Conservative Judaism maintains the traditional view that Jews must obey and observe the will of God through the Commandments. Conservative Judaism maintains that the Torah is of divine origin; however, there is debate within the movement as to how it was authored. Many American Jews affiliate with Conservative Judaism because they desire a satisfactory home "in between Orthodox and Reform." See Sarah E. Karesh and Mitchell M. Hurvitz, *Encyclopedia of Judaism* (New York: Infobase, 2006), 98–100.

95. Reform Judaism is the oldest of modern Jewish denominations. The leaders of the Reform movement began to argue that comprehensive changes in both the ideology and the practice of Judaism were needed in the modern world. These leaders instituted polite decorum in the synagogue. The rabbis donned vestments like their Protestant colleagues, gave sermons in their vernacular, and developed prayer books that were shorter and included translations in the vernacular. They encouraged their congregants to pray in the vernacular, too, and some brought in organs for live instrumental music on the Sabbath. Reform Judaism believes in the autonomy of individuals in choosing their own path of Jewish expression, that the Jewish people is dedicated to the improvement of the world, that Reform Jews are part of the historical tradition embodied in Torah and rabbinic literature, that the principles of pluralism are important, and that all Jews are obligated to study the traditions, history, and *mitzvoth* that link them together. See Karesh and Hurvitz, 419–22.

96. Orthodox Judaism is the theology, ideology, customs, and social patterns of those Jews who strictly follow traditional Jewish law. The belief system rests on the idea that the Torah in its entirety was handed down from God to Moses. The

majority of Orthodox Jews accept divine authorship of both the oral law and the written law. Modern Orthodox Jews believe that one must adhere to traditional Jewish law. They do not see participation in the modern world and observance of Jewish law as mutually exclusive. See Karesh and Hurvitz, 368–71.

97. ORT is a nonprofit and nonpolitical organization whose mission is to work for the advancement of Jewish and other people through training and education; to provide communities wherever they are, with the skills and knowledge necessary to cope with the complexities and uncertainties of their environment; to foster economic self-sufficiency, mobility, and a sense of identity through use of state-of-the-art technology. Through international cooperation programs, ORT supports nonsectarian economic and social development in underdeveloped parts of the world, with vocational training and the provision of technical assistance.

98. An Iranian Jewish fundraising organization based in Los Angeles.

99. The Women's Zionist Organization of America, a volunteer women's organization whose members are motivated and inspired to strengthen their partnership with Israel, ensure Jewish continuity, and realize their potential as a dynamic force in American society.

CHAPTER THREE

1. This is a scene from an Iranian Jewish wedding held at the Downtown Marriot Hotel, June 2006.

2. Ramesh Sanghvi, Clifford German, and David Missen, *Revolution of the Shah and the People* (London: Transorient Books, 1967); Paidar.

3. Nahid Yeganeh, "Women, Nationalism and Islam in Contemporary Political Discourse in Iran." *Feminist Review* 44 (Summer 1993): 3–18.

4. Paidar; Yeganeh.

5. Paidar, 8.

6. Ibid., 9.

7. Mehrdad Amanat, "Nationalism and Social Change in Contemporary Iran," in *Irangeles: Iranians in Los Angeles*, ed. Ron Kelly (Los Angeles: University of California Press, 1993), 17–20.

8. Ibid.

9. Yeganeh, 6.

10. Ibid.

11. David Mladinov, "Iranian Jewish Organization: The Integration of an Émigré Group into the American Jewish Community," *Journal of Jewish Communal Service* (Spring 1981): 245–48.

12. Michael Reichel, *Persian American Jewry at a Crossroads: Will the Traditions Continue?* (New York: LV, 2004), 64.

13. Leah Baer, "The Challenge of America," in *Padyavand*, ed. Amnon Netzer (Los Angeles: Mazda, 1996), 98.

14. Ellen M. Umansky, "Feminism and the Revolution of Women's Roles within American Jewish Life," in *Women, Religion, and Social Change*, ed. Yvonne Yazbeck Haddad and Ellison Banks Findly (New York: State University of New York, 1985), 480–81.

15. Jacob Katz, "German Culture and the Jews," in *The Jewish Response to German Culture: From the Enlightenment to the Second World War*, ed. Jehuda Reinharz and Walter Schatzberg (Hanover: University Press of New England, 1985), 85.

16. David Sorkin, "The Invisible Community: Emancipation, Secular Culture, and Jewish Identity in the Writings of Berthold Auerbach," in *The Jewish Response to German Culture: From the Enlightenment to the Second World War*, ed. Jehuda Reinharz and Walter Schatzberg (Hanover: University Press of New England, 1985), 100.

17. Katz 1985, 85–86.

18. Chelo-kabob restaurants serve beef, lamb, and chicken kabobs, usually accompanied with rice, grilled tomatoes, salad, bread, and stews.

19. Modern.

20. Parvin Paidar, *Women and the Political Process in Twentieth-Century Iran* (Cambridge: Cambridge University Press, 1995), 147.

21. Ibid., 148.

22. Arabic word, generally regarded as very difficult to translate but at the same time considered to be an all-encompassing word referring to schism, secession, upheaval, and anarchy all at once.

23. Nayareh Tohidi, "Iranian Women and Gender Relations in Los Angeles," in *Irangeles: Iranians in Los Angeles*, ed. Ron Kelly (Los Angeles: University of California Press, 1993), 185.

24. Sanghvi, German, and Missen, 5.

25. Ibid., 6.

26. Paidar, 149.

27. Tohidi, 180.

28. Camron Michael Amin, "The Attentions of the Great Father: Reza Shah, 'The Woman Question,' and the Iranian Press, 1890–1946" (PhD diss., University of Chicago, 1996), 352.

29. Amanat, 12.

30. Paidar, 151.

31. Amin, 79.

32. Ibid., 83.

33. Ibid.

34. Women's Organization of Iran, *The Employment of Women* (Tehran: Women's Organization of Iran, 1975), 37–42.

35. Paidar, 165.

36. Avishai Margalit, *The Ethics of Memory* (Cambridge, Harvard University Press, 2002), 61–62.

37. Ibid., 64.

38. Ibid., 550.

39. *Najes* refers to anything that is considered to be impure for Shi'i Muslims. Dogs, pigs, Christians, and Jews were put under this category.

40. *Juhud* is a derogatory term for a Jew in Persian.

41. The Persian word for nonkosher.

42. Kaveh Safa-Isfahani, "Female-Centered World Views in Iranian Culture: Symbolic Representations of Sexuality in Dramatic Games," *Signs* 6, no. 1 (Autumn 1980): 43.

43. Afsaneh Najmabadi, "Crafting an Educated Housewife in Iran," in *Remaking Women: Feminism and Modernity in the Middle East*, ed. Lila Abu-Lughod (Princeton: Princeton University Press, 1998), 102.

44. Ibid., 103.

45. Ibid.

46. Ibid.

47. Yeganeh, 4.

48. The Hebrew word for prayers.

49. Jewish day school located in Tehran.

50. Reichel, 57.

51. Ibid., 58.

52. Ibid.

53. Ibid.

54. Ibid., 59.

55. Ibid.

56. Male suitors.

57. Elaine Sciolino, "Iran's Well-Covered Women Remodel a Part That Shows," *New York Times* (September 22, 2000): 1.

58. Ibid.

59. Frances C. Macgregor, "Social and Cultural Components in the Motivations of Persons Seeking Plastic Surgery of the Nose," *Journal of Health and Social Behavior* 8, no. 2 (June 1967): 126–27.

60. Ibid., 128.

61. Ibid., 129.

62. Ibid.

63. Ibid., 130.

64. Sciolino, 3.

65. B. Hemation, "To Be or Not to Be Thankful," *Megillah* 47 (January 1995): 28.

66. Safa-Isfahani, 49.

67. Ibid., 50.

CHAPTER FOUR

1. Tohidi, 175.

2. Ibid., 191.

3. Reichel, 74.

4. Tohidi, 178.

5. Ibid., 195.

6. *Sheereeni-khorun* is a party celebrating the bride's family bringing sweets to the groom's family as a gesture of accepting the groom's proposal for marriage.

7. Anne H. Betteridge, "Gift Exchange in Iran: The Locus of Self-Identity in Social Interaction," *Anthropological Quarterly* 58, no. 4 (October 1985): 193.

8. Ron Kelley,"Interview with Homa Mahmoudi, Clinical Psychologist," in *Irangeles: Iranians in Los Angeles*, ed. Ron Kelly (Los Angeles: University of California Press, 1993), 166.

9. Tohidi, 213.

10. Before a wedding, the women would gather in the home of the bride's family and put henna on the bride's hair and on the hands of all the women for good luck. This is a *hennah-bandan*.

11. A temporary hut constructed for use during the week-long Jewish festival of Sukkot.

12. *Tefillin* are phylacteries that are worn to morning prayer services.

13. Umansky, 478–79.

14. Reichel, 68.

15. *Shema* is the first word of a section of the Torah (Hebrew Bible) that is a centerpiece of the morning and evening Jewish prayer services. The first verse encapsulates the monotheistic essence of Judaism: "Hear, O Israel: the Lord our God, the Lord is one," found in Deuteronomy 6:4.

16. The Sinai Temple Sisterhood is a group of Jewish women of different backgrounds and ages who gather to observe and promote Jewish values and traditions while enjoying warmth and friendship in the process. The Sisterhood offers classes and programs and is involved in board positions and community service. It supports Israel and many local Jewish organizations.

17. Women's League for Conservative Judaism is the largest synagogue-based women's organization in the world. As an active arm of the Conservative/Masorti movement, they provide service to hundreds of affiliated women's groups in synagogues across North America and to thousands of women worldwide.

18. Members of Nessah describe it as a synagogue that upholds the traditions and customs of Iranian Jews according to Orthodox, Sephardic law.

19. A *minyan* in Judaism refers to the quoraum of ten male Jewish adults required for certain religious obligations.

20. A *get* is a divorce document, which, according to Jewish law, must be presented by a husband to his wife to effect their divorce.

21. Lynn Davidman, *Traditions in a Rootless World: Women Turn to Orthodox Judaism* (Los Angeles: University of California Press, 1991), 26.

22. Recitation of seven blessings at a Jewish wedding.

23. Reichel, 68.

24. Karmel Melamed, "Iranian Jews Trying to Choose from the Cornucopia of Judaism in America," *The Jewish Journal of Greater Los Angeles*, August 13, 2007.

25. Davidman, 45.

26. Woman who adopt Orthodox Judaism as an adult.

27. Ibid., 195.

28. Negative disparaging but truthful remarks about a person or party who is not present.

29. Baer 1996, 103.

30. Amnon Netzer, "*Yehudai Iran B'Artzot Habrit* (Iranian Jews in America)," *Gesher Journal of Jewish Affairs* 1, no. 110 (Spring 1984): 79–90.

31. Baer 1996.

32. Tohidi, 212.

33. Baer 1996, 98.

34. Reichel, 68.

35. Baer 1996, 109.

36. Ibid., 106.

37. Kelley, 162–66.

38. Tohidi, 211.

CHAPTER FIVE

1. This is a description of one of the numerous Iranian Jewish parties the author attended in Beverly Hills in the past four years.

2. Herbert J. Gans believes symbolic ethnicity can be expressed in numerous ways, especially by a nostalgic allegiance to the culture of the immigrant generation, or that of the old country. Symbolic ethnicity is a love for and a pride in a tradition that can be felt without having to be incorporated into everyday behavior.

3. Gans, 204.

4. Ibid.

5. Ruben G. Rumbaut and Alejandro Portes, *Ethnicities: Children of Immigrants in America*, ed. Ruben G. Rumbaut and Alejandro Portes (Berkeley: University of California Press, 2001), 4.

6. Nilan and Feixa, 1.

7. Bhabha, 2.

8. Nilan and Feixa, 2.

9. Ibid.

10. Anne Marie Tupuola, "Talking Sexuality through an Insider's Lens: The Samoan Experience," in *All about the Girl: Culture, Power, and Identity*, ed. Anita Harris (New York: Routledge, 2004), 115.

11. Bianca L. Guzman, Elise Arruda, and Aida L. Feria, "Los Papas, La Familia y La Sexualidad," in *Latina Girls: Voices of Adolescent Strength in the United States*, ed. Jill Denner and Bianca L. Guzman (New York: New York University Press, 2006), 17.

12. Karen Isaksen Leonard, *The New American: The South Asian Americans* (London: Greenwood, 1997), 150.

13. Karen Pyke, "The Normal American Family" as an Interpretive Structure of Family Life among Grown Children of Korean and Vietnamese Immigrants," *Journal of Marriage and Family* 62, no. 1 (February 2000): 5.

14. Francis K. Goldscheider and Calvin Goldscheider, "Family Structure and Conflict: Nest-Leaving Expectations of Young Adults and Their Parents," *Journal of Marriage and the Family* 51, no. 1 (February 1989): 87–88.

15. Leonard, 146.

16. Pegah Hendizadeh Schiffman, "How Najeeb Are You? Reflections on Persian-American Girlhood," *Lilith* 24, no. 4 (January 31, 2000): 33.

17. Ibid., 35.

18. Leonard, 156.

19. Ibid.

20. Schiffman, 35.

21. Ibid.

22. Nedim Karakayali, "Duality and Diversity in the Lives of Immigrant Children: Rethinking the 'Problem of the Second Generation' in Light of Immigrant

Autobiographies," *Canadian Review of Sociology and Anthropology* 42, no. 3 (August 2005): 332.

23. Ibid., 333.

24. Joanne Entwistel, *The Fashioned Body: Fashion, Dress, and Modern Social Theory* (Cambridge: Polity, 2000), 187.

25. Kate Gleeson and Hannah Frith, "Pretty in Pink: Young Women Presenting Mature Sexual Identities," in *All about the Girl: Culture, Power, and Identity*, ed. Anita Harris, (New York: Routledge, 2004), 105.

26. Joanne B. Eicher, "Dress, Gender, and the Public Display of Skin," in *Body Dressing*, ed. Joanne Entwistle and Elizabeth Wilson (Oxford: Berg, 2001).

27. Gleeson and Frith, 106.

28. Ibid.

29. Patricia Zavella, "Talkin' Sex: Chicanas and Mexicans Theorize about Silences and Sexual Pleasures," in *Chicana Feminist: A Critical Reader*, ed. G. E. Arredondo, A. Hurtado, N. Klahn, O. Najera-Ramirez, and P. Zavelly (Durham: Duke University Press, 2003), 248.

30. An unmarried female who does not have physical contact.

31. Schiffman, 34.

32. Ibid., 32.

33. Beverly Hills High School.

34. Anita Harris, "Jamming Girl Culture: Young Women and Consumer Citizenship," in *All about the Girl: Culture, Power, and Identity*, ed. Anita Harris (New York: Routledge, 2004), 164–65.

35. Ibid., 165.

36. Ibid., 166.

37. Ibid., 167.

38. Lisa Jervis, "My Jewish Nose," in *Body Outlaws: Young Women Write about Body Image and Identity*, ed. Ophira Edut (Seattle: Seal, 1998), 63–64.

39. Ibid.

40. Schiffman, 34.

41. Samuel C. Heilman, *Synagogue Life: A Study in Symbolic Interaction* (London: Transaction, 1998), 158.

42. Ibid., 158–59.

43. Ibid., 161.

44. Ibid., 159.

45. Ibid., 161–62.

46. This term designates men who belong to a wide range of ultra-Orthodox Jewish communities—both Hasidic and not Hasidic.

47. Debra R. Kaufman, *Rachel's Daughters: Newly Orthodox Jewish Women* (New Brunswick: Rutgers, 1991).

48. Janet O. Aviad, *Return to Judaism: Religious Renewal in Israel* (Chicago: University of Chicago Press, 1983).

49. Dorit Roer-Strier and Roberta G. Sands, "The Impact of Religious Intensification on Family Relations: A South African Example," *Journal of Marriage and Family* 63 (August 2001), 869.

50. According to the laws of *kashrut*, any meat prepared and served in one's home must have been slaughtered in a special way and certified as acceptable. Almost all food must be approved as kosher. Separate sets of dishes and cutlery are required for serving mean and dairy meals. See Roer-Strier, 869.

51. Andrea E. Wilson, Kim M. Shuey, Glan H. Elder Jr., "Ambivalence in the Relationship of Adult Children to Aging Parents and In-Laws," *Journal of Marriage and Family* 65, no. 4 (November 2003): 1060.

52. Ibid., 1061.

53. Vern L. Bengston, "Beyond the Nuclear Family: The Increasing Importance of Multigenerational Bonds," *Journal of Marriage and Family* 63, no. 1 (February 2001): 6.

54. Ibid., 7.

55. Carol J. Boyd, "Mothers and Daughters: A Discussion of Theory and Research," *Journal of Marriage and Family* 51, no. 2 (May 1989): 296.

56. Only one woman said she feels closer to her mother when she takes on a maternal role with her.

CHAPTER SIX

1. Paidar, 149.

2. Ibid., 8.

3. This is the feminine plural form of *shomeret negiah*.

4. Tohidi, 194.

5. Shideh Hanassab, "Acculturation and Young Iranian Women: Attitudes toward Sex Roles and Intimate Relationships," *The Journal of Multicultural Counseling and Development* (1991): 19:11–21.

6. Shideh Hanassab, "Caught between Two Cultures: Young Iranian Women in Los Angeles," in *Irangeles: Iranians in Los Angeles*, ed. Ron Kelly (Los Angeles: University of California Press, 1993), 224.

7. Bruce A. Phillips and Mitra Kahrizi Khalili, "The Iranian Jewish Family in Transition," *Journal of Jewish Communal Services* (Winter/Spring 1995): 198.

8. Tohidi, 207.

9. Only one woman said that she feels closer to her mother when she takes on a more maternal role with her.

10. Tohidi, 194.

11. Kelley, 167.

12. Bernard Malamud, *The Assistant* (New York: Farrar, Straus and Giroux, 1957), xi.

GLOSSARY

abe: Persian word translated as something bad, wrong, or negative.

abji: Sister.

Abji Golbahar: Sister Golbahar, a game.

Aid-e-Nissan: Persian for "holiday of Nissan." Passover takes place during the month of Nissan.

aliyah: Being called up to read the Torah in the syngagogue.

Anusim: The term for Iranian Jews who were forced to convert to Islam, yet secretly remained Jewish.

ba'alat teshuvah (pl. *ba'alot teshuvah*): A woman who adopts Orthodox Judaism as an adult.

bar/bat mitzvah: According to Jewish law, when Jewish children reach the age of thirteen for boys and twelve for girls they become responsible for their actions, and "become a *bar* (boy) or *bat* (girl) mitzvah."

bazi (pl. *baziha*): Persian word for game.

Beit Knesset: Synagogue.

bimah: Stage, theater.

"black hat": A man who belongs to an ultra-Orthodox Jewish community.

chador: A loose robe.

charoset: Traditional Passover food that has a symbolic role in the ceremonial seder meal.

chastegaree: When a mother of a boy approaches a mother of a girl and asks permission for her son to meet her daughter in order to date for marriage.

chasterghar: Male suitors for marriage.

chashm ham cheshmi: Competition.

chelo-kabob: National dish of Iran consisting of basmati rice and kabob.

Chosen Mishpat: Laws about judges and witnesses, etc.; part of the Shulhan Arukh.

dorehs: Social gatherings.

esphan/esphand: Wild rue, a sacred herb whose smoldering fumes are said to ward off the evil eye.

ettefaqh: Jewish elementary and high school in Tehran.

Even Ha-Ezer: Laws of procreation, marriage, and divorce, part of the Shulhan Arukh.

Farangi: Persian word for a foreigner. A person from Europe.

fitna: Arabic word, generally regarded as very difficult to translate but at the same time is considered to be an all-encompassing word referring to schism, secession, upheaval, and anarchy.

Gemara: Discussion of the Mishnah and related writings that often ventures onto other subjects and expounds broadly on the Bible.

get: A divorce document, which, according to Jewish Law, must be presented by a husband to his wife to effect their divorce.

ghondi: Persian meatballs.

glatt kosher: Meat from animals with smooth or defect-free lungs; today the term is often used informally to imply that a product was processed under a stricter standard of *kashrut*.

haftorah: A short selection from the Prophets read on every Sabbath in a Jewish synagogue following a reading from the Torah.

haftsin: The Seven S's is a traditional table setting of Nowruz, the traditional Iranian spring celebration.

halakhah (**pl. *halakhot***): Jewish law.

Hamadanian Jews: Jews from Hamadan, Iran (did not live in ghettos and were, thus, more integrated into the community).

hames: Persian term referring to anything that is forbidden to eat during Passover. Not to be confused with the Hebrew *chametz*, leavened bread.

hammams: Public bath houses.

hennah-bandan: Before a wedding, the women would gather in the home of the bride's family and put henna on the bride's hair and on the hands of all the women for good luck.

Hozrei-bi-tshuvah: "Those who return." Becoming a religiously observant Jew.

Hillula: An annual celebration commemorating the saint's death anniversary.

Ishalah aroos beshi: Persian phrase meaning "God willing, you will be a bride."

Juhud: A derogatory way of calling someone a Jew in Persian.

kadosh: Holy.

kashrut: System of Jewish dietary laws.

ketubah: Jewish marriage contract.

khanevadeh: Family.

knisa: Persian word for synagogue.

kosher: Foods that conform to the rules of the Jewish religion.

kurosh: Jewish Day school located in Tehran.

Lag b'Omer: A Jewish feast celebrated on the thirty-third day of the counting of the Omer (the forty-nine days between the Jewish holidays of Passover and Shavuot).

lashon ha-ra: "Evil speech." One is prohibited, in Jewish Law, of telling gossip—negative disparaging of truthful and untruthful remarks about a person or party who is not present.

Maghreb: A term generally applied to all of Morocco, Algeria, and Tunisia.

Mahaleh: Jewish ghetto in Iran.

Majles: A place of "sitting," used to describe various types of special gatherings among common interest groups.

mikveh: Ritual bath that a woman immerses herself in seven days after she stops menstruating.

minyan: Quoraum of ten male Jewish adults required for certain religious obligations.

Mishnah: The first written compendium of Judaism's Oral Law.

mitzvah: A commandment of the Jewish law. A worthy deed.

mollah/mullah: Religious leader. Although *mullah* is referring to a Muslim religious leader, many Iranian Jews referred to their Hebrew teachers as *mullahs*, as well.

najeeb: Persian word which refers to someone who is simplistic and a bit naïve to the world. In regards to a woman, it means she does not interact with men, maintains her virginity, and is extremely sheltered.

najeebness: Virginity and innocence.

najes: Refers to anything that is considered to be impure for Shi'i Muslims. Dogs, pigs, Christians, and Jews were put under this category.

Namaz: The process of praying to God, making a sacred pilgrimage, and giving a monetary donation.

nejasat: Unbelievers' ritual impurity.

niddah: Jewish regulations and rituals concerning menstruation.

Nowruz: Persian New Year.

ob-ghoosh: Persian stew.

Orach Chayim: Daily, Sabbath, and Holiday Laws, part of the Shulhan Arukh.

ORT: A nonprofit and nonpolitical organization whose mission is to work for the advancement of Jewish and other people through training and education.

paziraeeh: Persian word for hospitality; it encompasses all aspects of hosting a party.

roshan–fekr: Enlightened thinker; an intellectual.

Rosh Hashanah: Jewish New Year.

sabze: Sprouts.

samanu: Creamy pudding.

sanjed: Dry fruit of the lotus tree.

seer: Garlic.

serkeh: Vinegar.

Shabbat: Hebrew word for the Jewish Sabbath.

shaitel: The Yiddish word for a wig worn by certain Orthodox Jewish married women in keeping with an old rabbinical precept that forbids a woman to leave her hair uncovered in the sight of a man other than her husband. This Ashkenazi practice is part of the modesty-related dress standard called *tzniut*. The Shulchan Aruch cites the opinion of Rabbi Joshua Boaz ben Simon Baruch, (d. 1557), who permitted the wearing of wigs.

shalom: Peace.

sheereeni-khorun: Party celebrating the bride's family bringing sweets to the groom's family as a gesture of accepting the groom's proposal for marriage.

Shema: A shortened version of "Shema Israel," the first two words of Deuteronomy 6:4–9. This passage is a centerpiece of daily prayers.

sheva berakhot: Recitation of seven blessings at a Jewish wedding and at postwedding celebratory feasts.

shoma: Polite form of "you."

shomeret negiah: The concept in Jewish law that forbids or restricts physical contact with a member of the opposite sex (except for one's spouse, children, grandchildren, parents, and grandparents). A boy who observes it is *shomer negiah*; a girl who observes it is *shomeret negiah*.

shomeret Shabbat: Observing the Jewish laws in regards to the Sabbath.

sib: Apple.

siddur: Jewish prayer book.

sofreh: A cloth on which food and other objects are displayed, the purpose of which is to heal the sick, solve sterility problems, and achieve desired marriages.

sofrey-ye-haft-sinn: Ceremonial setting, literally "seven dishes."

somaq: Sumac berries.

sufreh: A charitable table for the poor and hungry to thank God for fulfilling a wish. Each of the several different kinds of *sufreh* is dedicated to and named after a female or male figure from an Islamic legend.

sukkah: A temporary hut constructed for use during the week-long Jewish festival of Sukkot.

Sukkot: Feast of Tabernacles.

Sukkoth: A biblical pilgrimage festival that occurs in autumn on the fifteenth day of the month of Tishrei (late September to late October).

Talmud: A central text of mainstream Judaism, in the form of a record of rabbinic discussions pertaining to Jewish law, ethics, philosophy, customs, and history. The Talmud has two components: the Mishnah (c. 200 CE), the first written compendium of Judaism's oral law; and the Gemara (c. 500 CE), a discussion of the Mishnah and related writings that often ventures onto other subjects and expounds broadly on the Bible.

tasliyat: Persian word for condolences.

Tu B'Shvat: Jewish Arbor Day.

tefillah: The Hebrew word for prayer.

tefillin: Phylacteries.

tefillin bandan: Young men in Iran did not have *bar mitzvahs*, but were given a set of *tefillin* (phylacteries) at the age of thirteen, which they wore to morning prayer services.

tefillot: The Hebrew word for prayers.

Tehillim: Psalms.

Tishrei: Late September to late October.

Torah she-be'al-peh: Oral tradition of the Torah, which was given concurrently with the Hebrew Bible.

Torah she-be-ketav: The written Torah consists of the books of the Hebrew Bible.

Tu b'shvat: A minor Jewish holiday in the Hebrew month of Shevat, usually sometime in late January or early February, that marks the "New Year of the Trees."

tzedakah: Hebrew word for charity.

yas: Persian word for the jasmine flower.

Yom Kippur: Jewish Day of Atonement.

Yoreh De'ah: Laws about food and life issues, part of the Shulhan Arukh.

zagh o boor: Having light eyes and light hair.

zarchoobeh: Persian word for tumeric.

ziyarat: The ritual of pilgrimage.

REFERENCES

Amanat, Mehrdad. "Nationalism and Social Change in Contemporary Iran." In *Irangeles: Iranians in Los Angeles*, edited by Ron Kelly. Los Angeles: University of California Press, 1993.

Amin, Camron Michael. "The Attentions of the Great Father: Reza Shah, 'The Woman Question,' and the Iranian Press, 1890–1946." PhD diss., University of Chicago, 1996.

Aviad, Janet O. *Return to Judaism: Religious Renewal in Israel*. Chicago: University of Chicago Press, 1983.

Ayala, Jennifer. "Confianza, Consejos, and Contradictions: Gender and Sexuality Lessons between Latina Adolescent Daughters and Mothers." In *Latina Girls: Voices of Adolescent Strength in the United States*, edited by Jill Denner and Bianca L. Guzman, 29–43. New York: New York University Press, 2006.

Baer, Leah. "The Challenge of America." In *Padyavand*, Volume 3, edited by Amnon Netzer. Los Angeles: Mazda, 1996.

———. "Life's Events: Births, Bar Mitzvah, Weddings, and Burial Customs." In *Esther's Children: A Portrait of Iranian Jews*, edited by Houman Sarshar, 311–36. Beverly Hills: The Center for Iranian Jewish History, 2002.

Bahloul, Joelle. *Le Culte de la Table Dresse, Rites et Traditions de la Table Juive Algerienne*. Paris: A.-M. Metailie, 1983.

Banerji, Chitrita. *The Hour of the Goddess: Memories of Women, Food, and Ritual in Bengal*. Calcutta: Seagull Books, 2001.

Batmanglij, Najimieh Khalili. *New Food of Life: Ancient Persian and Modern Iranian Cooking and Ceremonies*. Los Angeles: Mage, 1998.

Bauer, Janet. "Demographic Change, Women and the Family in a Migrant Neighborhood of Tehran." In *Women and the Family in Iran*, edited by Asghar Fathi, 158–86. Netherlands: E. J. Brill, 1985.

Bell, Catherine. *Ritual Theory, Ritual Practice*. New York: Oxford University Press, 1992.

Ben-Ami, Issachar. *Saint Veneration among the Jews in Morocco*. Detroit: Wayne State University, 1998.

Bengston, Vern L. "Beyond the Nuclear Family: The Increasing Importance of Multigenerational Bonds." *Journal of Marriage and Family* 63, no. 1 (February 2001): 1–16.

Berger, Peter. *The Sacred Canopy: Elements of a Sociological Theory of Religion*. Garden City: Anchor Books/Doubleday, 1969.

Betteridge, Anne H. "Gift Exchange in Iran: The Locus of Self-Identity in Social Interaction." *Anthropological Quarterly* 58, no. 4 (October 1985): 190–202.

Bhabha, Homi. *The Location of Culture*. London: Routledge, 1994.

Biale, Rachel. *Women and Jewish Law*. New York: Schocken Books, 1984.

Bilu, Yoram. "The Inner Limits of Communitas: A Covert Dimension of Pilgrimage Experience." *Ethos* 16, no. 3 (September 1988): 302–25.

Boyd, Carol J. "Mothers and Daughters: A Discussion of Theory and Research." *Journal of Marriage and Family* 51, no. 2 (May 1989): 291–302.

Bozorgmehr, Mehdi. "*Internal Ethnicity: Armenian, Bahai, Jewish, and Muslim Iranians in Los Angeles*." PhD diss., University of California, Los Angeles, 1992.

———, and Pyong Gap Min. "Immigrant Entrepreneurship and Business Patterns: A Comparison of Koreans and Iranians in Los Angeles." *International Migration Review* 34, no. 3 (Autumn 2000): 707–38.

Cernea, Ruth Fredman. "Flaming Prayers: *Hillula* in a New Home." In *Between Two Worlds: Ethnographic Essays on American Jewry*, edited by Jack Kugelmass, 162–91. Ithaca: Cornell University Press, 1988.

Chaichian, Mohammad A. "First Generation Iranian Immigrants and the Question of Cultural Identity: The Case of Iowa." *IMR* 31, no. 3 (Fall 1997): 612–27.

Dallalfar, Arlene. "Iranian Immigrant Women in Los Angeles: The Reconstruction of Work, Ethnicity, and Community." PhD diss., University of California, Los Angeles, 1989.

Danforth, Loring M. *Death Rituals of Rural Greece*. Princeton: Princeton University Press, 1982.

———."Worlds Apart: Mothers, Daughters, and Family Life." In *Esther's Children: A Portrait of Iranian Jews*, edited by Houman Sarshar, 403–14. Beverly Hills: Center for Iranian Jewish History, 2002.

Datan, Nancy, Aaron Antonovsky, and Benjamin Moaz. *A Time to Reap: The Middle Age of Women in Five Israeli Subcultures*. Baltimore: Johns Hopkins University Press, 1981.

Davidman, Lynn. *Tradition in a Rootless World: Women Turn to Orthodox Judaism*. Berkeley: University of California Press, 1991.

Debold, Elizabeth, Marie Wilson, and Idelisse Malave. *Mother Daughter Revolution: From Betrayal to Power*. New York: Addison-Wesley, 1993.

Douglas, Mary, and Steven M. Tipton. *Religion and America: Spirituality in a Secular Age*. Boston: Beacon, 1982.

Durkheim, Emile. *The Elementary Forms of Religious Life*. Translation by Karen E. Fields. New York: Free, 1995.

Ebtami, Houshang. "The Impure Jew." In *Esther's Children: A Portrait of Iranian Jews*, edited by Houman Sarshar, 95–102. Beverly Hills: The Center for Iranian Jewish History, 2002.

Eicher, Joanne B. "Dress, Gender and the Public Display of Skin." In *Body Dressing*, edited by Joanne Entwistle and Elizabeth Wilson, 233–25. Oxford: Berg, 2001.

Eliade, Mircea. *Cosmos and History*. Princeton: Princeton University Press, 1954.

———. *The Sacred and the Profane*. Translated by Willard R. Trask. New York: Harcourt Brace and World, 1959.

Entwistel, Joanne. *The Fashioned Body: Fashion, Dress and Modern Social Theory*. Cambridge: Polity, 2000.

Espin, Oliva. "Race, Racism, and Sexuality in the Life Narratives of Immigrant Women." In *Latina Realities: Essays on Healing, Migration and Sexuality*, edited by Oliva Espin, 171–85. Boulder: Westview, 1997.

————. *Women Crossing Boundaries: A Psychology of Immigration and Transformation of Sexuality*. New York: Routledge, 1999.

Espiritu, Yen Le, and Diane L. Wolf. "The Paradox of Assimilation: Children of Filipino Immigrants in San Diego." In *Ethnicities: Children of Immigrants in America*, edited by Ruben G. Rumbaut and Alejandro Portes, 157–86. Berkeley: University of California Press, 2001.

Gabbay, Elias Yassi. "Esther's Tomb." In *Esther's Children: A Portrait of Iranian Jews*, edited by Houman Sarshar, 19–30. Philadelphia: Jewish Publication Society, 2002.

Gallagos-Castillo, Angela. "La Casa: Negotiating Family Cultural Practices, Constructing Identities." In *Latina Girls: Voices of Adolescent Strength in the United States*, edited by Jill Denner and Bianca L. Guzman, 44–58. New York: New York University Press, 2006.

Gans, Herbert J. "Symbolic Ethnicity: The Future of Ethnic Groups and Cultures in America." In *On the Making of Americas: Essays in Honor of David Reisman*, edited by Herbert J. Gans, Nathan Glazer, Joseph R. Gusfield, and Christopher Jencks, 193–220. Pennsylvania: University of Pennsylvania Press, 1979.

Gilad, Lisa. *Ginger and Salt: Yemeni Jewish Women in an Israeli Town*. Boulder: Westview, 1989.

Gleeson, Kate, and Hannah Frith. "Pretty in Pink: Young Women Presenting Mature Sexual Identities." In *All about the Girl: Culture, Power, and Identity*," edited by Anita Harris, 103–14. New York: Routledge, 2004.

Goldin, Farideh. *Wedding Song: Memoirs of an Iranian Jewish Woman*. Hanover: Brandeis University Press, 2003.

Goldscheider, Calvin. "Demographic Transitions, Modernization and the Transformation of Judaism." In *Events and Movements in Modern Judaism*, edited by Raphael Patai and Emanuel S. Goldsmith, 39–64. New York: Paragon House, 1995.

Goldscheider, Francis K., and Calvin Goldscheider. "Family Structure and Conflict: Nest-Leaving Expectations of Young Adults and Their Parents." *Journal of Marriage and the Family* 51, no. 1 (February 1989): 87–98.

Guzman, Bianca L., Elise Arruda, and Aida L. Feria. "Los Papas, La Familia y La Sexualidad." In *Latina Girls: Voices of Adolescent Strength in the United States*, edited by Jill Denner and Bianca L. Guzman, 17–28. New York: New York University Press, 2006.

Hanassab, Shideh. "Acculturation and Young Iranian Women: Attitudes toward Sex Roles and Intimate Relationships." *The Journal of Multicultural Counseling and Development* 19, no. 1 (1991): 11–21.

————. "Caught between Two Cultures: Young Iranian Women in Los Angeles." *Irangeles: Iranians in Los Angeles*, edited by Ron Kelly, 223–32. Los Angeles: University of California Press, 1993.

Hancock, Mary. *Womenhood in the Making: Domestic Ritual and Public Culture in Urban South India*. Boulder: Westview, 1999.

Harbottle, Lynn. *Food for Health, Food for Wealth: The Performance of Ethnic and Gender Identities by Iranian Settlers in Britain*. New York: Berghahn Books, 2004.

Harris, Anita. "Jamming Girl Culture: Young Women and Consumer Citizenship." In *All about the Girl: Culture, Power, and Identity*, edited by Anita Harris, 163–72. New York: Routledge, 2004.

Heilman, Samuel C. *Synagogue Life: A Study in Symbolic Interaction*. London: Transaction, 1998, 158.

Hemation, B. "To Be or Not to Be—Thankful." *Megillah* 47 (January 1995): 28.

James, William. *The Varieties of Religious Experience*. New York: Macmillan, 1961.

Jamzadeh, Laal, and Margaret Mills. "Iranian Sofreh: From Collective to Female Ritual." In *Gender and Religion: On the Complexities of Symbols*, edited by Caroline Walker Bynum, Steven Harrell, and Paula Richmon. Boston: Beacon, 1986.

Jervis, Lisa. "My Jewish Nose." In *Body Outlaws: Young Women Write about Body Image and Identity*, edited by Ophira Edut, 62–67. Seattle: Seal, 1998.

Johansson, Thomas. *The Transformation of Sexuality: Gender and Identity in Contemporary Youth Culture*. Burlington: Ashgate, 2007.

Johnson, Colleen Leahy. "Interdependence, Reciprocity, and Indebtedness: An Analysis of Japanese American Kinship Relations." *Journal of Marriage and Family* 39, no. 2 (May 1977): 351–63.

Karakayali, Nedim. "Duality and Diversity in the Lives of Immigrant Children: Rethinking the 'Problem of the Second Generation' in Light of Immigrant Autobiographies." *Canadian Review of Sociology and Anthropology* 42, no. 3 (August 2005): 325–43.

Karesh, Sarah E., and Mitchell M. Hurvitz. *Encyclopedia of Judaism*. New York: Infobase, 2006, 98–100.

Katz, Jacob. "German Culture and the Jews." In *The Jewish Response to German Culture: From the Enlightenment to the Second World War*, edited by Jehuda Reinharz and Walter Schatzberg, 85–99. Hanover: University Press of New England, 1985.

———. *The "Shabbes Goy."* Philadelphia: Jewish Publication Society, 1989.

Kaufman, Debra R. *Rachel's Daughters: Newly Orthodox Jewish Women*. New Brunswick: Rutgers, 1991.

Kelley, Ron. "Interview with Homa Mahmoudi, Clinical Psychologist." In *Irangeles: Iranians in Los Angeles*, edited by Ron Kelly, 162–74. Los Angeles: University of California Press, 1993.

Kerns, Virginia. *Women and the Ancestors*. Urbana: University of Illinois Press, 1983.

Klein, Isaac. *A Guide to Jewish Religious Practice*. New York: Jewish Theological Seminary of America, 1979.

Leonard, Karen Isaksen. *The New American: The South Asian Americans*. London: Greenwood, 1997.

Levi, Habib. *Comprehensive History of the Jews of Iran: The Outset of the Diaspora*. Costa Mesa: Mazda, 1999.

Loeb, Laurence D. *Outcast: Jewish Life in Southern Iran*. New York: Gordon and Breach, 1977, 224.

Lutske, Harvey. *The Book of Jewish Customs*. Northvale: Jason Aronson, 1986.

Macgregor, Frances C. "Social and Cultural Components in the Motivations of Persons Seeking Plastic Surgery of the Nose." *Journal of Health and Social Behavior* 8, no. 2 (June 1967): 125–35.

Malamud, Bernard. *The Assistant*. New York: Farrar, Straus, and Giroux, 1957.

Margalit, Avishai. *The Ethics of Memory*. Cambridge, Harvard University Press, 2002.

Mauss, Marcel. *The Gift*. Translated by Ian Cunnison. London: Cohen and West, 1954.

Melamed, Karmel. "Iranian Community Mourns Its Anchor." *The Jewish Journal of Greater Los Angeles*, September 23, 2005.

———. "Iranian Jews Trying to Choose from the Cornucopia of Judaism in America." *The Jewish Journal of Greater Los Angeles*, August 13, 2007.

Menashri, David. "The Pahlavi Monarchy and the Islamic Revolution." In *Esther's Children*, edited by Houman Sarshar, 379–402. Beverly Hills: Center for Iranian Jewish Oral History, Beverly Hills, 2002.

Mernissi, Fatima. *Woman, Saints, and Sanctuaries*. Lahore: Simorgh, 1987.

Mladinov, D. "Iranian Jewish Organization: The Integration of an Émigré Group into the American Jewish Community." *Journal of Jewish Communal Service* (Spring 1981): 245–49.

Mora, Pat. *Houses of Houses*. Boston: Beacon, 1997.

Najmabadi, Afsaneh. "Crafting an Educated Housewife in Iran." In *Remaking Women: Feminism and Modernity in the Middle East*, edited by Lila Abu-Lughod, 91–125. Princeton: Princeton University Press, 1998.

Netzer, Amnon, "Yehudai Iran B'Artzot Habrit (Iranian Jews in America)." *Gesher Journal of Jewish Affairs* 1, no. 110 (Spring 1984): 79–90.

Nikbakht, Faryar. "As with Moses in Egypt: Alliance Israelite Universelle Schools in Iran." In *Esther's Children: A Portrait of Iranian Jews*, edited by Houman Sarshar. Beverly Hills: Center for Iranian Jewish History, 2002.

Nilan, Pam, and Carles Feixa. *Global Youth? Hybrid Identities, Plural Worlds*. Edited by Pam Nilan and Carles Feixa. New York: Routledge, 2006.

Otto, Rudolph. *The Idea of the Holy*. Oxford: Oxford University Press, 1917.

Paidar, Parvin. *Women and the Political Process in Twentieth-Century Iran*. Cambridge: Cambridge University Press, 1995.

Patai, Raphael. *Jadid Al-Islam: The Jewish "New Muslims" of Meshhad*. Detroit: Wayne State University Press, 1997.

Phillips, Bruce A., and Mitra Kahrizi Khalili. "The Iranian Jewish Family in Transition." *Journal of Jewish Communal Services* (Winter/Spring 1995): 198.

Pilcher, Jeffrey. *Que Vivan los Tamales!: Food and the Making of Mexican Identity*. Albuquerque: University of New Mexico, 1998.

Pyke, Karen. "The Normal American Family" as an Interpretive Structure of Family Life among Grown Children of Korean and Vietnamese Immigrants." *Journal of Marriage and Family* 62, no. 1 (February 2000): 240–55.

Quicklists. http://www.thearda.com/QuickLists/QuickList_189.asp.

Reichel, Michael. *Persian American Jewry at a Crossroads: Will the Traditions Continue?* New York: LV, 2004.

Roer-Strier, Dorit, and Roberta G. Sands. "The Impact of Religious Intensification on Family Relations: A South African Example." *Journal of Marriage and Family* 63 (August 2001): 860–80.

Rumbaut, Ruben G., and Alejandro Portes. *Ethnicities: Children of Immigrants in America*. Edited by Ruben G. Rumbaut and Alejandro Portes. Berkeley: University of California Press, 2001.

Safa-Isfahani, Kaveh. "Female-Centered World Views in Iranian Culture: Symbolic Representations of Sexuality in Dramatic Games." *Signs* 6, no. 1 (Autumn 1980): 33–53.

Sanghvi, Ramesh, Clifford German, and David Missen. *Revolution of the Shah and the People.* London: Transorient Books, 1967.

Schifman, Pegah Hendizadeh. "How Najeeb Are You? Reflections on Persian-American Girlhood." *Lilith* 24, no. 4 (January 31, 2000): 30–34.

Sciolino, Elaine. "Iran's Well-Covered Women Remodel a Part That Shows." *New York Times* (September 22, 2000).

Sered, Susan Star. "Food and Holiness: Cooking as a Sacred Act among Middle-Eastern Jewish Women." *Anthropological Quarterly* 61, no. 3 (July 1988): 129–39.

———. *Women as Ritual Experts.* New York: Oxford University Press, 1992.

Shokeid, Moshe. *The Predicament of Homecoming: Cultural and Social Life of North African Immigrants in Israel.* Ithaca: Cornell University Press, 1974.

Simon, Rachel. *Change within Tradition among Jewish Women in Libya.* Seattle: University of Washington Press, 1992, 21.

Smith, Jonathan Z. *Imagining Religion* Chicago: University of Chicago Press, 1982, 54.

———. *To Take Place: Toward Theory in Ritual.* Chicago: University of Chicago Press, 1987.

Soomekh, Saba. "Between Religion and Culture: Three Generations of Iranian Jewish Women from the Shahs to Los Angeles." PhD diss., University of California, Santa Barbara, 2009.

Sorkin, David. "The Invisible Community: Emancipation, Secular Culture, and Jewish Identity in the Writings of Berthold Auerbach." In *The Jewish Response to German Culture: From the Enlightenment to the Second World War*, edited by Jehuda Reinharz and Walter Schatzberg, 100–119. Hanover: University Press of New England, 1985.

Taylor, Paul C. "Malcom's Conk and Danto's Colors; or, Four Logical Petitions concerning Race, Beauty, and Aesthetics." In *Beauty Matters*, edited by Peg Zeglin Brand, 57–64. Bloomington: Indiana University Press, 2000.

Tohidi, Nayareh. "Iranian Women and Gender Relations in Los Angeles." In *Irangeles: Iranians in Los Angeles*, edited by Ron Kelly, 174–84. Los Angeles: University of California Press, 1993.

Tupuola, Anne Marie. "Talking Sexuality through an Insider's Lens: The Samoan Experience." In *All about the Girl: Culture, Power, and Identity*, edited by Anita Harris, 115–26. New York: Routledge, 2004.

Umansky, Ellen M. "Feminism and the Revolution of Women's Roles within American Jewish Life." In *Women, Religion, and Social Change*, edited by Yvonne Yazbeck Haddad and Ellison Banks Findly, 477–94. New York: State University of New York, 1985.

Ungar, Sanford J. *Fresh Blood: The New American Immigrants.* New York: Simon and Schuster, 1995.

U.S. Department of Homeland Security, Office of Immigration Statistics. *Yearbook of Immigration Statistics, 1970–2004.*

Weintraub, D., and M. Shapiro. "The Traditional Family in Israel in the Process of Change—Crisis and Continuity." *British Journal of Sociology* 19, no. 2 (1968): 284–99.

Werbner, Pnina. "Economic Rationality and Hierarchical Gift Economies: Value and Ranking among British Pakistanis." *Man* 25, no. 2 (June 1990): 266–85.

Wilson, Andrea E., Kim M. Shuey, and Glan H. Elder Jr. "Ambivalence in the Relationship of Adult Children to Aging Parents and In-Laws." *Journal of Marriage and Family* 65, no. 4 (November 2003): 1055–72.

Women's Organization of Iran. *The Employment of Women.* Tehran: Women's Organization of Iran, 1975.

Yeganeh, Nahid. "Women, Nationalism and Islam in Contemporary Political Discourse in Iran." *Feminist Review*, no. 44 (Summer 1993): 3–18.

Zavella, Patricia. "Talkin' Sex: Chicanas and Mexicans Theorize about Silences and Sexual Pleasures." In *Chicana Feminist: A Critical Reader*, edited by G. F. Arredondo, A. Hurtado, N. Klahn, O. Najera-Ramirez, and P. Zavelly, 228–53. Durham: Duke University Press, 2003.

Zenner, Walter. *Syrian Jewish Identification in Israel.* New York: Columbia University, 1965.

INDEX